Chaucer
and the Making of
English Poetry

By the same author

The Pearl: an Interpretation (1967)

Chaucer
and the Making of
English Poetry

Shortened edition

P. M. KEAN

Routledge & Kegan Paul

London, Boston, Melbourne
and Henley-on-Thames

First published in 1972
by Routledge & Kegan Paul Ltd
Shortened edition published in 1982
by Routledge & Kegan Paul Ltd
39 Store Street, London WC1E 7DD,
9 Park Street, Boston, Mass. 02108, USA,
296 Beaconsfield Parade, Middle Park,
Melbourne, 3206, Australia
and Broadway House, Newtown Road,
Henley-on-Thames, Oxon RG9 1EN
Printed in Great Britain by
Unwin Brothers Limited,
Old Woking, Surrey

Library of Congress Cataloguing in Publication Data

Kean, P. M. (Patricia Margaret)
Chaucer and the making of English poetry.
Includes bibliographical references and index.
1. Chaucer, Geoffrey, d. 1400—Criticism and
interpretation. I. Title.
PR1924.K36   1982   821'.1   82–469

ISBN 0–7100–0898–8   AACR2

Contents

Plates

Preface

It will be obvious to anyone who reads this book that the debt it owes to previous writers on Chaucer is a very great one. It is easy to acknowledge particular obligations, but there remains a large and nebulous area, of which I can only say that the shape of these chapters would have been different if other critics had not been in the field before me. I have tried to keep the detailed tally of agreements and disagreements with other writers to the minimum – without, I hope, failing to acknowledge direct debts – because, where footnotes are in any case all too numerous, the piling up of such references can become irritating. I must, of course, add that not all agreements are necessarily plagiarisms; nor are all omissions of references which might have been useful deliberate. My copies of the voluminous bibliographies of works on Chaucer could well have Isidore of Seville's lines written on their fly-leaves:*

> Mentitur qui totum te legisse fatetur,
> Aut quis cuncta tua lector habere potest?

I have tried, too, to keep annotation within bounds by referring to the best starting point for further reading on any topic, where other references will be found collected. In the process, of course, I have necessarily omitted individual reference to many important books and papers. In dealing with quotations from Latin authors I have used English translations where the content only is of importance, but I have usually given the Latin text when the exact

* Inscribed above the cupboard containing the works of St Augustine in the library of Seville (Migne, *PL* 83, 1109).

wording is of interest or in cases where Chaucer knew, or might have known, the work. It will be appreciated that I have not been able to use work on Chaucer which has appeared since this book was sent to the press.

I owe a special debt to various friends who have made numerous suggestions and corrections, to say nothing of pupils with whom I have discussed many of the ideas. Miss E. G. W. Mackenzie and Mrs D. R. Sutherland have both helped me greatly by reading parts of my typescript, and by patiently answering innumerable questions. I also owe a great, but less definable, debt to the late Dorothy Everett. Here I can only acknowledge a pervading influence – I do not think that without it I should write about Chaucer as I have done. None of these friends, however, is to be held responsible for my mistakes – I must say, with Chaucer, that 'what I drye, or what I thynke, / I wil myselven al hyt drynke',* and the responsibility for the final form of the book, and for all its deficiencies, is my own.

My thanks are due to the Houghton Mifflin Company of Boston for permission to quote from *The Works of Geoffrey Chaucer*, edited by F. N. Robinson; to the editor of *Medium Aevum* for permission to use parts of a paper which originally appeared in that journal, in chapter 4; and to the following for permission to use photographs of manuscripts in their possession as illustrations: the Master and Fellows of Corpus Christi College, Cambridge; the Bibliothèque Nationale and the Bibliothèque de l'Arsenal, Paris; the Metropolitan Museum of Art, New York; and the Fitzwilliam Museum, Cambridge.

* *House of Fame*, 1879–80.

Preface to the shortened edition

This shortened edition aims at presenting in convenient and less expensive form those parts of the original edition which my experience as a teacher suggests are most useful to students. The method of reproduction has made it impossible to revise the text, and I have, therefore, apart from some shortening and simplification, not tried to put new references in the notes. To do so would have been to give the book a somewhat split personality. I have, however, added at the end of the notes a short list of the books on Chaucer published from 1972 onwards which seem to me of special interest. I should have liked to extend this list to include articles, but it would have become very long and unwieldy. It is, too, easy for anyone with access to a large library to use works like *The Year's Work in English Studies* which list, and in this case also discuss, the year's publications on Chaucer. It seems to me unlikely that anyone who does not use a library of this kind would want to extend their reading from books to periodicals.

Reference to the original, two-volume edition is given where necessary in the notes. The shortened version is not, in any sense, intended to cancel the longer one.

My thanks are again due to all those who are cited in the Preface to the original edition as giving permission for the use of quotations and photographs.

Abbreviations

CT   *Canterbury Tales* (passages quoted from F. N.
      Robinson, ed., *The Works of Geoffrey Chaucer*,
      2nd edn, 1957, Houghton Mifflin Co., Boston)

EETS Early English Text Society (O.S. = Old Series;
      E.S. = Extra Series)

ELH   *English Literary History*

MLN   *Modern Language Notes*

MPh   *Modern Philology*

OED   *The Oxford English Dictionary*

PL   J.-P. Migne, *Patrologiae Cursus Completus . . .*
      Series Latina

PMLA *Publications of the Modern Language Association of
      America*

RES   *Review of English Studies* (N.S. = New Series)

SATF Société des Anciens Textes Français

1

The urbane manner

Chaucer wrote poems of the kind he disowned in the *Retractions* as 'worldly vanitees' throughout his working life, if we can judge from our scanty information about the dates of composition of 'many a song and many a leccherous lay'. His probable last work is the frivolous (but not lecherous) *Complaint to his Purse*, dated, we can assume, between the coronation of Henry IV on 30 September 1399 and Chaucer's reception of a grant from the king on 3 October of the same year.[1] The Envoys to Scogan and to Bukton, both humorous and both concerned with love and marriage (among other things), also belong to the 1390s; that to Scogan has been dated 1393 and that to Bukton, 1396.[2] The other surviving short poems, most of them less personal, are not easy to date, but it is likely that they were scattered throughout the poet's career. *The Complaint to his Lady*, for example, shows Italian influence in its use of *terza rima* and belongs, therefore, to the period after the Italian journeys. The reference in the *Retractions* and also that in the Prologue to the *Legend of Good Women* to the writing of

> many a ympne for your halydayes,
> That highten balades, roundels, virelayes,[3]

support the impression that such poems were not just youthful exercises but continued to be written and to find favour with Chaucer's audience throughout his life.

Most of these poems are quite fairly to be called 'minor' or 'occasional' – terms which by no means fit the much greater scope and weight of the two more mature love visions, the *Parlement of*

Foules and the *House of Fame*. The third and, almost certainly, the earliest love vision, the *Book of the Duchess*,[4] was in fact written for a specific occasion and is less ambitious in plan than the other two. I shall, therefore, include it here among those poems which seem to me to have been the vehicle, above all, for the development of a new manner of writing in English – a manner which can best be characterized as 'urbane'. Urbanity, it is true, is to be found everywhere in Chaucer's writing, but we can see it most clearly evolving as a new poetic technique in the group of poems which have as their *raison d'être* the need to communicate directly with a clearly defined and known audience of a well-bred and sophisticated type.[5] In some of the short poems, especially in the two addressed to his actual friends, Bukton and Scogan, this sense of communication is both direct and vivid. To devise a humorous verse-letter to a friend in terms which give the illusion of the closest intimacy, while at the same time they also allow a like-minded and like-mannered audience to share both in the intimacy and in the joke, is something entirely new in English. This new kind of communication with the audience means two things for Chaucer in these shorter poems. First, and most striking and pleasing to a modern reader, it means the development and exploitation of a naturalistic, conversational manner. This manner, which, as we shall see, was to become the basis of much of his comic writing, is by no means absent from his mature serious works. Secondly, in poems which are also *divertissements* designed for a circle that, it is evident, shares with the poet certain definite expectations and experiences in literature, it means the use of accepted literary forms and topics. Since most of these are unknown in English before Chaucer, what poet and audience have in common to begin with is a taste for continental poetry, principally in French.[6] Experimentation and innovation on this basis were, no doubt, welcomed; it is notable that, throughout his life, Chaucer makes his adaptations from Italian in a way which would be intelligible to an audience that knew only French or English poetry. It is most unlikely that anyone else in England in his day – or at least in his audience – shared his first hand knowledge of the Italian poets.[7] His attempt at *terza rima*, for example, in the *Complaint to his Lady* is only one of many experiments with metrical forms in this group of poems, all of which would be of interest to those who knew of the virtuosity of contemporary French poetry in this respect.

2

It is, of course, by no means easy to define the relation of poet and audience in Chaucer's day, and much must be conjecture. We can only say that much of his work would be quite unintelligible unless we can regard it as a response to literary interests and enthusiasms which, no doubt, grew and perhaps altered as a result of his writing, but which must have existed to call it forth. If, as we may suppose, the latter part of the fourteenth century saw the development of an interest in poetry in English which was comparable to that of Italians in writing in their own language or even to the attitude of the Elizabethans to the work of their own age, then we can only say that they were fortunate in finding a poet perfectly equipped to foster and develop their taste. The greatest works, the *Troilus* and the whole elaborate structure of the *Canterbury Tales*, are uncompromising: the poet has the last word, and they must be taken or left as he has formed them. But in the short, often experimental, poems we can sense poet and audience working together, so that an occasion or a personality must often have given life to a work which may seem to us less successful than those in which Chaucer comes a little nearer to the fifteenth-century conception of him as a 'master' of poetry, to be looked up to and closely imitated. This, it is true, makes of these smaller works minor poetry, in the full sense of the term; but it must have been, in part at any rate, through the existence of minor poetry of this sort that the milieu was created in which the major works could grow and flourish.

The *Envoy to Scogan* provides a good example, towards the end of Chaucer's career, of this kind of poetic sensitivity, operating in both spheres – the naturalistic-familiar and the purely literary. It opens with a magnificent set-piece of the mock-sublime, somewhat reminiscent of the Squire's overambitious and abortive openings, but also, of course, within recognizable reach of Chaucer's serious proems in, for example, the *Troilus*:

> Tobroken been the statutz hye in hevene
> That creat were eternally to dure,
> Syth that I see the bryghte goddis sevene
> Mowe wepe and wayle, and passion endure,
> As may in erthe a mortal creature.
> Allas, fro whennes may thys thing procede,
> Of which errour I deye almost for drede?

By word eterne whilom was yshape
That fro the fyfte sercle, in no manere,
Ne myghte a drope of teeres doun escape,
But now so wepith Venus in hir spere
That with hir teeres she wol drenche us here.
Allas! Scogan, this is for thyn offence;
Thow causest this diluge of pestilence.

(1–14)

We are (if we can range ourselves for a moment with Chaucer's
original audience) at once lured into the comfortable position not
only of appreciating our own quick awareness of the force of the
conceit, but also our realization that its true significance lies in the
inappropriateness of all this cosmic magnificence to Scogan's
distressing tendency to 'hop alwey behinde' in 'the olde daunce',
and even, it appears in the next stanza, to forswear it altogether.

It is, perhaps, to labour the obvious, but it is true that in all this
there is a fundamental assumption that poet and audience share
two things: first, the same literary awareness – the same capability
to judge of the decorum of the passage; and, secondly, the same
standard of manners – the same feeling for the distance a joke can
go and remain friendly. Thus in the next two stanzas Chaucer
plays with the idea that both he and his friend are grey-haired
lovers – and, moreover, somewhat plump – in a way which takes the
jest just far enough and no further:

And, Scogan, though his bowe be nat broken,
He wol nat with his arwes been ywroken
On the, ne me, ne noon of oure figure;
We shul of him have neyther hurt ne cure.

Now certes, frend, I dreede of thyn unhap,
Lest for thy gilt the wreche of Love procede
On alle hem that ben hoor and rounde of shap,
That ben so lykly folk in love to spede.
Than shal we for oure labour han no mede;
But wel I wot, thow wolt answere and saye:
'Lo, olde Grisel lyst to ryme and playe!'

(25–35)

4

The last line gives Chaucer a transition to the theme, always a favourite one with him, of his own poetry; and while the balance between jest and earnest is still a delicate one, the tone deepens a little:

> Nay, Scogan, say not so, for I m'excuse –
> God helpe me so! – in no rym, dowteles,
> Ne thynke I never of slep to wake my muse,
> That rusteth in my shethe stille in pees.
> While I was yong, I put hir forth in prees;
> But al shal passe that men prose or ryme;
> Take every man hys turn, as for his tyme.
>
> (36–42)

This is a gentle, and ambiguous reminder of human and poetic mutability. In his lament for a maker Chaucer is more outspoken, but we feel the same fundamentally serious mood behind both passages:

> Fraunceys Petrak, the lauriat poete,
> Highte this clerk, whos rethorike sweete
> Enlumyned al Ytaille of poetrie,
> As Lynyan dide of philosophie,
> Or lawe, or oother art particuler;
> But deeth, that wol nat suffre us dwellen heer,
> But as it were a twynklyng of an ye,
> Hem bothe hath slayn, and alle shul we dye.
>
> (*CT* IV, 31–8)

The envoy brings the real point of the poem: 'Mynne thy frend, there it may fructyfye!' Scogan, 'that knelest at the stremes hed / Of grace, of alle honour and worthynesse', is in a position to bring advancement to his friend. The whole elaboration, in fact, preserves the illusion of the quick shifts in subject of inconsequent talk with a friend and at the same time lets us pleasantly down from the world of high literary allusion of the opening into that of practical affairs at the end.

This is a complex example of a poem in which the poet, the friend addressed and a wider but congenial and known audience all participate. Everywhere, however, in these minor poems we become

5

aware of the same familiar voice, inviting us to overhear and enjoy a conversation which is alive and vividly of the moment, but which also conforms to accepted standards:

> My maister Bukton, whan of Crist our kyng
> Was axed what is trouthe or sothfastnesse,
> He nat a word answerde to that axing,
> As who saith, 'No man is al trewe', I gesse.
> *(Envoy to Bukton, 1–4)*

> To yow, my purse, and to noon other wight
> Complayne I, for ye be my lady dere!
> I am so sory, now that ye been lyght . . .
> *(Complaint to his Purse, 1–3)*

> Nas never pyk walwed in galauntyne
> As I in love am walwed and ywounde,
> For which ful ofte I myself devyne
> That I am trewe Tristam the secounde.
> *(To Rosemounde, 17–20)*

> But what availeth such a long sermoun
> Of aventures of love, up and doun?
> I wol returne and speken of my peyne:
> The poynt is this, of my distruccioun . . .
> *(Complaint of Mars, 209–12)*

> Adam scriveyn, if ever it thee bifalle
> Boece or Troylus for to wryten newe,
> Under thy long lokkes thou most have the scalle,
> But after my makyng thou wryte more trewe;
> So ofte a-daye I mot thy werk renewe,
> It to correcte and eek to rubbe and scrape;
> And al is thorugh thy negligence and rape.
> *(Chaucers Wordes unto Adam, his Owne Scriveyn)*

This is a plain, colloquial, sometimes blunt, conversational style. It is the style which Chaucer uses for most of his characters of high rank – for example in the *Knight's Tale* and the *Troilus* except, as we have seen, on the occasions when they address ladies as suppliant lovers. This situation calls for the use of another style, which an earlier English romance – *The Lay of Havelok the Dane* – calls 'speken of luuedrurye',[8] and the author of *Sir Gawain and the Green Knight* 'talkyng noble'. How far this was a purely literary device, proper to poems about love designed for courtly circles, or how far it was actually practised, we cannot tell. In the Elizabethan period, it would appear, some elaborate literary styles were actually carried over into fashionable speech, and the same may have been true of court circles in Chaucer's day. The minor poems, at any rate, make much use of this style: the Complaints, the poem to Rosemounde and *Wommanly Noblesse* all reflect the fashion, with varying degrees of seriousness. The opening of the latter provides a good example:

> So hath myn herte caught in remembraunce
> Your beaute hoole and stidefast governaunce,
> Your vertues alle and your hie noblessse,
> That you to serve is set al my plesaunce,
> So wel me liketh your womanly contenaunce,
> Your fresshe fetures and your comlynesse,
> That whiles I live, myn herte to his maystresse
> You hath ful chose in trewe perséveraunce
> Never to chaunge, for no maner distresse.
>
> (*Wommanly Noblesse*, 1–9)

This is writing in 'thise . . . termes alle / That in swich cas thise loveres alle seche' (*Troilus*, II, 1067–8), and we may, if we choose, condemn the poem as somewhat dull and uninspired. The same, however, is true of Troilus's formal utterances as a lover here in Book II, or even face to face with his mistress, for example in Book III, 106 ff. The point of the use of the style in the *Troilus* is, of course, that it is dramatically justified. Troilus *is* one of 'thise loveres', and he only speaks in character. The same defence holds for the minor poems, though it will not give them permanency or raise their absolute value. Their justification lies in the occasion for which they were written; they exist as part of an agreeable exchange between poet and audience, which forms their context just as much as the totality of the poem forms the context for Troilus's speeches of love. As such, these poems must have succeeded and must have given pleasure; but, like all occasional poetry, their range is necessarily limited to an audience which accepts and shares in the convention. They are not, however, to be dismissed as bad 'lyrics' or failures to achieve art of a more ambitious kind. On the contrary, they perfectly fulfil a function which is primarily social, and which poetry is now no longer called on to fulfil – perhaps to its ultimate loss.

Not all the short poems were concerned with love. There was also a fashion for moral or philosophical *ballades*, which demonstrates that poet and audience, besides their interest in love and in light conversation, had intellectual interests in common.[9] This fashion is well attested in both France – where, for example, Deschamps contributed many poems in a style which probably provides the model for Chaucer's[10] – and in England – where, besides Chaucer, Gower wrote the *Cinkante Balades* (in French) and the Scottish and English Chaucerians took up the genre. Chaucer's achievement in his poems of this type – *The Former Age, Fortune, Truth, Gentilesse, Lak of Stedfastnesse* are all that survive, although similar themes are important in the *Complaint of Mars* – is to carry into this kind the same ease and familiarity in the conversational style which we have found characteristic of his less serious short poems. He uses an undogmatic way of writing, in which a philosophical point or a moral *sentence* is put forward for general consideration. No hard and fast conclusion is necessarily reached, though it may suggest itself to the experienced reader, and the total impression is of a free and equal interchange between poet and audience.

Sometimes, it is true, a more emphatic note is sounded. *Truth* achieves a metrical control in the imperative mood which is hardly to be met with again before the close of the sixteenth century in, for example, the poetry of Sir Walter Ralegh:

> Her is non hoom, her nis but wildernesse:
> Forth, pilgrim, forth! Forth, beste, out of thy stal!
> Know thy contree, look up, thank God of al;
> Hold the heye wey, and lat thy gost thee lede.
>
> (17–20)

The main theme, however, usually dealt with in a more leisurely way, is that of the consolation of philosophy, developed, inevitably, in Boethian terms, but with overtones of the familiar Senecan style and, I think, with the use of subject matter often more characteristic of Seneca than of Boethius.

Both Deschamps and Chaucer, in the short moral poems, use a

style which is unlike the rather discursive one of Boethius, but which is very reminiscent of the short, pithy, familiarly turned, and at times epigrammatic, sentences of Seneca. The resemblance might, of course, be accidental and due to the shortness of the *ballades* and the need to fit the thought to the verse line and the limits of stanza form. As far as subject matter is conerned there is, too, a considerable overlap between Boethius and Seneca. Both transmit the Stoic ideal of the philosophical good man who triumphs, by his inner victory over himself, over fortune and mutability. The *de Consolatione Philosophiae* however, is necessarily closely organized round Fortune as its main topic, while Seneca, in the short moral epistles and essays, discusses a wider range of topics – among them the advantages of poverty, the right attitude to riches, moderation and self-rule. All these are compatible with Boethius's thought, but are not always given separate or extensive treatment by him. As we shall see, while it has puzzled critics to find close parallels to *Truth* in Boethius, it is quite easy to do so in the writings of Seneca. These were equally available and popular in Chaucer's day, and there is no reason to suppose that he had not actually read an author to whom he refers more than once.

Both *Truth* and *Fortune* provide good examples of this style and these themes:

> Tempest thee noght al croked to redresse,
> In trust of hir that turneth as a bal;
> Gret reste stant in litel besinesse;
> Be war also to sporne ayeyns an al;
> Stryve not, as doth the crokke with the wal.
> Daunte thyself, that dauntest otheres dede,
> And trouthe thee shal delivere, it is no drede.
>
> (*Truth*, 8–14)

> Yit is me left the light of my resoun,
> To knowen frend fro fo in thy mirour
> So muchel hath yit thy whirling up and doun
> Ytaught me for to knowen in an hour.
> But trewely, no force of thy reddour
> To him that over himself hath the maystrye!
> My suffisaunce shal be my socour;
> But fynally, Fortune, I thee defye!
>
> (*Fortune*, 9–16)

9

Deschamps expresses himself in much the same way, though there are important differences. We could, for example, compare:

> Je ne requier a Dieu fors qu'il me doint
> En ce monde lui servir et loer,
> Vivre pour moy, cote entiere ou pourpoint,
> Aucun cheval pour mon labour porter,
> Et que je puisse mon estat gouverner
> Moiennement, en grace, sans envie,
> Sanz trop avoir et sanz pain demander,
> Car au joir d'ui est la plus seure vie.
>
> *(Balade* ccxl, 1–8)

This is, again, the Stoic ideal of an independent moderation, which is not, in fact, the same as the Christian one of patient poverty in the service of God.[11] Deschamps, through his opening lines, does, however, attempt to link it to the Christian service of God, and this is characteristic of his attitude in his *ballades*.[12] Chaucer, however, although some of the proverb-type sentences of *Truth* are derived from the Bible,[13] does not overtly attempt to Christianize the Stoic good man who has passed beyond the reach of Fortune. In *Fortune* as in the *Book of the Duchess*,[14] he puts forward Socrates as the supreme instance of such a man:

> O Socrates, thou stidfast champioun,
> She never mighte be thy tormentour;
> Thou never dreddest hir oppressioun,
> Ne in hir chere founde thou no savour.
> Thou knewe wel the deceit of hir colour,
> And that hir moste worshipe is to lye.
>
> (17–22)

Chaucer is probably remembering the *Roman de la Rose* (5845–50) here; but there is no reason why he should not also be aware of Seneca's repeated use of Socrates as the type of the man whose resignation is perfect and unshaken in the face of the worst that Fortune can do.[15]

The first stanza of *Truth* is particularly Senecan in its ideas:

> Flee fro the prees, and dwelle with sothfastnesse,
> Suffyce unto thy good, though it be smal . . .
> Savour no more than thee bihove shal;
> Reule wel thyself, that other folk canst rede;
> And trouthe thee shal delivere, it is no drede.
>
> (1–7)

It is not, of course, necessary to seek specific 'sources' in Seneca for these lines: it is rather that Chaucer (and, it would seem, the fashionable French poets of his day) writes from a general knowledge and recollection of his characteristic ideas. Thus, the first line of *Truth* contains the same idea as the seventh of the *Epistulae Morales*:[16]

> Quid tibi vitandam praecipue existimes, quaeris? Turbam.
>
> (Do you ask me what you should regard as especially to be avoided? I say crowds.)

The opening of the next epistle is even closer:

> 'Tu me', inquis, 'vitare turbam iubes secedere et conscientia esse contentum?'
>
> ('Do you bid me,' you say, 'shun the throng and withdraw from men, and be content with my own conscience?')

The next line is an imitation of the following Latin sentence:

> Si res tue tibi non sufficiant, fac ut rebus tuis sufficias.
>
> (If your goods don't accommodate you, accommodate yourself to your goods.)

Now this does not derive from Seneca, although it is entirely in keeping with his teaching, but from the *de Nugis Philosophorum* of Caecilius Balbus. The same sentence is quoted by Gower ir the *Confessio Amantis*, V, 7735 ff.; and there it is glossed in the margin as being from Seneca.[17] It may be, therefore, that Chaucer was not only using a tag thoroughly Senecan in tone, but one which he actually thought of as by Seneca. The rather similar idea of the next line is, again a common one in Seneca. Epistle xlii pursues it at length, especially in paragraph 6:

Hoc itaque in his, quae adfectamus, ad quae labore magno contendimus, inspicere debemus, aut nihil in illis commodi esse aut plus incommodi. Quaedam supervacua sunt, quaedam tanti non sunt.

(Therefore, with regard to the objects which we pursue and for which we strive with great effort, we should note this truth; either there is nothing desirable in them, or the undesirable is preponderant. Some objects are superfluous; others are not worth the price we pay for them.)

This epistle ends with a reference to the idea of self-rule:

Qui se habet, nihil perdidit. Sed quoto cuique habere se contingit?

(He that owns himself has lost nothing. But how few men are blessed with the ownership of self!)

Epistle viii recommends philosophy (Chaucer's 'truth') as of more value than the gifts of fortune. Epistle ii, paragraph 1, discusses 'besinesse' – another favourite subject of Seneca's:[18]

Non discurris nec locorum mutationibus inquietaris. Aegri animi ista iactatio est. Primum argumentum conpositae mentis existimo posse consistere et secum morari.

(You do not run hither and thither and distract yourself by changing your abode; for such restlessness is the sign of a disordered spirit. The primary indication, to my thinking, of a well-ordered mind, is a man's ability to remain in one place and linger in his own company.)

It would be possible to multiply examples of correspondences in thought, if not in expression, between Chaucer's moral poems and Seneca's writings. What is, I think, most interesting about these correspondences is that, for Chaucer, such ideas provided not only the basis for short epigrammatic poems in the familiar style, but also for much that he incorporates in his longer works, especially the *Troilus* and the *Knight's Tale*. Some understanding of the moral and philosophical themes pursued with such urbanity in the short poems, and of their background, is, therefore, of great importance to our understanding of the major works.

to a poetic activity which was, above all, social. Some are directed
at known persons, although they are to be shared by a wider circle.
Others, like the *Complaint of Mars*, are not occasional in this sense,
but are designed to give pleasure through the satisfaction of well-
known and clearly defined tastes and interests. To say of the Squire
'He koude songes make and wel endite' is to state a social accom-
plishment and a reason for popularity in a certain circle. From
Chaucer, as a professed poet, something more ambitious was obviously expected, in the form of longer and more elaborate *divertissements*. There is no reason to believe that these were not aimed at the
same circle which accepted and enjoyed the greater and more
independent works; but, like Lydgate after him, Chaucer continued
throughout his life to satisfy the more intimate taste for the smaller
things.

The *Book of the Duchess*, among the minor poems, impresses me as
Chaucer's longest and most successful essay in pure urbanity.
This is a judgement, however, with which by no means all critics
would agree. For Muscatine, as we have seen, there is discordance
in the range and variation of the style; and for some readers the
subject matter and its handling also seem discrepant.[21] I have
suggested that much of the variation in style can be accounted for
by Chaucer's use of a common narrative idiom. The problem of
subject matter, and the wider issues of its treatment in the *Book of
the Duchess*, cannot be understood without considering the nature
and aims of the poem as a whole. It is a love vision and owes much
to French handling of the genre. But it is also, it seems to me,
a poem in which Chaucer does two important things. In the first
place he develops and sustains the scope of the easy, civil, conversational method within a pleasantly literary, but not too dramatic
form: this method we found to be characteristic of the minor poems.
In the second place, something else evolves, which was of the
greatest importance to Chaucer as a narrative poet and which was
to be eagerly imitated:[22] this characteristic, necessarily absent from
the small-scale poems, was the ability to give a vivid impression,
not only of the persons of the narrative themselves, but also of their
relations to each other within the wider setting of the society of
which they form a part. The reader, in fact, is able to experience
the sensitive and yet controlled contact between human beings,

arising out of the personalities before us and their immediate situation, but conditioned by and fitted to the special demands and special manners of the world to which they belong. This is what is new and striking in the *Book of the Duchess*, in its precise and realistic handling of the encounter between the Dreamer and the Man in Black. It is an encounter – provided, of course, that we accept the traditional interpretation of the poem – between two persons of predetermined, known standing and relationship. The Dreamer, the reflection of Chaucer the poet and civil servant, is an ordinary person – a 'wyght' (530) – while the Man in Black, called a 'knight' and addressed at all times with great respect and caution by the Dreamer, is the image of a great and powerful prince, well able either to harm or advance the real Chaucer. We know from the facts of Chaucer's life that he had every opportunity of meeting John of Gaunt in person. We cannot tell whether he actually formed a definite relationship with him, either of friendship or patronage, but the fact remains that, through his position as a young man in the household of the Countess of Ulster, Chaucer became a part of the kind of society to which John of Gaunt belonged and was trained to appreciate and participate in the nuances of its manners and characteristic behaviour.[23] The basic situation of the poem, then, is a meeting between two people of fundamentally different origins and social status, who are yet bound together through the fact that each has his appointed place in a social scheme which had plenty of room for both. This provides for a constant tension between the areas of experience in which they meet as equals and those in which established convention decrees that they do not – and this results in a subtle interplay of respect and caution, combined with a surprising degree of directness when they find themselves on common ground.

Chaucer's greatest achievement in this field of complicated social relationships is undoubtedly the way in which in the *Troilus*, largely through the medium of the figure of Pandarus, he builds up a picture of the world of Troy as a close social unit, which does more to condition the development of the love story than the stars ever did. It is also, of course, one of the many reasons why the comic tales are more than mere hilarious anecdotes – although the churl's world is necessarily more limited in extent, and less subtle in its reactions and interactions, it is still densely structured. Even in minor episodes this kind of perceptiveness is often of great structural importance. In the *Squire's Tale*, for example, it is the familiarity with which

members of the crowd treat each other which anchors the im-
probabilities of the story in a more sober world – and also, on
another level, helps to cast something of a gently ironic light over
both the fairy tale and the youthful exuberance of the Squire:

> 'Myn herte,' quod oon, 'is everemoore in drede; . . .'
> Another rowned to his felawe lowe,
> And seyde, 'He lyeth, for it is rather lyk
> An apparence ymaad by som magyk . . .'
>   Another answerde, and seyde it myghte wel be
> Naturelly, by composiciouns
> Of anglis and of slye reflexiouns . . .
>
> $\qquad\qquad\qquad\qquad\qquad$ (*CT* V, 212–30)

Or, again, in the *House of Fame*, towards the end, the Dreamer's
momentary contact with a very ordinary person, obviously of
his own rank, with whom he has a civil but commonplace exchange,
plays an important part in a denouement which very thoroughly
completes the progression from the world of the great poets of
the past, represented by the summary of the *Aeneid*, to that of
'shipmen and pilgrimes, / With scrippes bret-ful of lesinges'.[24]

> With that y gan aboute wende,
> For oon that stood ryght at my bak,
> Me thoughte, goodly to me spak,
> And seyde, 'Frend, what is thy name?
> Artow come hider to han fame?'
> 'Nay, for sothe, frend,' quod y . . .
>
> $\qquad\qquad\qquad\qquad\qquad$ (1868–73)

The conversation continues on the same easy terms up to line
1915 and does much to emphasize that the poem has now left
Jove's eagle – a bird of more arbitrary habits of speech, standing
in a less natural relation to the Dreamer – behind.

  This kind of perception, so familiar to us from much later developments in narrative art, particularly in the novel, is almost entirely
lacking in earlier English narrative poetry, in spite of its undoubted
realism. It is not, of course, absent from contemporary French
literature, but I do not think that it would be easy to parallel in any
French love vision either the structural function of the relationship

between the Dreamer and the Man in Black or the complexity with which it is described.[25] Some idea of the difference can perhaps be given by a glance at the passage from Machaut's *Jugement dou Roy de Behaingne*[26] on which, it is generally agreed, Chaucer based his account of the meeting of the Dreamer and the Man in Black and, indeed, the whole opening of the dream in the *Book of the Duchess*. In Machaut's poem the matter is somewhat differently organized, since the poet-dreamer does not play a part in the dialogue which takes place between a solitary and sorrowful lady and a knight 'de moult trés noble arroy'. The situation is thus, from the start, a more expected and conventional one than that of Chaucer's poem: the relation between knight and lady explains itself to the experienced reader without the need of much elaboration on the poet's part. Nor is the lady such a strikingly tragic figure as the Man in Black. Her solitude is mitigated by a 'chiennet' and a 'pucelette', and there are none of the severe symptoms of bodily weakness, described in uncompromisingly medical terms, from which Chaucer's mourner suffers:

Mais tout einsi, com je me delitoie
En son trés dous chanter que j'escoutoie,
Je vi venir par une estroite voie,
   Pleinne d'erbette,
Une dame pensant, toute seulette
Fors d'un chiennet et d'une pucelette;
Mais bein sambloit sa maniere simplette
   Pleinne d'anoy.
Et d'autre part, un petit loing de moy,
Uns chevaliers de moult trés noble arroy
Tout le chemin venoit encontre soy
   Sans compaingnie;
Si me pensay qu'amis yert et amie,
Lors me boutay par dedens la feuillie
Si embrunchiez qu'il ne me virent mie.
   Mais quant amis,
En qui Nature assez de biens a mis,
Fu aprochiez de la dame de pris
Com gracieus, sages et bien apris
   La salua.

Et la dame que pensée argua,
Sans riens respondre a li, le trespassa.
Et cils tantost arriere rappassa,
      Et se la prist
Par le giron, et doucement li dist:
'Trés douce dame, avez vous en despit
Le mien salut?' Et quant elle le vit,
      Se respondi
En souspirant, que plus n'i attendi:
'Certes, sire, pas ne vous entendi
Pour mon penser qui le me deffendi;
      Mais se j'ay fait
Riens ou il et villenie ou meffait,
Veuilliez le moy pardonner, s'il vous plait.'
Li chevaliers, sans faire plus de plait,
      Dist doucement:
'Dame, il n'affiert ci nul pardonnement,
Car il n'y a meffait ne mautalent:
Mais je vous pri que vostre pensement
      Me veuilliez dire.'
Et la dame parfondement souspire
Et dist: 'Pour Dieu, laissiez m'en pais, biau sire;
Car mestier n'ay que me faciez plus d'ire
      Ne de contraire
Que j'en recoy.' Et cils se prist a traire
Plus près de li, pour sa pensée attraire,
Et li a dit: 'Trés douce debonnaire,
      Triste vous voy.
Mais je vous jur et promet par ma foy,
S'a moy volez descouvrir vostre anoy,
Que je feray tout le pooir de moy
      De l'adrecier.'
Et la dame l'en prist a merciër,
Est dist: 'Sire, nuls ne m'en puet aidier . . .'

                (41–94)

and so the dialogue continues until she is persuaded to relate her grief.

Neither party to this dialogue can really be accused of 'making it quaint'; and the possibility of 'making it tough' is of course entirely excluded by the nature of the pair.[27] The degree of tension in Chaucer's dialogue, where we are kept aware of the difference in status between the speakers, one of whom is a great enough man to be approached with a blend of daring and caution as well as with courtesy by the Dreamer, is therefore neither aimed at nor achieved in Machaut's. It is of interest here to compare another passage, in the *Dit dou Vergier*,[28] where Machaut's Dreamer does approach one of the figures of the Dream, who turns out to be the God of Love, with a similar blend of feelings. His misgivings are allayed, in much the same way as Chaucer's Dreamer's, by the courtesy of the reply he gets:

> Mais cils qui sëoit au deseure
> Seur l'arbre entreprist le parler
> Et encommença a parler,
> Et me rendi si doucement
> Mon salu, que le hardement
> Qui estoit en moy tous perdus
> Me fu par son parler rendus.
>
> (212–18)

Chaucer's Dreamer says very much the same:

> Loo! how goodly spak thys knyght,
> As hit had be another wyght;
> He made hyt nouther towgh ne queynte.
> And I saw that, and gan me aqueynte
> With hym, and fond hym so tretable,
> Ryght wonder skylful and resonable,
> As me thoghte, for al hys bale.
>
> (529–35)

The difference, it seems to me, is that, for Chaucer, the passage serves a structural purpose – it is a definite part of the evolution of the dialogue, which in turn is the vehicle of much of the significant content of the poem. For Machaut, it is part of the description of the gracious God of Love. Dialogue, it turns out, is not important in the *Dit* as a whole, which largely consists of indefatigable self-descriptive speeches on the part of the deity. Lastly the relation of the god and his worshipper is self-evident; and, again, of little structural importance in the poem. It is, too, not a relation which has any 'real' meaning – that is, it does not, like that of the Dreamer and the Man in Black, reflect any of the complexities of the natural world.

Again, the variety of style and diction, which Chaucer can use to express a more complicated situation, is hardly possible to the French poet. In the *Jugement*, the lady must be addressed with uniform gentleness by a knight 'de moult trés noble arroy'. We may perhaps detect a slight sharpness in her 'laissiez m'en pais', but this is not a note that is at all sustained.

Chaucer, therefore, makes a very free adaptation of his French model and is bound by it neither in the overall plan of the situation nor in style. In fact, we could say that while smoothness and uniformity of treatment is characteristic of the French passage, Chaucer, on the other hand, makes a point of contrasts. The figure of the fainting Man in Black is an abrupt invasion of the idyllic landscape; the appearance of a beautiful lady, however sad, with a little dog and a little maid to accompany her, even before she meets a knight fully equipped to take charge of the situation, is not really disturbing. It is not, of course, the case that Machaut never disturbs. There is much in the *Jugement dou Roy de Navarre*, for example, which is extremely disturbing – but this is, overall, a poem of a different sort, with its own consistency.

The love vision, in fact, as the French poets handle it, is not designed to carry a great weight either of meaning or of feeling. The *Roman de la Rose* continuation contains a great variety of material, much of it serious; and Gower successfully imitates this variety in the *Confessio Amantis*, a poem built on as large a scale as the *Roman*. Chaucer, on the contrary, keeps the graceful, manageable proportions of the love vision as he found it in the work of Machaut or Froissart. In the Prologue to the *Legend of Good Women*, especially, he gives us a perfect example of the advantages of a restricted content coupled with graceful treatment. Increasingly, however, as we shall see in the case of the *Parlement of Foules* and the *House of Fame*, he extends the range of the content and the variety of feeling and meaning to be expressed, with the result that it is a curious and unexpected fact of literary history that Chaucer actually used the essentially stylized form of the love vision to develop characteristics which are more typical of naturalism. This was not what the form as a whole, traditionally and even in Chaucer's own hands, was aimed at. It does not, for example, depend on the development of naturalistic, consecutive narrative order: the choice of the dream as a framework for what little story there is allows of a good deal of arbitrary scene-shifting. The main theme is usually a simple statement or situation, not a development involving naturalistically conceived characters in a continuous action. The slight story of the *Book of the Duchess* comes nearer to our idea of the naturalistic treatment of characters in action than do most of the love visions, but in the *Parlement* and the *House of Fame*, as the weight of content increases, so Chaucer actually decreases the realism of his handling of the narrative as a whole, although he increases it greatly in the treatment of incidents and details. This, however, is to anticipate.

The *Book of the Duchess*, indeed, is linked to actuality in so far as it is an elegy; it mourns the death of a real person and offers consolation to her husband, who, only slightly disguised, is brought within the frame of the poem as one of the protagonists. It has, thus, much in common with the shorter poems we have been considering – the poet writes of and to someone known to him, with whom he stands in a definite relationship; but he writes in such a way that a wider circle can share their communication. The choice of the love vision for the form of his poem actually aids such communication; it is a form in which a courtly circle can be assumed to take pleasure; it is known as a suitable vehicle for fine and serious, though not exalted or disproportionately intense, writing; it traditionally uses dreams and disguises and thus lends itself to the humane distancing of grief which is a necessary part of the consolation, as well as of conversational good manners. As we have seen, Chaucer brings to the French form an additional intimacy and variety of style which, particularly in the dialogue, gives him the chance of developing the relationship of the protagonists with great subtlety and flexibility.

Chaucer begins the poem, as he does his other two love visions, with an introductory section in which he writes of himself, his sleep, and his dreams. He addresses his audience familiarly and abruptly, very much in the manner of the short poems and, in this case, in close imitation of the opening lines of Froissart's *Paradys d'Amour*:[29]

> I have gret wonder, be this lyght,
> How that I lyve, for day ne nyght
> I may nat slepe wel nygh noght;
> I have so many an ydel thoght,

> Purely for defaute of slep,
> That, by my trouthe, I take no kep
> Of nothing, how hyt cometh or gooth . . .
>
> (1–7)

He continues for some fifty lines in this vein, in a passage dominated by the constantly repeated word 'sleep',[30] and by words denoting sorrow and sickness – 'sorowe', 'sorwful', 'melancolye', 'drede', 'hevynesse', 'sicknesse'. But, as a kind of counterpoint to these ominous words, counteracting any tragic effect they might have, the whole passage maintains an easy, conversational tone, avoiding both outright humour and an exclusive concentration on personal emotion, which, in the context would be unmannerly and overserious.

> For there is phisicien but oon
> That may me hele; but that is don.
> Passe we over untill eft;
> That wil not be mot nede be left;
> Our first mater is good to kepe.
>
> (39–43)

Chaucer, in fact, holds his audience's attention for the description of his uneasy, sorrowful state as the very opposite to the Ancient Mariner – his art ensures that they will not escape him, but he deals pleasantly with his troubles and suggests that they belong to a world in which consolation is not impossible – where a 'spirit of quycknesse' and of 'lustyhede' (24–5), though extinguished for the moment, may be rekindled, and where there are physicians capable of healing if they will.

This opening is important because, through its style and content, it sets the tone of the poem as a whole and shows us what Chaucer is about. He writes of grief which exists and which is pitiful and serious, but which is only one aspect of the world. It is, too, grief softened by recollection and told to others – it is not the urgent and personal outcry of immediate suffering, which he gives us in the *Troilus* and in the *Knight's Tale*. It is, in fact, grief brought down to a sympathetic and intimate conversational level, which allows for a modulation not, it seems to me, to the purely comic (which could not fail to be discordant) but to a tone of pleasant apology to a friend – the good manners which ensure that the communication is not permitted to become too painful.

The introduction leads into the story of Ceix and Alcyone, since it is related in the book which Chaucer finally takes up to while away his sleeplessness. This is a sad story of the death of kings, and of an inconsolable wife who is unable to live with her sorrow. The actual story is plainly and soberly told; and Chaucer suppresses the ending, which he must have known from Ovid, in which the parted lovers are reunited as sea-birds. Death is final, as Ceix tells Alcyone:

> 'For, certes, swete, I nam but ded;
> Ye shul me never on lyve yse . . .
> To lytel while oure blysse lasteth!'
>
> (204–11)

As part of the consolation, the story merely makes the point that bereavement is not a unique experience, but is shared with all mankind, and even with the great kings of the past. Emotionally it preserves and deepens the sorrowful tone of the opening and gives a more objective and uncomplicated, though still distanced and muted presentation of grief:

> Anon her herte began to erme;
> And for that her thoughte evermo
> It was not wele [he dwelte] so,
> She longed so after the king
> That, certes, it were a pitous thing
> To telle her hertely sorowful lif
> That she had, this noble wif,
> For him she loved alderbest.
>
> (80–7)

Alcyone's feelings rise in a gentle crescendo from an uneasiness comparable to the narrator's in the opening section, to outright sorrow; and even this is presented to the reader in the most tolerable terms – it is the feeling of a 'noble wif' and arises from her true and loyal love for her husband. In fact, as in the opening, the positive aspects of life are tactfully brought forward and juxtaposed to its more sorrowful ones – 'To lytel while oure blysse lasteth'; but we may expect some bliss.

The simple narrative of the Queen's loss and her sorrow and death is extended by a long passage describing the intervention of the gods: briefly, Juno, in answer to Alcyone's prayer for information concerning her husband's fate, sends a messenger to the Cave of Sleep to obtain a dream, through which Alcyone may learn the truth. Chaucer maintains the easy, conversational, and at times colloquial tone throughout this passage. Juno commands her messenger in familiar terms:[31]

> 'Go bet,' quod Juno, 'to Morpheus, –
> Thou knowest hym wel, the god of slep,
> Now understond wel, and take kep!
> Sey thus on my half, . . .'
>
> (136–9)

The arrival of the messenger, and his difficulty in awakening the God of Sleep, takes the same technique to the verge of outright comedy:

> This messager com fleynge faste
> And cried, 'O, ho! awake anoon!'
> Hit was for noght; there herde hym non.
> 'Awake!' quod he, 'whoo ys lyth there?'
> And blew his horn ryght in here eere,
> And cried 'Awaketh!' wonder hyë.
> This god of slep with hys oon yë
> Cast up, axed, 'Who clepeth ther?'
> 'Hyt am I,' quod this messager . . .
>
> (178–86)

It may be that in this passage Chaucer misjudged his effect, and that he allowed the complex and subtle attitude to his subject matter, which he has maintained so far with success, to harden into mere poking fun. On the other hand, our comprehension of his colloquialisms may be at fault. To take one certain case: 'Hyt am I', which may seem, to an age used to the telephone, a peculiarly pointless and maddening response was, to judge from Chaucer's use of it elsewhere, common form in polite but familiar conversation in his day.[32] Nevertheless the tone of the whole description is a light one, and it contrasts sharply, in its enjoyment in the elaboration of improbable detail, with the bare references to the King's corpse:

> Seys body the kyng,
> That lyeth ful pale and nothyng rody;
> (142–3)

and:

> Took up the dreynte body sone
> And bar hyt forth to Alcione.
> (195–6)

There is no decoration or elaboration over the core of the story, but Chaucer does allow himself, and his audience, a little light relief when it comes to the marvels of the land of sleep. And he continues to elaborate on the theme of sleep in much the same way in the next section, in which, much struck by the account of 'the goddes of slepyng' (230) which he has just read, he determines to profit by the example of Queen Alcyone, whose vows brought her sleep, and to promise:

> I wil yive hym the alderbeste
> Yifte that ever he abod hys lyve.
> And here on warde, ryght now, as blyve,
> Yif he wol make me slepe a lyte,
> Of down of pure dowves white
> I wil yive hym a fether-bed,
> Rayed with gold, and ryght wel cled
> In fyn blak satyn doutremer,
> And many a pilowe, and every ber
> Of cloth of Reynes, to slepe softe.
> (246–55)

No sooner are the words spoken than sleep comes to him and with it:

> so ynly swete a sweven,
> So wonderful, that never yit
> Y trowe, no man had the wyt
> To konne wel my sweven rede.
> (276–9)

A pattern begins to emerge. The sadness of the story of Ceix and Alcyone has been set aside, and Chaucer concentrates on another part of the tale – on the healing powers of sleep. Like Alcyone's, however, his sleep is to be visited by a dream of sorrow. But we are not to think of the sorrow as entirely bitter or unalloyed. The dream will be 'ynly swete' and will have a deeper meaning than one might at first imagine. In fact, this whole section maintains the impression of a sorrow, seen and pondered over from a little distance, which is also part of a wider scheme, and which, in the long run, does admit of consolation.

The dream itself is set in all the brightness of a May morning, with sunshine and birdsong. Its first scene, after the Dreamer has left his bed, is a hunt through a green and flowery woodland. It is, the Dreamer is told, the Emperor Octovyen who is pursuing the hart. The hunt, however is unsuccessful:

> and so, at the laste
> This hert rused, and staal away
> Fro alle the houndes a privy way.
> The houndes had overshote hym alle,
> And were on a defaute yfalle.
> Therwyth the hunte wonder faste
> Blew a forloyn at the laste.
>
> (380–6)

It seems quite likely that in describing this loss of the 'hert' (hart) Chaucer intends a punning preparation for the loss he is about to describe which concerns the 'herte' (heart). The chase as a figure of the pursuit of love is, after all, a commonplace.[33] Certainly the lack of success of the hunt helps to maintain, even within the beauty of the dream, the feeling of uneasiness which dominated the opening. It also, since it is not, after all, an irremediable loss, helps to keep grief at a distance. The Dreamer wanders on through the wood and it is only at line 445 that he finally meets the main personage of the poem, the Man in Black.

In his dealings with the Man in Black, the Dreamer has been accused by some critics of clumsiness and lack of tact.[34] As it seems to me that the effect is the very reverse of this, and that it is here that Chaucer's urbane manner, in the sense in which I have been using the term, is most fully developed, it will be necessary to look

carefully at this section of the poem. In the first place, the Dreamer
has been accused of obtuseness and failure to comprehend the sorrow
before him. Now, Chaucer devotes a long passage to making it
clear that his Dreamer does in fact know, first, how great the sorrow
is, and secondly, exactly what has caused it. In the course of his
description of the Man in Black, the Dreamer comments:

> Hit was gret wonder that Nature
> Myght suffre any creature
> To have such sorwe, and be not ded.
>
> (467–9)

And he also overhears the mourner's 'compleynte', which has no
ambiguity about it:

> 'I have of sorwe so gret won
> That joye gete I never non,
> Now that I see my lady bryght,
> Which I have loved with al my myght,
> Is fro me ded and ys agoon.
>   Allas, deth, what ayleth the,
> That thou noldest have taken me,
> Whan thou toke my lady swete,
> That was so fair, so fresh, so fre,
> So good, that men may wel se
> Of al goodnesse she had no mete!'
>
> (475–86)

The Man in Black is reduced to a state of considerable physiological
danger:

> Hys sorwful hert gan faste faynte,
> And his spirites wexen dede;
> The blood was fled for pure drede
> Doun to hys herte to make hym warm –
> For wel hyt feled the herte had harm –
> To wite eke why hit was adrad
> By kynde, and for to make hyt glad;
>
> (488–94)

It is at this dangerous moment, while nature is struggling to reassert control over the mourner's bodily mechanisms,[35] that the Dreamer intervenes.

The stages by which contact is established are carefully described. At first the Man in Black is not even aware of the Dreamer's presence – his preoccupation and bodily weakness 'Made hym that he herde me noght' (510). Then, as he does become conscious that he is being spoken too, the attitudes and good manners of both characters are delicately but clearly depicted:

> But at the last, to sayn ryght soth,
> He was war of me, how y stood
> Before hym, and did of myn hood,
> And had ygret hym as I best koude,
> Debonayrly, and nothyng lowde.
> He sayde, 'I prey the, be not wroth.
> I herde the not, to seyn the soth,
> Ne I sawgh the not, syr, trewely.'
> 'A, goode sir, no fors,' quod y,
> 'I am ryght sory yif I have ought
> Destroubled yow out of your thought.
> Foryive me, yif I have mystake.'
> 'Yis, th'amendes is lyght to make,'
> Quod he, 'for ther lyeth noon therto;
> There ys nothyng myssayd nor do.'
>   Loo! how goodly spak thys knyght,
> As hit had be another wyght;
> He made hyt nouther towgh ne queynte.
>   (514–31)

Chaucer delightedly points out to his reader the excellence of the Man in Black's manners – and gives us plenty of material to form an equally favourable impression of his own. There is, however, a little more to the exchange than merely formal good manners. The Man in Black is neither 'tough' – brusque or snubbing – nor 'quaint' – that is he does not indulge in over-elaborate politeness. His is a sincere and plain courtesy which fits the Dreamer's sincerity of sympathy.

Finding one who is obviously a great man so 'tretable' (533), the

Dreamer looks for a conversational opening which will take him deeper into the matter:

> Anoon ryght I gan fynde a tale
> To hym, to loke wher I myght ought
> Have more knowynge of hys thought.
>
> (536–8)

His remark about the hunt (539 f.) gives him the opportunity he wants, and he cautiously and courteously puts forward his proffer of help:

> 'But, sir, oo thyng wol ye here?
> Me thynketh in gret sorowe I yow see.
> But certes, sire, yif that yee
> Wolde ought discure me youre woo,
> I wolde, as wys God helpe me soo,
> Amende hyt, yif I kan or may.
> Ye mowe preve hyt be assay;
> For, by my trouthe, to make yow hool,
> I wol do al my power hool.
> And telleth me of your sorwes smerte;
> Paraunter hyt may ese youre herte,
> That semeth ful sek under your syde.'
>
> (546–57)

The Dreamer, in fact, offers himself in the therapeutic rôle of sympathetic confidant, and the rest of the poem is a long process by which the Man in Black is at last brought to speak of his sorrow in plain terms. The poem, indeed, does not offer any easy solution to grief – to suggest one would be to insult the mourner's sense of genuine and serious loss. But the promises of healing and renewal in the opening sections are not unfulfilled. We see the mourner progress from a hopeless, solitary and uncontrolled grief which threatens him even with physical dissolution and which is contrary to nature's plan, to a stage at which he can clearly define his loss both to himself and to another person, and so stand back a little from it – a process which necessarily renders emotion more tolerable. Moreover, through his dealings with the Dreamer, he is brought back within the framework of social reference. At the end of the poem his solitary ramble in the wood is over.[36] He returns, just before the Dreamer awakens, homewards to a nearby castle; and, we feel, life is thereby taken up again.

The Dreamer's 'obtuse' comments can thus be seen as gently but firmly forcing the mourner to the full confession which will ease his sick heart. The Man in Black at first takes refuge in the figure of the game of chess with Fortune in which he loses his Queen. The Dreamer argues that a man should not regard the blows of Fortune and that, in any case:

> 'ther is no man alyve her
> Wolde for a fers make this woo!'
> (740–1)

Here Chaucer touches on the theme of the consolation of philosophy, as it is developed, for example, in *Fortune* and *Truth*, and puts before the mourner the example of Socrates:

> 'Remembre yow of Socrates,
> For he ne counted nat thre strees
> Of noght that Fortune koude doo.'
> (717–19)

But here, as in the opening section, where the consolation to be derived from the existence of a natural cycle of change and renewal is only hinted at, the subject is not developed at length; and Chaucer passes on to an elegant and learned list of examples of murder and suicide for grief (725 ff.). As in the passage, derived from Ovid, on the God of Sleep, he offers the attractions, and perhaps the dignity, of Classical poetry and story as a distraction to the mourner, rather than any reasoned argument to overcome grief.

The Dreamer's bluntness in this passage provokes the Man in Black to the admission that his sorrow has to do with a human mistress, not a mere chess piece. The effect of the momentary harshness of the Dreamer's probing is recovered in the brief exchange of courtesies which prefaces the long account of this lady, and of his courtship of her:

31

'Why so?' quod he, 'hyt ys nat soo.
Thou wost ful lytel what thou menest.
I have lost more than thow wenest.'
'Loo, [sey] how that may be?' quod y;
'Good sir, telle me al hooly
In what wyse, how, why, and wherfore
That ye have thus youre blysse lore.'
'Blythely,' quod he; 'com sytte adoun!
I telle the upon a condicioun
That thou shalt hooly, with al thy wyt,
Doo thyn entent to herkene hit.'
'Yis, syr.' 'Swere thy trouthe therto.'
'Gladly.' 'Do thanne holde herto!'
'I shal ryght blythely, so God me save,
Hooly, with al the wit I have,
Here yow, as wel as I kan.'
'A Goddes half!' quod he, and began.

(742–58)

His narrative continues uninterrupted for some three hundred lines, but the conversational interlude just quoted is long enough, and vivid enough, to keep the two speakers fresh in our minds.

This speech uses, in the main, the style and language of fashionable love poetry as we have seen it in the short poems and in the *Troilus*. The opening provides a good example of this manner:

'Dredeles, I have ever yit
Be tributarye and yiven rente
To Love, hooly with good entente,
And throgh plesaunce become his thral
With good wille, body, hert, and al.
Al this I putte in his servage,
As to my lord, and dide homage;
And ful devoutly I prayed hym to,
He shulde besette myn herte so
That hyt plesance to hym were,
And worship to my lady dere.'

(764–74)

Differences in style in the *Book of the Duchess* have already been discussed. We can now see that these more exalted flights are still carefully integrated into the context of the poem as a whole. This, I think, is achieved in two main ways. The paragraph openings are framed so that the reader is reminded that he is listening to a narrative within a narrative – that is to an account which the Mourner is giving to the Dreamer – for example:

> 'And thilke tyme I ferde ryght so . . .' (785)
> 'Hit happed that I cam on a day . . .' (805)
> 'I sawgh hyr daunce so comlily . . .' (848)

Another type of paragraph opening which also keeps the fact of the conversation before us is the exclamatory one – it is as if the speaker breaks off and starts again with a direct appeal to his hearer:

> 'But which a visage had she thertoo!' (895)
> 'And which a goodly, softe speche . . .' (919)

Again, the use of the formula 'to speak of' has much the same effect:

> 'To speke of godnesse, trewly she . . .' (985)
> 'And trewly, for to speke of trouthe . . .' (999)

Or there is the reminder of the circumstances of the speech:

> 'But wherfore that y telle my tale?' (1034)
> 'But wherfore that I telle thee . . .' (1088)

The paragraph endings are also used to remind us of the situation of speaker and hearer:

> 'And I wol telle sone why soo.' (816)
> 'I wil anoon ryght telle thee why.' (847)

Within the paragraphs, too, the style is not uniformly elevated. There is much that is simple and direct:

33

'I durste swere, thogh the pope hit songe,
That ther was never yet throgh hir tonge
Man ne woman gretly harmed.'
(929–31)

'Hyt was my swete, ryght as hirselve . . .'
(832)

'Hyt folowed wel she koude good.
She used gladly to do wel.'
(1012–13)

The Man in Black, too, uses exclamations and asseverations – 'I dar swere wel' (924, *cf.* 929, 962, 971, etc.) – and references to his own situation in the past – 'as I have now memoyre' (945); 'I was ryght yong, soth to say' (1090) – all of which combine to give an easy, even colloquial, flow to his speech and to bring it down to the general stylistic level of the poem, in spite of his use of many of the terms of 'thise loveres alle.' 'This', C. S. Lewis said, roundly, 'is the old bad manner'.[37] I would see it rather as a serious, and by no means unsuccessful, attempt to solve a problem of modulation in a poem whose occasion, and whose intimate contact with a particular audience, requires the treatment of material of different kinds in different ways.

The Man in Black dwells on the beauties and virtues of his mistress and the happiness of time past until the Dreamer once more gives him a push towards the easing of the heart which is the object of the confessional (the figure is used in lines 1112–14, where the Dreamer speaks of 'schryfte wythoute repentaunce'). Once again, he speaks with some bluntness:

'Now, goode syre,' quod I thoo,
'Ye han wel told me herebefore,
Hyt ys no nede to reherse it more
How ye sawe hir first, and where.
But wolde ye tel me the manere
To hire which was your firste speche,
Therof I wolde yow beseche;
And how she knewe first your thoght,
Whether ye loved hir or noght.
And telleth me eke what ye have lore,
I herde yow telle herebefore.'
(1126–36)

The Man in Black still winces away from the clear statement of his
loss:

> 'Yee!' seyde he, 'thow nost what thow menest;
> I have lost more than thou wenest.'
>
> (1137–8)

and he continues the history of his successful courtship, ending with
a description of an ideal union:

> 'Oure hertes wern so evene a payre,
> That never nas that oon contrayre
> To that other, for no woo.
> For sothe, ylyche they suffred thoo
> Oo blysse and eke oo sorwe bothe;
> Yliche they were bothe glad and wrothe;
> Al was us oon, withoute were.
> And thus we lyved ful many a yere
> So wel, I kan nat telle how.'
>
> (1289–97)

The Dreamer now puts the pertinent question, from which there is
no ultimate escape:

> 'Sir,' quod I, 'where is she now?'
> (1298)

Even now the Man in Black hesitates for a moment:

> 'Now?' quod he, and stynte anoon.
> Therwith he wax as ded as stoon,
> And seyde, 'Allas that I was bore!
> That was the los that here-before
> I tolde the that I hadde lorn.
> Bethenke how I seyde here-beforn,
> "Thow wost ful lytel what thow menest;
> I have lost more than thow wenest" –
> God wot, allas! ryght that was she!'
>
> (1299–307)

The Dreamer's final question is more an exclamation of sympathetic grief than an enquiry, and it brings, at last, the plain admission which resolves all the tension that has been building up and sends both the 'hert-hunting' and the poem quietly into its final phase:

> 'Allas, sir, how? what may that be?'
> 'She ys ded!' 'Nay!' 'Yis, be my trouthe!'
> 'Is that youre los? Be God, hyt ys routhe!'
> And with that word ryght anoon
> They gan to strake forth; al was doon,
> For that tyme, the hert-hunting.
>
> (1308–13)

The figure of the hunt has shifted its meaning from the dream-Emperor's unsuccessful pursuit of the hart, through the lover's conquest of his lady's heart, to illuminate the real aim of the poem – the restoration to some ease and health of the mourner's sick heart.

The *Book of the Duchess* does not offer any profound solution, either philosophical or religious, to the problem of mortality. Christian consolation, as a matter of fact, is not proposed; and the consolation of philosophy remains a minor theme. What it does provide is an offering from one human being to another, within the strict framework of agreed manners and of an accepted social scale, of sympathetic understanding of an unhappy situation. It also provides a means of return to human contacts, and to life which continues as nature intends it to do, in spite of loss, for one whom the intensity of grief has temporarily cut off. The emphasis on social forms and on the comparative rank of the two speakers is thus by no means inappropriate to the theme of the poem as a whole – and it also arises naturally from the fact that, like most of the shorter poems we have been considering, this work is actually written to meet an existing situation and is addressed to a known person, who stands in an established relation to the poet. Chaucer has made of his poetry a vehicle perfectly adapted to the expression of all these nuances; and, even if parts of the praise of the lady read a little mechanically, the poem lives for its accurate delineation of the relationship within which the two main figures stand, both to each other and to the society which is glimpsed in the background as giving form and meaning to their encounter.

2

New themes in the love vision

The philosophical ideas which were an important part of the material of Chaucer's poetry throughout most of his working life, not only in the short poems, but also in some of his most ambitious works, played, as we have seen, only a peripheral part in the *Book of the Duchess*. In the *Parlement of Foules*, however, this philosophical material is brought into the foreground and is fully deployed in both sections of the poem, in the introductory one based on the *Somnium Scipionis*, and in the vision itself.[1] Yet, there is a great deal more to the *Parlement* than philosophical exposition. In spite of Chaucer's emphasis, at the beginning and end, on his dependence on books and his lack of personal experience – 'al be that I knowe nat Love in dede' (8) – his philosophy of Love and Nature is certainly put to some kind of practical test when it meets the varied reactions of the living birds. His disclaimers, in fact, although they reflect a poem which is weighted on the side of theory against practice, also give ironical point to an ending which decides nothing and in which the voice of the pragmatical duck is challenged, but by no means silenced. The theme of experience *versus* authority, which is so often important for Chaucer, is a major one in this poem.

The *Parlement of Foules*, according to its opening stanzas, is a poem about love as it is experienced in life, as well as described in books:

> The lyf so short, the craft so long to lerne,
> Th'assay so hard, so sharp the conquerynge,
> The dredful joye, alwey that slit so yerne,

37

> Al this mene I by Love, that my felynge
> Astonyeth with his wonderful werkynge
> So sore, iwis, that whan I on hym thynke,
> Nat wot I wel wher that I flete or synke.
>
> (1–7)

So far life, 'preue', experience. The next stanza turns to 'authority', books:

> For al be that I knowe nat Love in dede,
> Ne wot how that he quiteth folk here hyre,
> Yit happeth me ful ofte in bokes reede
> Of his myrakles and his crewel yre.
> There rede I wel he wol be lord and syre;
> I dar nat seyn, his strokes been so sore,
> But 'God save swich a lord – I can na moore!'
>
> (8–14)

The poet's attitude is one of awe and fascination. We are prepared for a discussion of love seen as a great natural phenomenon, with all the complexity and relentless force of Nature. We are also prepared for something ambiguous and contradictory – the *dredful joye*. It is true that phrases of this kind are a conventional part of the description of profane love – for some poets, no more than a rhetorical trick. Nevertheless, as we shall see, in this poem the contradictory nature of love is something more than a neat turn of phrase. It is one of the main themes. It is, indeed, one of the great themes, always raising questions to be searchingly explored, but never finally answered, which recurs again and again in Chaucer's poetry. It is the question posed by Mars:

> To what fyn made the God that sit so hye,
> Benethen him, love other companye,
> And streyneth folk to love, malgre her hed?
> (*Complaint of Mars*, 218–20)

and also by Troilus:

> If love be good, fro whennes cometh my wo?
> (I, 407)

38

Here, in the *Parlement*, the tone is lighter. The poet speaks as an
observer, in much the same way as Theseus, who also looks at
love with some sympathy, but from the outside:

> 'The God of Love, a *benedicite*!
> How myghty and how greet a lord is he!
> Ayeyns his myght ther gayneth non obstacles.'
>
> (*CT* I, 1785-7)

Through the half-humorous picture of the bewildered reader,
helpless in the face of so much complexity, we find ourselves once
more in the urbane, undictatorial world of the minor poems. We
are not dealing with a poet who professes to offer infallible instruction, whether his reader likes it or not. We are, once again, invited
to share the experience and form our own judgement of its meaning,
of a poet who quickly modulates from the crisp rhetorical arrangement of his first stanza to the more conversational and diffuse tone
of the second, ending in pure colloquialism – 'But "God save swich
a lord" – I can na moore!'

The book to which Chaucer now turns for information about
the subject is not, to our way of thinking, about love at all; it is,
in fact, an encyclopedic volume, a mixture of science and metaphysics, with a strong bias towards cosmology. This is 'Tullyus of
the Drem of Scipioun', that is, the sixth book of Cicero's otherwise
lost *Republic*, with the famous commentary of Macrobius. It was
through this commentary that so much of the peculiar late Latin
blend of Platonic and Stoic philosophical material was transmitted
to the Middle Ages, together with much which we should call (as
does Chaucer) scientific, rather than philosophical in the strict
sense. It is, paradoxical as it may seem to the modern reader,
precisely because of this blend of science and metaphysics that
Chaucer is able to link the book to the poet's proper subject of love.[2]
He gives us his reasons. First, 'out of olde bokes' (presumably including this one) 'Cometh al this newe science that men lere'[3]
(24-5); and secondly:

> Chapitres sevene it hadde, of hevene and helle
> And erthe, and soules that therinne dwelle.
>
> (32-3)

It is, thus, a book which deals with descriptive cosmology (or, as we should say, provides a model of the universe) and also with the rewards and punishment of human conduct after death. Given that this is its subject matter, how is it possible to say, with Chaucer, 'al this mene I by Love'? The answer is that Macrobius, drawing heavily on the *Timaeus* and on neoplatonic elaborations of its doctrines, describes a system in which a concept of love plays a leading rôle. Furthermore, an important theme of the *Somnium Scipionis* is that of the 'common profit', as the principal aim and justification of human endeavour. As we shall see, even in Cicero's treatment of the idea, it has a link with love; and to a poet familiar with the *Roman de la Rose* as Jean de Meun concluded it, the implications can become even more precise. We could, in fact, see in the *Parlement* a brilliant rehandling of the treatment of Venus and Nature, as we find it at the conclusion of the *Roman de la Rose*, in which an effective variation on the theme is achieved, partly by a bold reorganization of the material so as to lay it out in a quite different pattern, partly by juxtaposing it to the philosophical ideas of Macrobius and Boethius. Chaucer allows these ideas to remain clear-cut by separating them from the main body of the poem; Jean de Meun inserted them as digressions into the speeches of the personifications. In fact, Chaucer attacks the weak point of the love vision: he gives independent existence and life to the matter of its interminable speeches.

The *Somnium Scipionis*, as we have said, is full of descriptive cosmology. But it is also a work with a strong moral bias. It is concerned with the whole duty of man while on earth and, since human existence is not bounded by earth – 'Know thyself first immortal' – with the rewards and punishments which come to man after death. It is this aspect of the book which is brought out in Chaucer's brief summary in lines 36–84. The key phrase, used in lines 47 and 75, is 'commune profyt': those who make this the object of their lives will be rewarded by entry after death into a 'blysful place' in heaven. Those who sin, on the other hand, will be condemned to 'whirle aboute th'erthe alwey in peyne.' The sinners, however, are not merely those who neglect the common profit – Cicero's life of service to the state, as Chaucer must have realized – but those who indulge in lust – 'likerous folk'. By the 'law' that they break (78), Chaucer almost certainly means the law of nature: they indulge their passions unnaturally, or even merely unproductively.[4] They are the victims, in the phrase which he uses of Troilus, and also of Tarquin and the would-be ravisher of Constance, of 'the blinde lust'.[5] This too, is well within the spirit, if not the letter, of Cicero. The reason why Cicero opposes service to the state to self-indulgent passion is that he is thinking in terms of the Stoic good man, whose goodness consists, precisely, in the conquest of all passion.

In giving his good man the reward of stellification in return for his services to the community, Cicero is pursuing a definite line of argument, which is not taken up by Macrobius. This, as we can see from other passages in his writings, relates to the explanation of the gods as originally men, who benefited their fellows and were rewarded with divine status.[6] Macrobius does not comment on this aspect of the idea, but leaves the rewards and punishments of mankind as a loosely attached excursus within the frame of his cosmological survey, where they are juxtaposed to, but not actually incorporated in, the account of the platonic creation, originating in love and sustained by harmony.[7] Chaucer takes over these ideas for his vision of Venus and Nature, but with a difference. The common profit is now linked more directly to love; and, in keeping with the *Roman de la Rose*, it is associated with Nature's task of replenishing the earth and so maintaining the divine order of created beings.

The idea that the creation is brought about by divine love flowing outward from the godhead and that divine perfection necessarily implies the full realization of every possible variety of created being, in unbroken continuity from the highest and most perfect, which are nearest to God, to the lowest and least, which are furthest from him, is certainly present in Macrobius, in a passage like the following one:

> Secundum haec ergo cum ex summo Deo mens, ex mente anima sit; anima vero et condat, et vita compleat omnia, qui sequuntur, cunctaque hic unus fulgor illuminet, et in universis appareat, ut in multis speculis per ordinem positis vultus unus, cumque omnia continuis successionibus se sequantur, degenerantia per ordinem ad imum meandi, invenietur praescius intuenti a summo Deo usque ad ultimam rerum faecem una se mutuis vinculis religans, et nusquam interrupta connexio.

> (Accordingly, since Mind emanates from the Supreme God and Soul from Mind, and Mind, indeed, forms and suffuses all

below with life, and since this is the one splendour lighting
up everything and visible in all, like a countenance reflected
in many mirrors arranged in a row, and since all follow on in
continuous succession, degenerating step by step in their
downward course, the close observer will find that, from the
Supreme God even to the bottommost dregs of the universe there
is one tie, binding at every link, and never broken.)

(*Somnium* I, xiv; Stahl trans.)

Chaucer never elaborates this idea in precisely this form, but it
is implied in his treatment of a cosmic love descending through all
creation in the *Troilus*, in the proem to Book III and in the *Knight's
Tale*.[8] In the *Parlement*, we have only the suggestion of the 'principle
of plenitude' (to use Lovejoy's phrase) in the description of Nature's
abundantly thronging creatures and in the emphasis on the fulfilment of the command of Genesis to go forth and replenish the earth.
Nature, as a personification of the creative energy, takes the place
of love – or rather expresses that aspect of it which is most closely
linked to the preservation of the species. Chaucer, indeed, gives
us her full significance in a single, economical stanza, which represents a long section of Macrobius's book. Her power, like that of
Venus Cytheria in other contexts,[9] is a cosmic one, which, under
God, whose 'vicaire' she is, extends over the whole created world
of matter.[10] This is, of course, not to depreciate her function of
presiding over the marriages of the lesser creatures, but only to
bring the perpetuation of the individual species into the total,
all-embracing scheme.

> Nature, the vicaire of the almyghty Lord,
> That hot, cold, hevy, lyght, moyst and dreye
> Hath knyt by evene noumbres of acord,
> In esy voys began to speke and seye,
> 'Foules, tak hede of my sentence, I preye,
> And for youre ese, in fortheryng of youre nede,
> As faste as I may speke, I wol me speede.'

(379–85)

The first three lines condense Macrobius; the last four somewhat
modify the augustness of a being on whom the whole fabric of the

world depends, and for these Chaucer draws on another and different tradition.

From Macrobius, to take the first part of the stanza first, Chaucer takes the idea of a creative energy which holds together the opposing elements; and thus continues the theme of the dual nature of love, consisting in both conflict and its resolution, with which the poem began. Macrobius writes of the chain, or bond, of the elements in the following terms:

Deus mundanae molis artifex conditorque mutuatus insolubili inter se vinculo elementa devinxit sicut in Timaeo Platonis assertum est.

(The Creator of the Universe bound the elements together with an unbreakable chain, as was affirmed in Plato's *Timaeus*.)

(I vi)

For Boethius, as for Theseus, the bond is love: 'Haec concordia' (the 'amor' of line 17) 'temperat aequis / Elementa modis' (*de Consolatione*, IV, m. vi, 19–20). For both, God, as Creator, acts directly, without an intermediary. In making Nature the intermediary who actually applies the chain, Chaucer follows most closely the *Roman de la Rose*:

Si gart, tant m'a Deus enouree,
La bele chaiene doree
Qui les quatre elemenz enlace
Trestouz enclins devant ma face.

(Thus I control – God has so greatly honoured me – the fair golden chain which binds the four elements, all of which bow down before my presence.)

(16785–8)

Chaucer's use of these ideas elsewhere, however, shows that, although the framework of the *Parlement*, as a vision of Venus and Nature, requires the emphasis to be placed on the latter at this point, he is well aware of their associations with love. Thus, at the end of Book III of the *Troilus* it is Love 'that of erthe and se hath governaunce', and

> So wolde God that auctour is of kynde,
> That with his bond Love of his vertu liste
> To cerclen hertes alle and faste bynde.
>
> (1765–7)

Here Love and Nature are brought together, and, once more, the basis of this earthly stabilization of conflicting forces is the binding of the elements:

> That elementz that ben so discordable
> Holden a bond perpetuely durynge.
>
> (1753–4)

The state that Troilus hymns in this song is that tragically temporary one in which the lovers are 'in lust and in quiete' (1819), and his use of this phrase of love, in close proximity to a passage on the chain, suggests yet another source for the enrichment of Chaucer's ideas on the subject. This is the very influential *de Divisione Naturae* of John Scotus Eriugena.[11] Here a chain of Love is described, with particular emphasis on the idea of ascent and descent – an idea which is found in Macrobius, as we shall see, and which is also important in Theseus's speech in the *Knight's Tale*.[12] Eriugena writes:

> Amor est connexio ac vinculum quo omnium rerum
> universitas ineffabili amicitia insolubili unitate copulatur.
>
> (Love is a bond and chain by which the totality of all things
> is bound together in ineffable friendship and indissoluble unity.)
>
> (pp. 210–11)

Of the descent from and ascent into love he says:

> Idem in eisdem: 'Age nunc, et has iterum,' hoc est amoris
> virtutes, 'in unum congregantes dicamus quia una quidam est
> simplex virtus se ipsam movens ad unitivam quandam
> temperantiam ex optimo usque existentium novissimum et ab
> illo iterum consequenter per omnia usque ad optimum ex se ipsa
> et per se ipsam et ad se ipsam se ipsam revolvens et in seipsam
> semper eodem modo revoluta.'

(The same [author] says in the same [Hymns: Eriugena is quoting from Ps. Dionysius] 'Come now, and gathering these', that is the virtues of love, 'again into one, let us say that there is one simple virtue which moves itself to a unitive mingling [of all things] from the Best to the lowest of beings, and back from that through all things in order to the Best again, spinning itself out from itself, through itself, towards itself and ever winding itself up again into itself in the same way.'

(pp. 212–13)

A further definition of love, according to Eriugena is,

Amor est naturalis motus omnium rerum quae in motu sunt finis quietaque statio, ultra quam nullus creaturae progreditur motus.

(Love is the end and quiet resting place of the natural motion of all things that are in motion, beyond which no motion of the creature extends.)

(pp. 210–11)

This, I think, gives Chaucer a phrase he uses in various forms, again and again, of the realization of the bliss of love[13] – a phrase which gains poignancy as well as intensity from the fact that he uses it to refer, not to the ultimate return to the One, but to a moment which is only part of the temporal progressions of the natural world and which necessarily shares their transience.

In the *Troilus* and in the *Knight's Tale*, ideas such as these play a major part. In the *Parlement*, however, they are only present by implication, as part of the nexus of ideas to which the description of Nature's power belongs. The most important aspect of love, in the *Parlement*, as we have said, is its duality; and, just as it is a force which can produce opposite results in human life, so that Venus presides over a temple with pictures of differing import on the opposing walls, even Nature is shown presiding over a world of matter which contains a fundamental core of conflict. This is the 'quatuor elementorum concors discordia' of which Alanus writes in his *de Planctu Naturae*, Chaucer's other main source for this part of the poem.[14] In the case of the creatures, Nature brings together the opposites, male and female. The elements, too, according to Macrobius are kept together in a kind of marriage, since their ordering

45

depends on the odd and even numbers. These too are 'male' and 'female', and the whole creation depends on their union.[15]

Chaucer follows Macrobius closely in his account of the elemental bond. He correctly names, not the elements themselves, but their attributes, since it is through these that the actual 'knitting' takes place. Macrobius describes this in two different ways, both of which Chaucer combines in his condensed account. First, because each element has two attributes, they can be linked in a kind of circular chain by the quality they have in common, i.e., the attributes hot, cold, moist, dry in Chaucer's list:[16]

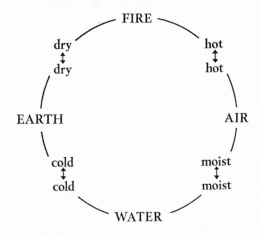

Secondly, there is another arrangement, by which the light is drawn downwards and the heavy forced upwards. This depends on the attributes of weight and lightness, the 'hevy' and 'lyght' of Chaucer's list. In this arrangement three intermediate linking factors are involved and are named 'obedience', 'harmony', and 'necessity' by Macrobius.[17]

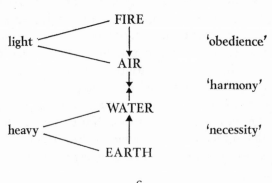

46

It is, I think, in this second arrangement, rather than in the first, that we have the clue to Chaucer's phrase 'by evene noumbres of accord'. These numbers are 'even' in the sense of 'exact' and are three and four.[18] As Macrobius explains, to join together four things it is necessary to have three intermediate terms. These are the numbers which make possible the realization of tangible and visible matter, as Macrobius learnt from the *Timaeus* and its neo-Platonic commentators.[19] As he reminds us, Cicero had already said of their sum, the number seven: 'qui numerus rerum omnium fere nodus est' (*Somnium* I, vi). It would thus not, I think, be possible for anyone to write of the creative stabilization of the opposing elements in terms of 'even' numbers in the sense of the opposite of odd.

The harmony which nature imposes on the elements, the building bricks of creation, is mirrored through the natural order: in his description of the surroundings of Venus's temple, the same natural landscape in which Nature later holds court, Chaucer twice indicates this. In line 191 the birds sing 'with voys of aungel in here armonye' and in lines 197–200:

> Of instruments of strenges in acord
> Herde I so pleye a ravyshyng swetnesse,
> That God, that makere is of al and lord,
> Ne herde nevere beter, as I gesse.

God, of course, hears the divine harmony of the angels and also the music of the spheres, both dependent on 'evene noumbres'.[20] Finally:

> And whan this werk al brought was to an ende,
> To every foul Nature yaf his make
> By evene acord.
>
> (666–8)

The basic harmony of creation is thus also expressed in Nature's provision for the continuance of the species.

In order to understand in more detail how these ideas are worked out in a vision of Venus and Nature, we need to look at Chaucer's other sources for this latter part of the poem and at the way in which he transforms the material he took over from them. The formative influence on the *Parlement* in this section is the device of the Complaint

of Nature, as Chaucer knew it from the *de Planctu Naturae* of Alanus
and from the *Roman de la Rose*. It is on this kind of material that the
second half of the stanza describing Nature, which we have been
discussing, is based.

Nature's complaint is that, alone among her subjects, mankind
does not obey her laws. They disrupt her whole fabric by their
perversity and sinfulness, instead of carrying out her purpose and
helping, through an ordered and reasonable love, to keep the earth
filled with good creatures. This is the central theme of Alanus's
work. He does not exclude Venus, but he distinguishes between her
unfallen state, in which she is an ally of Nature, and her fallen one,
in which, as 'blind lust', she assists the perverse and barren loves of
sinful mankind.[21] Alanus does not exclude chastity either. There is
a place for her among Nature's followers, as well as for marriage:
marriage, indeed, is incompatible with virginity, in the strict sense,
but not with chastity.[22] In the *Roman*, Venus is drawn into Nature's
orbit in a rather different way. She is, emphatically, at war with
chastity, and when she is in danger of defeat in her attempt to bring
to fruition the love of Amans for the Rose, Nature comes to her
rescue; and through her speeches and those of her priest, Genius,
Jean de Meun is able to incorporate much of the material of the
Complaint of Nature – besides a great deal more.[23] Since, however,
his treatment of love is a complex one, the figure of Nature is not
as clearcut for him as it is for Alanus. Nature repudiates falsehood
and hypocrisy, whom Love had accepted as supporters, and thus
makes it clear that she will have nothing to do with the most dubious
aspects of the love to which Amans is victim. Nevertheless this love
is, as Jean de Meun makes clear from the beginning of his part
of the *Roman*, contrary to reason and therefore, even shorn of its
worst excesses, not entirely admirable. Nature, accordingly, is made
to explain that though she is God's vicar on earth, and therefore,
we must assume, a force for good, she has no control whatsoever
over man's intelligence; she did not make that part of him to which
he will owe eternal life – indeed, she says, none of her creatures
are anything but mortal. It is for this reason, to keep death at bay,
that she is in alliance with love.[24] It will be clear that Jean de Meun
has ingeniously sidestepped the problem of reconciling the love
which he satirizes in much of his work with a Nature of whom he
clearly approves – as far as she goes. What Nature favours is legitimate sexuality used to perpetuate the species. But she cannot go

beyond this. Reason also favours natural love as a part of the world God made, but Reason can, and does, go a good deal further. So, I think, can, and does, Chaucer. Jean de Meun's Nature and Venus together (as that poet was well aware, since such limitations were for him part of the comedy of the misguided Amans) get no further than passion, legitimate or illegitimate. At its worst this is what, as we have said, Chaucer stigmatizes as 'the blinde lust'. At its best, it is a noble thing, but only a part of the complexity of human contacts and human relationships which are included in the concept of love. This, I think, is what emerges from the debate of the birds. The common birds get immediate satisfaction for their uncomplicated impulses, and this is right and good. The more sensitive creatures have to grapple with the problems set them by their more complicated relationships with each other – and it follows that it will be even more true that human beings, with their endowment of a mind which is not the work of Nature, will not be able to solve all their problems by Nature's light, any more than they could do so by Venus's.

Chaucer shows us Venus and Nature in the same beautiful and natural setting, and thus suggests the fundamental link between them. But, within the park full of plants and creatures, Venus is to be found inside an artifact – her temple – described after the manner of the *Teseida*, its immediate surroundings peopled with personifications, not with natural creatures. Within the temple, too, love is, in the main, shown as out of step with Nature. The break with Nature is not, I believe, complete, but the emphasis falls on what is contrary to natural love – that is on jealousy and frustration:

> Withinne the temple, of sykes hoote as fyr
> I herde a swogh that gan aboute renne,
> Whiche sikes were engendered with desyr,
> That maden every auter for to brenne
> Of newe flaume, and wel espyed I thenne
> That al the cause of sorwes that they drye
> Cam of the bittere goddesse Jelosye.
>
> (246–52)

The stories depicted on the temple walls, however, are not all tragic. They are of two kinds, which occupy different positions in the building. Lines 281–7 describe the trophies won from Diana in the war with chastity:

49

> in dispit of Dyane the chaste,
> Ful many a bowe ibroke heng on the wal
> Of maydenes swiche as gonne here tymes waste
> In hyre servyse.

These conquests are in accord with Nature; just as, in the *Knight's Tale*, Diana's refusal to grant Emely's prayer 'not to ben a wyf and be with childe' is not regarded as tragic. Significantly, too, the maidens were wasting their time. This stanza, however, is counterbalanced by one (287–94) describing loves which were contrary to nature. The first group (except for Hercules) is of unnatural lovers, who indulged in incest.[25] The second, like Hercules, were brought to death by love instead of to fruition. The names from Dido to Troilus, are those of typical heroes and heroines of romantic tales of love. If this is contrary to nature, it is because it is unproductive. The last two names are of criminals in love – Silla, who betrayed her father to gain Minos's love and was repulsed by him in consequence, and the vestal virgin, Rhea, who broke her vows and gave birth to Romulus and Remus. Clearly, since her story is depicted on 'that other side', i.e., on the opposite wall of the temple to that which holds the spoils of Diana, Chaucer regards her in a different light to the conquered nymphs.[26] This division between the spoils of Venus's temple bears out the impression we gain from the mixture of figures, good and bad, pleasant and unpleasant, who guard its approaches:

> Tho was I war of Plesaunce anon-ryght,
> And of Aray, and Lust, and Curteysie,
> And of the Craft that can and hath the myght
> To don by force a wyght to don folye –
> Disfigurat was she, I nyl nat lye;
> And by hymself under an ok, I gesse,
> Saw I Delyt, that stod with Gentilesse.

> I saw Beute withouten any atyr,
> And Youthe, ful of game and jolyte;
> Foolhardynesse, Flaterye and Desyr,
> Messagerye, and Meede, and other thre, –
> Here names shul not here be told for me –
> (218–29)

50

This is a temple of human love, with all its advantages and disadvantages. There are the trophies of victories won in the war waged equally by Venus and Nature against a chastity which would deny the world the continuance of its fill of creatures. But there are also all the causes of Nature's complaint against mankind. There are the perverse and unproductive loves which only lead to suffering and death.

Chaucer has here introduced much that is unlike either Alanus or Jean de Meun – in the main, because he is using quite different visual types in the descriptions. In the case of Venus, instead of the allegory of the *Roman*, he borrows the much richer description of the temple from Boccaccio, which, in spite of its abstractions and personifications, is conceived, visually speaking, in fully naturalistic terms. In the case of Nature and her creatures, the result is much the same. Once again consistent allegory is rejected: we have neither the somewhat heated figure of Nature hammering away in her forge, from the *Roman*, nor the device of the figured robe on which all the creatures are depicted, from Alanus. Instead, we have the gracious figure in the beautiful landscape, which impressed Spenser, surrounded by the jostling, living, highly individualistic birds, who can, and do, speak for themselves. Moreover, Chaucer makes another important change when he removes the actual material of complaint from Nature's speeches to the world around her, where it is enacted, in a detailed way, in Venus's temple and, by implication, in the only partially successful love story of the noble birds. A tranquil, confident Nature is both better suited to Chaucer's purpose of avoiding too clearcut answers to the problems he poses and a more effective goddess.

The serenity and, as it were, broad daylight, of Nature is, indeed, in obvious contrast to the sighs and semi-darkness of Venus's temple – but we must remember, before we overemphasize the contrast, that Peace was Venus's doorkeeper and that, when even Nature encounters some difficulty with her more complex creatures, it is their refusal to enter into relations with Venus and her son which causes the trouble:

> 'I wol nat serve Venus ne Cupide,
> Forsothe as yit,'
>
> (652–3)

says the Formel Eagle. Like Emely, however, the implication is
that she will submit to Nature's law after her year's respite and will
turn voluntarily from the service of Diana to the service of Venus.[27]
The relation, in fact, between Nature and Venus is both close and
beneficial, although the perversity of the human will can make a
sorry place of Venus's temple and, at the same time, invalidate
Nature's plan.

Nature, as we have said, is seen in full daylight and open air:

> Tho was I war wher that ther sat a queene
> That, as of lyght the somer sonne shene
> Passeth the sterre, right so ever mesure
> She fayrer was than any creature.
>
> And in a launde, upon an hil of floures,
> Was set this noble goddesse Nature.
> Of braunches were here halles and here boures
> Iwrought after here cast and here mesure.
>
> (298–305)

But, and the fact is important, this is part of the same landscape
in which Venus's temple stands – the landscape to which the Dreamer
came when he first entered the gate and to which he now, again,
refers:

> Whan I was come ayeyn into the place
> That I of spak, that was so sote and grene . . .
>
> (295–6)

The significance of the gate with its two inscriptions now becomes
clearer. Like the opposing walls of Venus's temple, this gate has
inscriptions on its opposite sides of different import,[28] again, set
out in two counterbalancing stanzas, so ordered as to lend great
importance to the subject matter, through the vigour and beauty
of the first, and the telling image of the dry tree and gasping fish
in the second:

> 'Thorgh me men gon into that blysful place
> Of hertes hele and dedly woundes cure;
> Thorgh me men gon unto the welle of grace,
> There grene and lusty May shal evere endure,
> This is the wey to al good aventure.

Be glad, thow redere, and thy sorwe of-caste;
Al open am I – passe in, and sped thee faste!'

'Thorgh me men gon,' than spak that other side,
'Unto the mortal strokes of the spere
Of which Disdayn and Daunger is the gyde,
Ther nevere tre shal fruyt ne leves bere.
This strem yow ledeth to the sorweful were
There as the fish in prysoun is al drye;
Th'eschewing is only the remedye!'

(134–47)

In fact, the two contradictory aspects of love are to be found in the same place and reached through the same gate. Those who pass through it will have both inscriptions to reckon with, and it is not surprising that the Dreamer is left like a piece of iron between two equal magnets (148–9). This state of conflict is further emphasized by the metaphor Africanus uses to encourage him. Even if a man does not take an active part, he likes 'at the wrastlyng for to be' (165). We therefore arrive at a picture in which Venus, unaided by Nature, lends herself to all the perversities and self-inflicted torments of which humanity is capable, but in which she still remains an essential part of Nature's plan for the perpetuation of the species. Both Venus and Nature are thus, in their different ways, involved in the irreducible core of conflict which underlies the material fabric of the universe; while at the same time, both are also the personifications of the energies which force strife into harmony. By replacing the moral-political theme of Cicero's book (with which, indeed, Macrobius does not have much to do) by a 'common profit' which concerns the maintenance of creation through the continuity of the species, Chaucer has been able to bring ideas which Jean de Meun often leaves as openly digressive to bear closely on his main theme of the duality of love.

Chaucer, in fact, like Nature, knits the elements of his poem in a firm bond; but, also like Nature, he does more than this – and a good deal more than Jean de Meun – and preserves their harmonious relationship to each other and the whole. Philosophizing does not mean exhaustive exposition at disproportionate length. Ideas which take up several pages of Macrobius's book are firmly but lightly sketched in a couple of lines. The reader is given the theme of

common profit in the first part and he is left to work out its application to the second for himself. Nature is not left at comparative
peace in the world of the elements, but is placed on her mound
among a troop of birds who are noisy, rude and contentious, as
well as capable of expressing the loftiest sentiments. Appropriately
enough, it is the noisy, rude ones who are most easily brought to
fulfil her laws, and the idealists who threaten trouble. From Nature's
point of view the duck is in the right of it:

> 'Wel bourded,' quod the doke, 'by myn hat!
> That men shulde loven alwey causeles,
> Who can a resoun fynde or wit in that?
> Daunseth he murye that is myrtheles?
> Who shulde recche of that is recheles?
> Ye quek!' yit seyde the doke, ful wel and fayre,
> 'There been mo sterres, God wot, than a payre!'
>
> (589–95)

From the point of view of maximum fecundity, this is, indeed,
spoken 'ful wel and fayre', and the retort of the gentil tercelet:

> 'Thy kynde is of so low a wrechednesse
> That what love is, thow canst nat seen ne gesse',
>
> (601–2)

is fraught with danger, although it also indicates the possibility
of a richer experience. Mankind, in fact, for whose dilemmas the
noble birds stand, is left to grapple with the problems set them by
an endowment which is not wholly Nature's and which, while it
places heaven or hell within their reach, makes the simple happiness
of the duck difficult to achieve. It is true that the human situation is
only lightly touched on in the *Parlement*. We have to wait for the
Troilus, and for the treatment of the problems of love and marriage
in all their variety in the *Canterbury Tales*, to learn how perceptively
Chaucer could explore the subject and how complete was his
awareness of the interest and importance of the variation which the
human factor introduces into philosophical schemata.

Nature, at any rate, once more like the poet, does not dogmatize.
She treats her more complex and wayward creatures sympathetically; and we are left with the impression that, although her law

of fecundity must triumph in the end, chastity properly precedes fulfilment and is not incompatible with it. The conclusion of the debate, however, remains a matter of impression. The poet does not commit himself:

> I wok, and othere bokes tok me to,
> To reede upon, and yit I rede alwey.
> I hope, ywis, to rede so som day
> That I shal mete som thyng for to fare
> The bet, and thus to rede I nyl nat spare
>
> (695–9)

A clearcut solution is indeed impossible because, just at the point when it seems about to become most abstract and definitive in its philosophizing, with the description of Nature, the poem un-expectedly explodes into a richness of life and movement which make abstract theorizing irrelevant. The noise of the birds effectively drowns any possible theoretical solution to the poet's problem, as he posed it in his opening stanza, and it is only on reflection that we realize how much light has been thrown on the themes, so casually suggested in the first section, of contradictory love and common profit.

When Africanus introduces the dreaming Chaucer into the park which contains the temples of Venus and Nature, his purpose in doing so is tersely expressed:

> 'I shal the shewe mater of to wryte'
> (168)

The matter turns out to be the application of the scientific and moral-philosophical ideas of Macrobius and Boethius to love in its various aspects. In the *House of Fame*, the poet's guide, now Jove's eagle, has the same preoccupation. It proposes to extend the material available to a poet who:

> 'hast no tydynges
> Of Loves folk yf they be glade,
> Ne of oght elles that God made.'
>
> (644–6)

This might lead us to expect an encyclopedic journeying among the wonders of creation – a popular form with which Chaucer was perfectly familiar. On the contrary, however, although the eagle does show Chaucer some natural phenomena of a marvellous kind in the course of his flight, the poet shows little interest in them:

> 'No fors,' quod y, 'hyt is no nede.
> I leve as wel, so God me spede,
> Hem that write of this matere.'
>
> (1011–13)

Books provide all the poet needs, so far as matter of this kind is concerned, as the *Parlement* demonstrates – and indeed, as Chaucer remarks, when it comes to the observation of 'ayerissh bestes', only thought, 'wyth fetheres of Philosophye', can fly high enough to contemplate them. The destination of the flight is, in fact, a specific one – the House of the goddess Fame; and its relevance to the eagle's purpose of giving the poet material to write about is soon made obvious. The renown of the most famous of all the heroes of old, Alexander and Hercules, is upheld by the goddess herself; but, apart from these, it is the writers and poets who 'bear up' the fame of peoples and places. In fact, for Chaucer, fame means primarily the reputation assigned to persons, races, or cities by written tradition. It is, therefore, very much the affair of an ambitious working poet. What he learns from it and from the contemplation of the house of the even more capricious Rumour is, characteristically, left for the reader to decide. It is not the result of the search for specific 'tidings' which is important, but the ideas which are explored on the way.

In the *Parlement*, the different blocks of material which are juxtaposed and examined in relation, or contrast, to each other are distinguished by differences in style and technique – the texture of the poetry is not the same in the opening section, in the description of Venus's temple or in the dialogue of the birds. These differences in texture are, of course, as much a part of the exposition as the structural organization of the material. By the differences in the language used, we are made to experience the difference in viewpoint between, say, the duck and the unhappy lovers of Venus's temple in a more direct way than would otherwise be possible. In the *House of Fame*, Chaucer uses the same method, but to a quite unprecedented degree, so that not only is the surface variety very much greater than that of the *Parlement*, but it would be hard to find a poem to set beside it for sheer technical brilliance. It is as though the theme of the complexity of Fame – who is, on the one hand, responsible for all the beauty, grandeur and importance of poetry, and on the other, absurdly capricious, untruthful and ultimately based only on the even more absurd and trivial Rumour – has been woven so closely through the whole surface of the poem that there is hardly a line, and certainly not a paragraph, which does not faithfully reflect it.

To speak so decidedly about the theme of the poem, however, is perhaps to anticipate, since critics are by no means agreed about it.[29] My view will, I hope, be sufficiently supported by what follows, but first more must be said about the technical virtuosity with which the poet presents his ambiguous subject-matter. A good starting point will be the first appearance of the Eagle – a figure, like Fame herself, part majestic, part grotesque – which forms the close of Book I and the opening of Book II.

At the end of Book I, Chaucer has just finished his résumé of the *Aeneid*, a long set piece in a serious style, with the interest centering on the story of Dido's unhappy passion.[30] No contemporary reader would be likely to question the importance and interest of this material, although its relevance to the main themes of the poem only gradually emerges.[31] After this impressive interlude, one might think that the poet would be hard put to it to end the book in a sufficiently striking way. Chaucer solves this problem by using material which would form the natural opening of the next book, that is, he introduces the figure which is to be the guide to the events of the next section:

> Thoo was I war, lo! at the laste,
> That faste be the sonne, as hye
> As kenne myghte I with myn yë,
> Me thoughte I sawgh an egle sore,
> But that hit semed moche more
> Then I had any egle seyn.
> But this as sooth as deth, certeyn,
> Hyt was of gold, and shon so bryghte
> That never sawe men such a syghte,
> But yf the heven had ywonne
> Al newe of gold another sonne;
> So shone the egles fethers bryghte,
> And somwhat dounward gan hyt lyghte.
>
> (496–508)

In spite of a certain sparseness in diction and rhythm, this is a description in the grand style, and its magnificent hyperbole of the heaven's new golden sun forms a fitting end to the book, not out of keeping with the splendours of the *Aeneid*. In fact, we are already in the presence of 'the beaute and the wonder' which is never far off in the *House of Fame*, even though it is often closely jostled by the grotesque and the trivial,[32] and which wrings from a highly critical poet the heartfelt tribute:

> 'O God!' quod y, 'that made Adam,
> Moche ys thy myght and thy noblesse!'
>
> (970–1)

After the interruption of the short proem, Chaucer takes up the description in Book II where he left it, using it to open the next narrative section. But now he treats it rather differently. After the first few lines, he leaves the purely pictorial aspect alone and concentrates on conveying a complicated impression of speed in movement, as the bird of prey stoops, gathers up its victim while still in flight and soars again, without a check:

> This egle, of which I have yow told,
> That shon with fethres as of gold,
> Which that so hye gan to sore,
> I gan beholde more and more,
> To se the beaute and the wonder;
> But never was ther dynt of thonder,
> Ne that thyng that men calle fouder,
> That smot somtyme a tour to powder,
> And in his swifte comynge brende,
> That so swithe gan descende
> As this foul, when hyt beheld
> That I a-roume was in the feld;
> And with hys grymme pawes stronge,
> Withyn hys sharpe nayles longe,
> Me, fleynge, in a swap he hente,
> And with hys sours ayen up wente,
> Me caryinge in his clawes starke
> As lyghtly as I were a larke,
> How high, I can not telle yow,
> For I cam up, y nyste how.
>
> (529–48)

We are still within the bounds of the grand style here – or, at any rate of the grand style as Chaucer found it in Dante – but we are to modulate, almost at once, into something different. Chaucer, like Dante in similar circumstances, is faint and afraid:

> For so astonyed and asweved
> Was every vertu in my heved,
> What with his sours and with my drede,
> That al my felynge gan to dede;
> For-whi hit was to gret affray.
>
> (549–53)

So far, although the description does not depend slavishly on the corresponding one in Dante's *Purgatorio* (indeed, most of the best things in it are new), there is nothing in the style or mood which is inconsistent with the seriousness which Dante maintains throughout his poem. His description runs thus:

> in sogno mi parea veder sospesa
>   un' aguglia nel ciel con penne d'oro,
>   con l'ali aperte ed a calare intesa;
> ed esser mi parea là dove foro
>   abbandonati i suoi da Ganimede,
>   quando fu ratto al sommo consistoro.
> Fra me pensava: 'Forse questa fiede
>   pur qui per uso, e forse d'altro loco
>   disdegna di portarne suso in piede.'
> Poi mi parea che, poi rotata un poco,
>   terribil come folgor discendesse,
>   a me rapisse suso infino al foco.
> Ivi parea che ella e io ardesse;
>   e sì lo 'ncendio imaginato cosse,
>   che convenne che 'l sonno si rompesse.
> Non altrimenti Achille si riscosse,
>   li occhi svegliati rivolgendo in giro
>   e non sappiendo là dove si fosse,
> quando la madre da Chirone a Schiro
>   trafuggò lui dormendo in le sue braccia,

là onde poi li Greci il dipartiro;
che mi scoss' io, sì come dalla faccia
mi fuggì 'l sonno, e diventa' ismorto
come fa l' uom che, spaventato, agghiaccia.

(I seemed in a dream to see above me stoop
    An eagle of golden plumage in the sky
    With wings strecht wide out and intent to swoop.
He seemed above the very place to fly
    Where Ganymede was forced his mates to lose
    When he was snatcht up to the assembly on high.
Within me I thought: Perhaps only because
    Of habit he strikes here, and from elsewhere
    Scorneth to carry up aught in his claws.
Then, having seemed to wheel a little, sheer
    Down he came, terrible as the lightning's lash,
    And snatcht me up as far as the fiery sphere.
Then he and I, it seemed, burnt in the flash,
    And I so scorched at the imagined blaze
    That needs must sleep be broken as with a crash.
Not otherwise Achilles in amaze,
    Not knowing whither he was come, did start
    and all around him turn his wakened gaze
When Scyros-wards from Chiron, next her heart,
    His mother bore him sleeping, to alight
    There where the Greeks compelled him to depart,
Than I now started as sleep fled me quite
    And my face turned to death-pale suddenly,
    Even as a man who freezes from affright.)
            (*Purgatorio* IX, 19–42; Binyon trans.)

Chaucer rejects the Classical similes, but what he does imitate from Dante, with great success, is the perfect control of the movement of the verse, in imitation of the movement of the bird in flight. The total effect, however, without the Classical allusions, is lighter, and the development is more rapid. We are carried along at a pace which makes easy the transition into a kind of writing which would be inconceivable in Dante's poem. When the eagle calls on the Dreamer of the *House of Fame* to awake, his first dazed reaction reminds us of Chaucer the dubiously successful lover – a person who could not appropriately be compared to Ganymede or Achilles (as he ruefully points out in line 589):

> And, for I shulde the bet abreyde,
> Me mette, 'Awak,' to me he seyde,
> Ryght in the same vois and stevene
> That useth oon I koude nevene;
> And with that vois, soth for to seyn,
> My mynde cam to me ageyn,
> For hyt was goodly seyd to me,
> So nas hyt never wont to be.
>
> (559–66)

With these lines, we find ourselves in a familiar, everyday world, in which it comes as no surprise when the eagle, for all its miraculous beauty, speaks with a familiar voice and is preoccupied with the difficulty of testing the pulse of a wriggling burden while in full flight:

> 'Seynte Marye!
> Thou art noyous for to carye,
> And nothyng nedeth it, pardee!
> For, also wis God helpe me,
> As thou noon harm shalt have of this;
> And this caas that betyd the is,
> Is for thy lore and for thy prow; –
> Let see! darst thou yet loke now?
> Be ful assured, boldely,
> I am thy frend.' And therwith I
> Gan for to wondren in my mynde.
> 'O God,' thoughte I, 'that madest kynde,
> Shal I noon other weyes dye?
> Wher Joves wol me stellyfye
> Or what thing may this sygnifye?'
>
> (573–87)

Whatever our view of Chaucer's purpose in this transition from the sublime to the broadly comic, we cannot but admire the ease and sureness of touch with which he makes it.

Contrasts of this kind, swift passages from the grand to the trivial, the sublime to the comic, and vice versa, are such a constant feature of this poem that we must regard them as a deliberate part of the poet's method. In, for example, the formal proems and invocations (surely in themselves a sign of ambitious craftsmanship) with which the books begin, we find the same jostling together of the apparently incongruous. The proem to Book II begins humbly with an imitation of the characteristic jingle of popular English romance:

> Now herkeneth, every maner man
> That Englissh understonde kan,
> And listeneth of my drem to lere.
> For now at erste shul ye here
> So sely an avisyon,
> That Isaye, ne Scipion,
> Ne kyng Nabugodonosor,
> Pharoo, Turnus, ne Elcanor,
> Ne mette such a drem as this!

Already, with the mention of famous dreamers, the jingling line has levelled out into the normal non-committal four-stress couplet which we have seen Chaucer using to good effect in transition passages in the *Book of the Duchess*. In the second half of the Prologue, however, it changes again, and the rhythm, with its calculated shifts of the pause in the line, gains a cumulative force which is quite unlike anything that has gone before:

> Now faire blisfull, O Cipris,
> So be my favour at this tyme!
> And ye, me to endite and ryme
> Helpeth, that on Parnaso duelle,
> Be Elicon, the clere welle.
> O Thought, that wrot al that I mette,
> And in the tresorye hyt shette
> Of my brayn, now shal men se
> Yf any vertu in the be,
> To tellen al my drem aryght.
> Now kythe thyn engyn and myght.
>   (518–28)

Surely an arrogant ending for a rhymer who started so diffidently with something very like the 'rym dogerel' of *Sir Thopas*.

New themes in the love vision

In the *Purgatorio*, after the description of the eagle, Dante addresses his reader and warns him that, as his matter becomes increasingly sublime, so his art must grow more exalted:

> Lettor, tu vedi ben com' io innalzo,
> la mia matera, e però con più arte
> non ti maravigliar s'io la rincalzo.
> (IX, 70–2)

It is as if Chaucer is determined to show not only the same discrimination in fitting the style to the subject matter, but also his ability to shift rapidly fron one level to another in such a way that his verse accurately mirrors each alteration in content. In the *House of Fame*, where poetry itself, according to his definition of Fame, is one of the main themes, we can see stylistic innovation – the bending, stretching, as it were elasticizing of the English poetic language – going on, if not quite for its own sake, at least as a major part of the brilliant display which is the poem's *raison d'être*. Whereas in the *Troilus*, for example, the juxtapositions and shifts of style – from the colloquialism of Pandarus to the deliberately conventionalized lover's plaints of Troilus or the grand style of the proems – all arise from the actual requirements of the story at a given point, in the *House of Fame* such changes (one or two obvious cases apart) reflect the shifting, ambiguous nature of the subject matter, which can best be handled by one who can run the whole gamut from 'drasty' rhyming to the 'rethorike sweete' of the great Italians. That this shifting style is the result of deliberate policy on the poet's part (if we were tempted to doubt it)[33] is shown by the Invocation which opens the third book, where, in a magnificent line, Apollo – 'O God of science and of lyght' – is called upon to guide the 'lytel laste bok', in spite of the fact that the 'rym ys lyght and lewed'. Here, it is true, Chaucer seems to distinguish between the form and subject-matter, since he adds:

> I do no diligence
> To shewe craft, but o sentence.
> (1099–100)

The closing lines of the invocation, however, show that we need not take this too seriously, since they refer to his total plan for form and content in this section:

And yif, devyne vertu thow
Wilt helpe me to shewe now
That in myn hed ymarked ys –
Loo, that is for to menen this,
The Hous of Fame for to descryve –
Thou shalt se me go as blyve
Unto the nexte laure y see,
And kysse yt, for hyt is thy tree.
Now entre in my brest anoon!

(1101–9)

Indeed, it is hardly likely that Chaucer would invoke the god of poetry without reference to 'art poetical', however modest his disclaimers. He could, no doubt, rely on his audience to share the joke of so noted a poet pretending to lack professional skill.

The figure of the goddess Fame is at the heart of the complexities of the poem, and in describing her rapid shifts of shape and mood Chaucer exploits to the full the stylistic variety which he has established in the earlier part. His initial description of 'this ilke noble quene' is a brilliant tour de force; in it the emphasis is on the wonder as well as the beauty of the strange figure, and also on the sheer dimension (little and great), number, or superlativeness of all her characteristics and associations:

Y saugh, perpetually ystalled,
A femynyne creature,
That never formed by Nature
Nas such another thing yseye.
For alther-first, soth for to seye,
Me thoughte that she was so lyte
That the lengthe of a cubite
Was lengere than she semed be.
But thus sone, in a whyle, she
Hir tho so wonderliche streighte
That with hir fet she erthe reighte,
And with hir hed she touched hevene,
Ther as shynen sterres sevene.
And therto eke, as to my wit,
I saugh a gretter wonder yit,

Upon her eyen to beholde;
But certeyn y hem never tolde.
For as feele eyen hadde she
As fetheres upon foules be,
Or weren on the bestes foure
That Goddis trone gunne honoure,
As John writ in th' Apocalips.
Hir heer, that oundy was and crips,
As burned gold hyt shoon to see;
And, soth to tellen, also she
Had also fele upstondyng eres
And tonges, as on bestes heres;
And on hir fet woxen saugh y
Partriches wynges redely.
     But, Lord! the perry and the richesse
I saugh sittyng on this godesse!
And, Lord! the hevenyssh melodye
Of songes, ful of armonye,
I herde aboute her trone ysonge,
That al the paleys-walles ronge!
So song the myghty Muse, she
That cleped ys Caliope,
And hir eighte sustren eke,
That in hir face semen meke;
And ever mo, eternally,
They songe of Fame, as thoo herd y:
'Heryed be thou and thy name,
Goddesse of Renoun or of Fame!'

                    (1364–1406)

    I have quoted this description at length because it is not only at the heart of the method of the poem but also of the matter. Among other things, Chaucer uses it to make two vital points: that, for him, Fame = Renown and does not have the Classical Latin sense of which he must have been perfectly well aware, and, secondly, that it is the Muses who sing eternal acclamations to Fame. The meaning of Renown, in fact, is more closely defined as the reputation handed down to posterity through written records and through the arts.[34]

    In his further handling of the goddess, Chaucer explores the question of the relationship of this recorded reputation to actual fact – to the real persons and events that it purports to describe. The result, for one who has been brought up to prefer other poets to Homer because Homer was a liar, is disquieting.[35] Fame, it appears, is a sister of Fortune (1547), and equally capricious. His first encounter with her method of treating her suitors leaves the poet wondering:

> They gonne doun on kneës falle
> Before this ilke noble quene,
> And seyde, 'Graunte us, Lady shene,
> Ech of us of thy grace a bone!'
> And somme of hem she graunted sone,
> And somme she werned wel and faire,
> And some she graunted the contraire
> Of her axyng outterly.
> But thus I seye yow, trewely,
> What her cause was, y nyste.
> For of this folk ful wel y wiste,
> They hadde good fame ech deserved
> Although they were dyversly served.
>
> (1534–46)

Moreover, this 'ilke noble quene', like the eagle, which was so impressive seen at a distance and which spoke with such a familiar voice close to, proves capable of as colloquial a turn of speech as any low-life character in the *Canterbury Tales*. In fact, she scolds like a fishwife:

> 'Fy on yow,' quod she, 'everychon!
> Ye masty swyn, ye ydel wrechches!
> Ful of roten, slowe techches!
> What? False theves! wher ye wolde
> Be famous good, and nothing nolde
> Deserve why, ne never ye roughte?
> Men rather yow to hangen oughte!
> For ye be lyke the sweynte cat
> That wolde have fissh: but wostow what?
> He wolde nothing wete his clowes.
> Yvel thrift come to your jowes,
> And eke to myn, if I hit graunte,
> Or do yow favour, yow to avaunte!'
>
> (1776–88)

New themes in the love vision

It is easy enough to follow the tracks of Chaucer's reading through the learned fluency of his initial description of Fame. It is not so easy to detect his models in a passage like the one just quoted. There is, however, a curious resemblance in the choppy rhythm and the energetic relish in vituperation between Fame's diatribe and the style of an earlier English romance – the *Lay of Havelok the Dane*:[36]

> Bernard stirt up, þat was ful big . . .
> Lep to þe dore, so he wore wode,
> And seyde, 'Hwat are ye, þat are theroute,
> þat þus biginnen forto stroute?
> Go henne swiþe, fule þeues,
> For bi þe Louerd þat man on leues,
> Shol ich casten þe dore open,
> Sum of you shal ich drepen,
> And þe oþre shal ich kesten
> In feteres, and ful faste festen!'
> 'Hwat haue ye seid?' quoth a ladde,
> 'Wenestu þat we ben adradde?
> We sholen at þis dore gonge,
> Maugre þin, carl, or ouht longe.'
>
> *(Havelok, 1774–89)*

Comparisons between the vigorous, thrusting style of parts of the *House of Fame* and *Havelok* could be multiplied; but, even if Chaucer did not know its energetic rhythms and vocabulary, and its somewhat unusual ability to sustain an effect through a long passage, he would have found in earlier English romances plenty of short passages, lines and turns of phrase, to serve as a basis and to give the general sound and ring of Fame's tirades. To give one brief example, the pattern of the opening of her speech is found in these vigorous lines of *Kyng Alisaunder*:

> 'Fitz a puteyne!' he seide, 'lecchoure!
> Thou schalt sterue so a tretour!'
>
> *(B, 3912–13)*

This matter is, perhaps, worth a moment's pause, because Chaucer's avowed preoccupation with the technique of poetry is so great in the *House of Fame* – and, as we shall see, he by no means excludes the humbler vernacular practitioners from her presence. We have already seen his exploitation of the familiar commonplace of the English romance jingle in the proem to Book II. It is at any rate worth conjecturing (as we have already done in chapter 1 [36a]) that he may have deliberately drawn on such technical achievements as his English predecessors could offer him, and that an important part of his preoccupation in this poem may have been how, from the 'grant translateur', to become, with equal greatness, the poet of 'every maner man / That Englissh understonde kan'. In the development of such a poet, a moment must certainly come when the fact has to be faced that for all the help afforded by the sophisticated poets of France and Italy, his particular medium is, for better or worse, his own language, with its own traditions and its own genius. In Chaucer's case, since the earlier English tradition was not one of exalted writing, but rather of a plain, vigorous style, the question would be how far its achievements could be incorporated in a wider stylistic range which also utilized the more varied achievements of the modern French and Italian poets, as well as that of the Classical ones. In the *House of Fame*, Chaucer seems to be still at the experimental stage. It is not so much a question of producing a homogeneous blend of different styles and techniques, but rather of exploiting first one and then another as it is appropriate to the subject-matter. The result may, at times, seem harsh, and the transitions abrupt, but in the case of Fame herself, it is fitting that the shifty, delusive goddess, so zestfully compounded out of a string of learned literary allusions, should, with equal zest, speak with such an unmistakably English accent.

The pinnacles of Fame's house are set with 'habitacles', each containing figures:

> Of alle maner of mynstralles,
> And gestiours, that tellen tales
> Both of wepinge and of game,
> Of al that longeth unto Fame.
>
> (1197–200)

The idea of recorded Fame, in fact, is stretched to cover poetry of all kinds. The same inclusiveness is shown when the musicians are described. The list starts with Orpheus, but we soon hear of the 'smale harpers with her glëes', who:

68

> Sate under hem in dyvers seës,
> And gunne on hem upward to gape,
> And countrefete hem as an ape,
> Or as craft countrefeteth kynde.
>
> (1210–13)

Nevertheless, these 'small' practitioners are just as much a part of the external adornment of Fame's House as the great ones, and the same is true of the musicians:

> Tho saugh I stonden hem behynde,
> Afer fro hem, al be hemselve,
> Many thousand tymes twelve,
> That maden lowde mynstralcies
> In cornemuse and shalemyes,
> And many other maner pipe,
> That craftely begunne to pipe,
> Bothe in doucet and in rede,
> That ben at festes with the brede;
> And many flowte and liltyng horn,
> And pipes made of grene corn,
> As han thise lytel herde-gromes,
> That kepen bestis in the bromes.
>
> (1214–26)

It is, no doubt, largely because they caught Spenser's eye that these last lines seem to us representative of a manner that is peculiarly English. But there is also no doubt that they reproduce a lilt that is to be found in earlier English romances which use the four-stress couplet and which like to interpose a lyrical movement in the more straightforward narrative progression. *Kyng Alisaunder*,[37] for example, has:

> Mery is the blast of the styuoure;
> Mery is the touchyng of the harpoure.
> Swete is the smellyng of the floure;
> Swete it is in maydens boure.
> Appel swete bereth fair coloure;
> Of trewe loue is swete amoure.
>
> (B, 2567–72)

Another romance which Chaucer certainly knew, and from which he elsewhere borrows,[38] has:

> Kniȝtes and leuedis com daunceing
> In queynt atire, gisely
> Queynt pas and softly;
> Tabours and trunpes ȝede hem bi,
> And al maner menstraci.
>
> (*Sir Orfeo*, 298–302)

With this lyrical insertion in the *House of Fame*, in the manner of romances such as these, Chaucer, it seems to me, is at once utilizing something he found as a part of an earlier poetic style and laying a foundation for much that was to come.

Chaucer, it is clear, thought of the 'little' poets and musicians as operating in and with the vernacular – not only, of course, in English. Apart from 'the Bret Glascurion', there are 'Pipers of the Duche tonge' (1234), and the minstrels of Spain. Even inside the House, although the positions of dignity on the pillars are given to the great authors of the past who wrote in Greek or Latin,[39] still:

> The halle was al ful, ywys,
> Of hem that writen olde gestes,
> As ben on treës rokes nestes.
>
> (1514–16)

All this emphasizes the connection of Fame with poetry; and, just as Fame herself gives no guarantee of the ultimate truth or importance of the event she helps to preserve in memory, so the poets are of all sorts and sizes. The trivial is not excluded either from the matter or the makers.

The *House of Fame* thus has a great deal to say which bears directly on the subject of poetry and art poetical. It remains to ask how far, and in what forms, this theme is consistently developed through the poem. If we look at the ground-plan of the work, we can, I think, see that, for all the surface elaboration, it is designed to set out one main theme in a fairly straightforward way. Chaucer, as a matter of fact, with the kind of economy of effort which is not rare in poets, uses the same basic plan for much the same basic purpose in all three of his love visions, although this is a little obscured by the very striking

70

differences between them in other respects. All three have four parts: (1) an introduction concerned with sleep; (2) a retold tale; (3) a first location and a first experience of the Dreamer; (4) a second location and a second experience.[40] To recapitulate briefly, the *Book of the Duchess* has an introduction lamenting Chaucer's inability to sleep; a retold tale, of Ceix and Alcyone, linked to the introduction, since it suggests a solution to the problem of sleeplessness – and to what follows, since it illustrates and highlights the problem of mortality and grief; a first location in which the Dreamer experiences an encounter with the Emperor Octovyen's unsuccessful hunting party, in a woodland described in terms of the *Roman de la Rose*. This part is linked, as a tactful and graceful conceit, to the last, the second location and experience, in which, deeper in the wood, the Dreamer encounters the Man in Black, and the real purpose of the poem is brought into the foreground. The *Book of the Duchess* thus shows a continuous development of its theme, although the links are of a tenuous kind. In the *Parlement*, they are much stronger; from the introduction on sleep, to the Dream, which forms a continuation to the retold tale of Africanus, and on to the twofold vision of Venus and Nature, which with all its contrasts, explores a single subject. The *House of Fame* repeats the introduction on sleep and dreams, but moves the retold tale, that of the *Aeneid*, into the dream itself and makes it a part of an extra location, the Temple of Venus. The two locations and experiences of the story proper follow in due order, though with much additional material in the form of the space-flight and the Eagle's informative discourses. These locations and experiences are, of course, the House of Fame itself, and the Dreamer's vision there, which gives him insight into the nature of Fame, and the House of Rumour, where he learns what rumour is like and where, if the poem had been finished, he might perhaps have learnt something more.

In the first part of the *House of Fame*, Chaucer brings into the foreground and develops at length one of the typical trophies of Venus's temple, which, in the *Parlement*, are only briefly mentioned as part of the general decoration of the place. In the *Parlement*, the main part of the description is the set piece depicting Venus herself. In the *House of Fame*, however, Venus is described almost cursorily, the repeated 'hers' suggesting no more than a brief reminder of attributes that every reader will readily call to mind (rather typically with Chaucer, the comb in her hand is not, in fact, an obvious one):

> Hyt was of Venus redely,
> The temple; for in portreyture,
> I sawgh anoon-ryght hir figure
> Naked fletynge in a see.
> And also on hir hed, pardee,
> Hir rose garlond whit and red,
> And hir comb to kembe hyr hed,
> Hir dowves, and daun Cupido
> Hir blynde sone, and Vulcano,
> That in his face was ful broun.
>
> (130–9)

In contrast to this, the story engraved on the tablet of brass – or possibly the series of wall paintings which accompany the inscription[41] – occupies lines 143–467. When the tale is told Chaucer leaves the temple, after only the briefest of recapitulations on the general excellence of its decoration:

> 'A, Lord!' thoughte I, 'that madest us,
> Yet sawgh I never such noblesse
> Of ymages, ne such richesse,
> As I saugh graven in this chirche.'
>
> (470–3)

Venus's temple, in fact, is here only of interest and importance as the setting for Virgil's poem.[42]

What, in fact, are the links between Venus and Virgil? One of the most obvious is, of course, that Venus is an important character in the *Aeneid* and the mother of its hero. Further, as Chaucer retells it, the *Aeneid* has all the ingredients which he himself seems to find essential to the poetry of love: a mixture of high policy and human passion, a machinery of the gods which can be brought to bear illuminatingly on human conduct;[43] and, of course, the tragic ending to a love story presided over by Venus alone, without Nature's cooperation. These, already touched on in the *Parlement*, are the stuff of which the *Troilus* and the *Knight's Tale* are made.

Chaucer retells the whole story, from the opening lines, which he translates and quotes, to its conclusion. But he gives more space to Dido and her abandonment by Aeneas than to any other part. This seems to justify the Eagle's reproach 'thou hast no tydynges / Of Loves folk yf they be glade'. It is not, however, the love story that is elaborated or commented on in the rest of the *House of Fame*. On the contrary, what makes this particular story appropriate to Chaucer's purpose and links it to the next two books is the special situation in which both the main figures are placed. Both are exposed to unpleasant gossip. Dido has lost her reputation, both for lack of virtue and because she is shamefully abandoned by her lover:

> 'O, wel-awey that I was born!
> For thorgh yow is my name lorn,
> And alle myn actes red and songe
> Over al thys lond, on every tonge.
> O wikke Fame! For ther nys
> Nothing so swift, lo, as she is!
> O, soth ys, every thing ys wyst,
> Though hit be kevered with the myst.
> Eke, though I myghte duren ever,
> That I have don, rekever I never,
> That I ne shal be seyd, allas,
> Yshamed be thourgh Eneas,
> And that I shal thus juged be . . .'
>
> (345–57)

Aeneas, too, will need to be 'excused' if his reputation is to survive unharmed, an office which Virgil performs for him:

> But to excusen Eneas
> Fullyche of al his grete trespas,
> The book seyth . . .
>
> (427–9)

Chaucer has dealt with his recapitulation of Virgil's story in a subtle way, so as to bring out his own theme. Just as, at the beginning, the inscription on the tablet of brass seems to dissolve and give way to a series of paintings, so, from about line 293 onwards, 'But let us speke of Eneas . . .', the graven images fade from view and the story is directly presented, with the characters moving and speaking. In this part, we are shown the actual events, which Virgil, and other upholders of Fame, are to hand down to posterity, together with their own particular colouring of the matter, and their own excuses for the conduct of their hero:

Whoso to knowe hit hath purpos,
Rede Virgile in Eneydos,
Or the Epistle of Ovyde.

(377–9)

The end of the story is told, rather hurriedly, in terms of what 'the book us tellis'. The result is, that out of a kind of frame of two-dimensional pictorial scenes, that part of the story which concerns love, and which also places the protagonists in a peculiarly equivocal position as regards their future repute, stands out in life and movement as the actual basis on which the great poets worked.

This, then, is what Chaucer finds in the Temple of Venus. He does not, as he does in the *Parlement*, see a living, breathing goddess, attended by Priapus as well as by Cupid. He finds a painting and a poem in which Venus is implicated in more ways than one. Moreover, it is the poem, not the goddess to which he gives most space, and his treatment of it is not calculated to bring out its relation to Venus and her worship, but to raise questions like that of the poet's relation to his subject-matter and to the basis of the story in history.

After expressing his appreciation of the 'noblesse' of what he has seen (470–2), Chaucer emerges in an uninhabited desert. This waste-land suggests some degree of frustration or dissatisfaction with what he has just experienced.[44] His praise of the temple is for its art, and the characteristic feature of the desert is that there is in it:

No maner creature
That ys yformed be Nature.

(489–90)

His second burst of enthusiastic praise for what he sees in the poem is for nature's creatures, not for art, and it is to their contemplation that the Eagle, plunging down into the desert, with all the brilliance of a new sun, brings him. His words then pick up and echo his praise of the temple, but with a difference:[45]

'O God!' quod y, 'that made Adam,
Moche ys thy myght and thy noblesse!'

(970–1)

Fame's house is certainly elaborately and richly ornamented, but she herself, however strange and unique, is one of Nature's creatures:

> A femynyne creature,
> That never formed by Nature
> Nas such another thing yseye.
>   (1365–7)

The negatives pile up, but this must mean that Fame, although unlike any of Nature's other creations, was made by her. The word 'creature' could hardly be used of anything except Nature's handi- work. There is, thus, a pattern in the way in which events follow one another. The Dreamer finds only art, and no creature of any kind, in Venus's temple. In the desert, a natural place, he finds neither art nor life; then, under the guidance of the Eagle he reaches a place which, while it displays great elaboration of art in the construction and adornment of Fame's house, is teeming with creatures.

The Eagle, certainly, seems to suggest that Chaucer ought to pay more attention to experience of the actual world around him, the work of Nature, than to what he learns from books or artifacts like the richly decorated temple:

> 'Wherfore, as I seyde, ywys,
> Jupiter considereth this,
> And also, beau sir, other thynges;
> That is, that thou hast no tydynges
> Of Loves folk yf they be glade,
> Ne of noght elles that God made;
> And noght oonly fro fer contree
> That ther no tydynge cometh to thee,
> But of thy verray neyghebores,
> That duellen almost at thy dores,
> Thou herist neyther that ne this.'
>   (641–51)

How exactly are we to take all this? Not, it is obvious, too naïvely, or we should find ourselves giving literal credence to the Eagle's aspersions on Chaucer's wit and morals. It is, of course, tempting to see the Eagle's criticism that too much time is being spent on books and too little on 'thy verray neyghebores' as a call for what we should think of as 'realism' in art and the exploitation of the familiar and the everyday – especially since we know (as Chaucer, at this time, presumably did not) what the poet was to make of such material in some of the *Canterbury Tales*. This would be to understand the Eagle's advice as a piece of purely literary criticism, rather like that of the great novelist to the beginner in Henry James's short story *The Lesson of the Master*:

> 'You must do England – there's such a lot of it.'
> 'Do you mean that I must write about it? . . .'
> 'Of course you must, and tremendously well, do you mind?
> That takes off a little of my esteem for this thing of yours –
> that it goes on abroad. Hang "abroad"! Stay at home and do
> things here – do subjects that we can measure.'

Although the Eagle does seem to favour the idea that Chaucer should 'do subjects that we can measure', he would obviously not be at home in this dialogue. What he does seem to be urging, if we can judge from his later summary of what Chaucer is to learn in Fame's house (672 ff.), is, merely, inclusiveness – the exploitation of the fact that life has greater variety than art, a fact which has already been indicated by the glimpse given in Book I of the actions and persons that lie behind the official 'excusing' versions of the great poets.[46] On the other hand, the Eagle's summary of the variety to be put at the poet's disposal is an undignified rigmarole, in which comedy and tragedy are not differentiated and in which one thing follows another like the disorderly crowd in the House of Rumour, when they 'troden fast on others heles, / And stampen, as men doon aftir eles' (2153–4):

> 'For truste wel that thou shalt here,
> When we be come there I seye,
> Mo wonder thynges, dar I leye
> And of Loves folk moo tydynges,
> Both sothe sawes and lesinges;
> And moo loves newe begonne,
> And longe yserved loves wonne,
> And moo loves casuelly
> That ben betyd, no man wot why,
> But as a blynd man stert an hare.'
> (672–81)

The variety is there, but life would seem to need the shaping hand of art. We have moved from the static, finished, 'official version' of the *Aeneid* to something so jumbled and confused as to have no significance. These, surely, are the two poles around which the *House of Fame* is organized: the finished work of art, which has its own beauty but is of doubtful validity in relation to actual fact, and the facts themselves, which, 'casuel' in their very nature, are made even more confused as they slip into the past and can only be known through Rumour and Fame. Certainly, the conclusion that renown is of little absolute value is unavoidable; but Fame's suppliants are not, as a matter of fact, asking for precisely this. The distinction is perhaps a nice one, but, as Chaucer phrases their requests, they ask for a certain version of their actions to be the accepted one, rather than for praise (or dispraise) *per se*. This is clear, for example, in the case of the wicked men who want to be known as wicked: ironically enough they want Fame's version to correspond to the truth:

> 'Wherefore we praye yow, a-rowe,
> That oure fame such be knowe
> In alle thing ryght as hit ys.'
>
> (1835–7)

Fame's activities, in fact, are, in the last analysis, only the putting out of versions – the summation of the work of the rookery of writers who people her house. It is only reasonable, therefore, that Chaucer should conclude that he has learnt nothing from her that he did not know already and that, as far as his own art is concerned, he will have nothing to do with her:

> 'I wot myself best how y stonde;
> For what I drye, or what I thynke,
> I wil myselven al hyt drynke,
> Certeyn, for the more part,
> As fer forth as I kan myn art.'
>
> (1878–82)

This is ostensibly an answer to the question 'Artow come hider to han fame?' (1872), and Chaucer does answer this in terms of personal reputation, in lines 1876–7:

77

'Sufficeth me, as I were ded,
That no wight have my name in honde.'

In lines 1878–82, however, the meaning of the Fame he does not
want seems to shift; and, although he speaks in terms that are almost
riddling, the sense of 'drinking' his own experience and thought in
accordance with his own knowledge of his art is, surely, that he will
assume full responsibility for his own handling of the matter of his
poetry and for the relation the finished product will bear to its
originating material, without concerning himself overmuch with
Fame in the sense of those traditions preserved by her rookery of
writers, or even by her more dignified upholders on their pillars.
'Thinking' here is likely to mean the special mental activity of the
poet, as 'thought' does in the proem to Book II, or, in the paraphrase
of the proem to the third book, 'That in myn hed ymarked ys'.

With this manifesto on his art, the poet sets off for the House of
Rumour and one more attempt to learn the tidings he was promised.
What he finds here is the raw material of Fame: the even more
haphazard basis of her haphazard judgements, since whatever is
spoken here:

> Thus out at holes gunne wringe
> Every tydynge streght to Fame,
> And she gan yeven ech hys name,
> After hir disposicioun,
> And yaf hem eke duracioun,
> Somme to wexe and wane sone,
> As doth the faire white mone,
> And let hem goon. Ther myghte y seen
> Wynged wondres faste fleen,
> Twenty thousand in a route,
> As Eolus hem blew aboute.
>
> (2110–20)

We have travelled a long way from the splendid monument of the
Aeneid, and yet not without Virgil's own authority for doing so. In
the passage on *Fama* in Book IV, which Chaucer uses as the basis for
his own portrait of Fame, Virgil describes the spread of rumours
about the lovers, which finally reach King Iarbas.[47] It is reasonable
enough to pass from Virgil's actual poem to the permanency of

Fame, and its uncertain and impermanent basis, and so on to the even more fleeting, unreliable rumours that feed Fame. Fame in this sense, of course, is not the same as Virgil's *Fama*, but once the new equation of *Fama = Laus* (Renown) is admitted, the whole progression is logical enough; and we can see why the story of Dido and Aeneas, in the setting of the *Aeneid*, forms the best possible starting point for a poem which plays at length with the implications for poets and poetry of the various senses of *Fama*.

The most wonderful thing about the House of Rumour, Chaucer tells us, is the distortion which every tale undergoes before it escapes to go on to the House of Fame:

> Thus north and south
> Wente every tydyng fro mouth to mouth,
> And that encresing ever moo,
> As fyr ys wont to quyke and goo,
> From a sparke spronge amys,
> Til al a citee brent up ys.
> And whan that was ful yspronge,
> And woxen more on every tonge
> Than ever hit was, [hit] wente anoon
> Up to a wyndowe out to goon.
>
> (2075–84)

Even then, in the struggle to get out, the thronging rumours cause more confusion by getting mixed up with each other:

> Thus saugh I fals and soth compouned
> Togeder fle for oo tydynge.
>
> (2108–9)

In spite of these apparent disadvantages, Chaucer hurries about with a satisfaction which the House of Fame did not afford him:

> I alther-fastest wente
> About, and dide al myn entente
> Me for to pleyen, and for to lere,
> And eke a tydynge for to here –
>
> (2131–4)

79

At this point, with the poem obviously nearing its end, the pace quickens into something like the *rym dogerel* of the Book II proem, and the style becomes a riddling one once more. Chaucer will not commit himself to a clear statement as to whether he has or has not in fact heard the tidings (although it sounds as if he has) and, still more, will give no inkling of what they might be:

> a tydynge for to here
> That I had herd of som contre
> That shal not now be told for me –
> For hit no nede is, redely;
> Folk kan synge hit bet than I;
> For al mot out, other late or rathe,
> Alle the sheves in the lathe.
>
> (2134–40)

This has every sign of a rapid retreat from his subject, leaving his readers to draw their own conclusions. It is, moreover, also a retreat from seriousness. There is no doubt, from many passages – the serious parts of the proems and the manifesto on Chaucer's own relation to Fame, for example – that the issues raised in the poem are of great importance to the poet. But it would not be in Chaucer's manner, or in keeping with that urbanity which we have seen as the key-note of so much of his work, to end the divertissement on too serious or definitive a note. Accordingly, even this riddling refusal to commit himself is interrupted by the crowd running and jostling to hear something new:

> For I saugh rennynge every wight,
> As faste as that they hadden myght;
> And everych cried 'What thing is that?'
> And somme sayde, 'I not never what.'
> And whan they were alle on an hepe,
> Tho behynde begunne up lepe,
> And clamben up on other faste,
> And up the nose and yën kaste,
> And troden fast on others heles,
> And stampen, as men doon aftir eles.
>
> (2145–54)

After this magnificent crescendo, in a style which, like Fame's scolding, seems reminiscent of the rhythms and methods of *Havelok*,[48] and which is certainly both colloquial and essentially English in tone, the poem breaks off, and the words of the 'man of gret auctorite' are lost to us. Caxton's solution, of a few lines telling how this loud voice woke the Dreamer up and ended his dream, is neat but, clearly, only a guess. Certainly, Chaucer can have had little more to say. He has fully explored the ideas of Fame and Rumour,[49] and it would be unlike him, as we have said, to end with any clearcut 'solution' to any of the problems he has raised.

To sum up: it seems to me that in the *House of Fame*, Chaucer has taken as his main theme the relation of poetry to the traditions which form its material. On one level, he writes in a jesting spirit which leads him to the *reductio ad absurdum* of rumours crying angrily, 'Lat me go first!' 'Nay, but let me!'; but on another he raises seriously many problems very relevant to the poet: the relation of art to nature, for example, and to other works of art as the objects of imitation; the question of the poet's personal responsibility to his own experience and creative powers. I think, too, that another basic theme emerges and another problem is examined. This is the problem of Chaucer's own, personal identity as a poet – his relationship to the great past, as represented by Virgil, and also his position in a line of descent which includes the little poets of the vernacular languages. The stylistic variations of the *House of Fame* certainly include, as we have seen, many imitations of more popular types of English writing, and it is perhaps not going too far to suggest that one of the underlying problems which Chaucer tries to thrash out in this strange poem is the exact relation of a poet of his day, with all France and Italy to draw on in addition to the Classical language of Virgil and Ovid, to his own roots in his own language. This, again, raises the even more important problem of the status of the vernacular poet: whether he was to remain among the little craftsmen, inhabiting an obscure and dusty rookery, or whether he could, as Chaucer hopes at the end of the *Troilus*, follow in the steps of the great past-masters. There seems little doubt of Chaucer's answer and no failure of confidence in the 'vertu', 'engyn and myght' of his poetic inspiration.

3

Troilus and Criseyde

The *House of Fame*, whenever we date it and however we understand it, forms an interlude in Chaucer's exploration of the theme of love. In the *Troilus*, with one of the stories that he found among the trophies in Venus's temple in the *Parlement of Foules*, he once more takes up the subject of love's problems and paradoxes. He does so, however, with a difference. In the *Parlement*, he writes as one who knows not 'love in dede', and the material for his discussion is largely drawn from books. What *is* presented as direct experience is still kept at a distance by the use of the birds to suggest and comment on the human problem, but not to represent it directly. In the *Troilus*, on the other hand, 'love in dede' is exactly what is put before us, in a story about human beings who make their impact on us with no veil of animal fable or allegory between. Moreover, although there is still much exploration of the theory of love, the tragedy lies, as much as anything, in the failure of theory, however complicated, to cope with the complexity of human reactions. In this respect, we could regard the *Troilus* as expanding the suggestion contained in the difficulties of the noble birds in love in the *Parlement*.[1]

It is true, of course, that all directness of impact is contained in the story itself: the poet is still cautious in claiming for himself knowledge derived from experience. But there is a difference between the total disclaimer of the *Parlement* and his cautious qualification of his own position at the beginning of the *Troilus*:

For I, that God of Loves servantz serve,
Ne dar to Love, for myn unliklynesse,
Preyen for speed, al sholde I therfore sterve,
So fer am I from his help in derknesse.

(I, 15–18)

There is a claim in the paraphrase of the papal title, as well as a
denial in the 'derknesse'; and we are left with an author who occupies
a more ambiguous, but also a more ambitious position than was the
case in the *Parlement*.

Again, it is true that, throughout the poem, Chaucer is careful to
disclaim personal responsibility for his story. He refers, again and
again, to his author – to what the book tells us, even to what people
say – with poignant effect in his reluctant report of Criseyde's
dealings with Diomede, at the end:

Men seyn – I not – that she yaf hym hire herte.

(V, 1050)

The result of the device, it seems to me, is not to build up the
theme – which is certainly present in the *Parlement* and, though with
a difference, in the *House of Fame* – of authority versus experience, but
rather to increase our sense of the objectivity of the story-telling.
This, we are told by a poet who is still, as he was in the *Parlement*,
'astonyed' by the 'wonderful werkynge' of love, is how it is all laid
down as having actually happened. Like most of Chaucer's interven-
tions as narrator, these statements have to be understood as guiding
us not as to the facts of composition, but as to the way in which we
are to regard the story at the moments in which its teller intervenes.
The line just quoted, for example, heightens our sense of the pathos
and the pity of Criseyde's failure, and does nothing else. The *Troilus*
is an ambitious work, probably Chaucer's first one to be laid out on
a really large scale and to show, fully absorbed into its texture and
structure, the impact of the new Italian models and the new ideas
concerning the scope and dignity of poetry which were, in part at
least, the fruit of the Italian journeys. Yet, in spite of all the assur-
ances that the poet is merely following his model, the most cursory
comparison of the *Troilus* with *Il Filostrato* shows Chaucer working
with great freedom, and with full control over his material.

The main differences between Boccaccio's *Il Filostrato* and Chaucer's *Troilus and Criseyde* have often been described[2] – only a brief summary will be needed here. In general plan and purpose the two poems are quite unlike. Boccaccio's is a poem straightforwardly concerned with love. It arises, he tells us, from the absence of his mistress, when, searching among old stories for the most suitable one to express his griefs, he finds that of Troilus. His retelling of it is aimed at provoking her pity. The setting is a courtly one. The prologue places the whole matter as arising out of discussion as to which of three things would give a lover most delight: sometimes to see his lady, sometimes to talk of her, or sometimes to think of her. This is spoken of as a formal discussion in Love's court among noble men and beautiful ladies.[3] Boccaccio says that he himself always maintained that thought gave most delight, until the actual absence of his lady convinced him of his error. His poem has two focal points: the rapid and complete satisfaction of Troilo's desires by a willing Criseida who takes torch in hand to light her lover to her bed,[4] and the complications of his grief at her absence and betrayal. She leaves Troy considerably sooner than Chaucer's Criseyde – half-way through Boccaccio's poem.

Boccaccio's treatment is not without its ironies and complexities; courtly ideals are sadly let down by his heroine, and his denial in the Prologue of an ambition so exalted as to hope to equal Troilo's success need not be taken wholly at its face value.[5] Nevertheless, in his conclusion, he merely warns lovers to choose more wisely than Troilo did when he set his heart on 'Criseida villana' (VIII, 28) – a phrase far too clearcut for Chaucer ever to use of his heroine. He makes no attempt to set the love story within any wider view of human life and achievement. His characters suit his story. Troilo is noble and brave, but is seen primarily as the amorous young man. Pandaro is young also; he is Criseida's cousin and guardian, but not a man of any greater standing or experience of life than the lovers themselves. Criseida is a young widow, easily won, and seeing no reason why she should not have a love affair like everybody else:

'Io non conosco in questa terra ancora
Veruna senza amante, e la più gente,
Com' io conosco e veggo, s'innamora.'

(II, 70)

The story, in fact, belongs to a world where almost everybody is in love, and where other activities are of little importance.

Chaucer's poem lacks the introductory courtly and personal setting. He takes from the Italian poem the large scale, the comparatively taut construction, and the simple story, which, making much of a few episodes and involving a concentration on the feelings and motives of a small group of people, contrasts sharply with the episodic type of romance. Instead of the exclusively personal frame of reference, he places much more emphasis on the historical setting of Troy and the Trojan War – his descriptions of life and of places in the city are much fuller than Boccaccio's, and often, indeed, are additions of his own. Within this much more three-dimensional, solidly constructed frame he places characters of a more complex kind than Boccaccio attempted; and in his handling of them we see the full flowering of the flexible, infinitely varied style of the minor poems, and of the descriptive and narrative technique which I have characterized as urbane – the ability to present the relations between characters within a naturalistically conceived social setting. Boccaccio's characters are comparatively simple in themselves, and their relationships are also simple and hardly extend beyond the love story. Chaucer's characters are complex, and their relationships depend to a large extent on their positions within a stable social scheme existing independently of the love affair which brings them all, for a time, closer together.

This is most clearly seen in the case of Pandarus's relationship to Criseyde. He is her uncle, not her cousin; he is an older man, and one on whom she habitually relies for help in conducting the ordinary affairs and business of her life. More than this, he stands in the kind of intimate relationship to her which allows them to share the same jokes and to be affectionately amused by each other – it is, in fact, from this most disarming of contacts that Chaucer makes the whole intrigue begin. In Book II, when we first see him with Criseyde, the conversation begins with the topic of love and with a joke. Pandarus asks about the book he finds her reading:

> 'For Goddes love, what seith it? Telle it us!
> Is it of love? O, som good ye me leere!'
> 'Uncle,' quod she, 'youre maistresse is nat here.'
> With that thei gonnen laughe . . .
>
> (II, 96–9)

It is because he occupies this position that Pandarus is able to work on Criseyde so effectively, and it is this familiarity and dependence that he exploits when he invents an imaginary lawsuit to frighten her into appealing to the royal princes of Troy. His familiar, colloquial introduction of the matter and her response keep the impression of their intimacy vividly before us:

> He seide, 'O verray God, so have I ronne!
> Lo, nece myn, se ye nought how I swete?'
> (II, 1464–5)

And she answers in terms of, first, her fears, and then, their relationship:

> 'What is he more aboute, me to drecche
> And don me wrong? What shal I doon, allas . . .
> But, for the love of God, myn uncle deere,
> No fors of that, lat hym han al yfeere.
> Withouten that I have ynough for us.'
> (II, 1471–8)

But, besides her involvement with Pandarus, Criseyde remains constantly involved in and aware of the dangers of her position in Troy. She does not forget that Troilus is 'my kynges sone' (II, 708) and a powerful protector.[6] The genuineness of her love, at the time, is not called in question, but her reactions are now more complicated than the simple decision of Criseida to be like all the other people whom she sees enjoying love; Criseyde's love is presented as the product of her whole experience of her world.

All this means that she is shown as sensitive to a much wider range of contacts and influences than Criseida. Chaucer, moreover, gives her the character of timidity and anxious calculation – Criseida's review of her circumstances before she decides to take Troilo as a lover is superficial compared to Criseyde's constant references back to her general situation and to the careful reservations which make her a willing victim of Pandarus's intrigue in the end.[7] These characteristics, of course, also lead her into Diomede's arms, and in the pathetically self-revealing speech in which she answers his proposals, we can follow her mind as it anxiously twists and turns in the feverish survey of her own difficulties which we have come to expect of her character.[8]

For the presentation of these complexities Chaucer needs a different narrative pace and a different inclusion of detail than Boccaccio. He takes much longer over the courtship, since his concern is primarily with the cumulative pressure of a series of small events on Criseyde's mind. What he takes over from Boccaccio tends to be lengthened, and two long sections are added: II, 1394–III, 231, in which Pandarus plans and brings about the meeting with Troilus at the house of Deiphebus, and III, 505–1309, the whole elaborate organization of the meeting at Pandarus's own house which brings about the final union of the lovers. Both these sections involve a great deal of detail of place, time and circumstance, which necessarily slows the pace of the narrative in comparison with the brisk, uninterrupted progress of Boccaccio's lovers towards their consummation.

Most of the changes in Pandaro when he becomes Pandarus have already been indicated: Chaucer gives him age and experience; puts him in the kind of intimate relationship with the other characters in which humour plays an important part; makes him essentially practical, a great deviser of all the little details which forward an intrigue; and, moreover, although his affectionate pity for Troilus is perhaps heightened, he is also given a kind of practical cynicism, in the last resort not reconcilable with the friendship and understanding he feels for Troilus. For Pandarus, love is a game – 'the olde daunce' – and there will always be as good fish in the sea as ever came out of it. It is the tragedy of Troilus's situation that, in a way which it is never given to Pandarus to understand, he does not share this view.[9]

Superficially at least, Troilus is the least altered from Boccaccio's conception of the character, in that he remains an ideal lover; but on analysis the changes are numerous and significant. From the start he is given a kind of innocence in love which Pandarus and Criseyde, both experienced, do not share. Unlike Troilo he loves for the first time. Secondly, although his great worthiness as a soldier and as a patriot are heightened, as a lover he is unable to act to help himself; he is fearful and introspective. He tries to analyse and explain his own fate, especially in the long speech on predestination, which is an addition of Chaucer's (IV, 957 ff.). Like Criseyde, he is worked on by Pandarus, but in a different way: where she is manœuvred into position largely through mental pressure, Troilus has to be moved about until he is physically in the right position – a state of affairs taken to the point of broad comedy in the consummation scene, where Pandarus actually strips him and casts him into bed. Pandarus's influence on his mind is, as a matter of fact, practically non-existent. His words are often received with flat contradiction, or at least set aside; and at one point Chaucer tells us they are not even heard – they go in at one ear and out at the other (IV, 432–4). In creating the character of this Trojan prince who is active and successful to the point of heroism in the field – he is second only to Hector – but who shows mental activity coupled with almost total physical inertia in the pursuit of his own affairs, Chaucer makes the crisis which removes Criseyde convincing. Just as Criseyde is, as he depicts her, necessarily the victim of Diomede, so Troilus is put in a position, when her removal from Troy is proposed, in which his active forceful character as a soldier and patriot is accurately balanced by his inability to act as a lover. On the one hand, he could retain her by force. On the other, this would mean the betrayal of his country and, also, the open, active prosecution of the love affair – and this, besides being harmful to the lady's reputation, is just what he has shown himself incapable of.[10] Both Troilus and Criseyde, as Chaucer shows them to us, are neatly caught, at their moments of crisis, by the net which circumstances cast round their own ruling characteristics.

All this is to suggest that more emphasis is to be placed on character and on personal responsibility in the unfolding of the story than is sometimes assumed. It is true, as Curry long ago pointed out, that Chaucer makes great play throughout the poem with the forces which destiny, fate, the influences of the stars, exert on his characters and their circumstances. Some of this was in Boccaccio's poem; but much is added by Chaucer. To get the proportion right between such forces and personal responsibility in the poem, we need to turn from analysis of the characters to a consideration of the story as a whole. It is, after all, not likely that Chaucer altered his original in order to present different characters; it is rather that, because he had a different conception of the significance of their story and of the issues involved in the action, the persons necessarily emerge as unlike those of Boccaccio.

Chaucer describes his own work at the beginning and at the end. In the first stanza he proposes: ,

The double sorwe of Troilus to tellen,
That was the kyng Priamus sone of Troye,
In lovynge, how his aventures fellen
Fro wo to wele, and after out of joie.

(1–4)

In the closing section he addresses his work:

Go, litel bok, go litel myn tragedye
(1786)

and contrasts it with the 'comedy' he hopes one day to write.[11]
Precisely what Chaucer meant by 'tragedy' is indicated by a gloss to
the *de Consolatione Philosophiae* which he duly included in his translation. This defines tragedy as a poem with a certain kind of content:

What other thyng bywaylen the cryinges of tragedyes but oonly
the dedes of Fortune, that with unwar strook overturneth the
realmes of gret nobleye? (*Glose. Tragedye is to seyn a dite of a
prosperite for a tyme, that endeth in wrecchidnesse*)

(II. pr. 2, 67–72)

The definitions of tragedy in the *Monk's Prologue and Tale* agree with
this and, within the tale at any rate, also link tragedy and Fortune.[12]
In the case of the *Troilus*, as Chaucer points out, a double movement
is present, since Troilus begins in happiness of a kind, before he falls a
victim to love. He then suffers misery, which gives way for a short
period to bliss, when his love is successful; and this, in turn, is followed
by the misery of his betrayal. This scheme does, in fact, give the work
its overall form. Where Boccaccio's poem is arranged in nine short
parts, Chaucer has a symmetrical arrangement of five books: two
for the first period of sorrow, one for the brief period of bliss, and two
more for the final sorrow and the tragic conclusion. If we look more
closely at the disposition of the material within this scheme, we shall
see that it is the basic concept of a doubly tragic love, which finally
destroys a great and worthy man, that shapes the characters. No
doubt the result is, as we should say, 'to bring them to life', and no
doubt Chaucer was as well aware of this as we can be. By deepening
and extending the scope and significance of Boccaccio's concept of
love he has, in fact, at the same time necessarily deepened and
extended the whole concept of characterization.

89

Tragedy, as we have said, implied for Chaucer a definite movement in human life – a pattern taken by the course of events; and, as
we read the *Troilus*, to say nothing of other works with similar
themes, it becomes clear that for him such patternings of events had
philosophical implications. These are often expressed through the
linking, which we have already seen, of the tragic pattern and the
Wheel of Fortune.[13]

For the reader of Boethius, or of Seneca, the phenomenon for
which the turning of Fortune's wheel is a figure is an inescapable
feature of all human and natural life.[14] The world is essentially
subject to change, and, indeed, it is only through change that it can
achieve any semblance of stability. This, however, is a stability of the
whole at the expense of the parts. Individuals, whether natural
objects or human beings, cannot expect material permanence, since
the continuity of nature depends on the completeness of the cycle of
birth, death, decay and rebirth which ensures the continuance of the
species. This cycle was, for Christian and Roman authors alike, an
expression of the beneficence of God's providence in the world below
the moon (according to Aristotle's widely followed view, which was
held, for example, by Macrobius, the moon forms the boundary
between the transitory and the intransitory). Theseus refers to this
in his speech on the First Mover and the Chain of Love.[15] It is also
in this sense that Nature in the *Parlement of Foules* presides as God's
vicaire over the pairing of the birds, that is over the continuity of the
species. She would also, although it does not happen to be a part of
the subject-matter of the poem, preside over the dissolution of the
individual fowl that make up her court.[16]

Although man on earth is ineluctably subject to change and to
changeful Fortune (and Chaucer knew from his reading of Boethius
that she is most dangerous and deceiving when she seems most
favourable, for then a reversal is sure to follow[17] – and this is the
pattern he in fact uses in the *Troilus*), it does not follow from this that
Chaucer's view was a deterministic one. In the first place, natural
change only applies below the moon, and it is possible for mankind to
mount beyond its sphere and exchange the values of time for those of
eternity; both Chaucer and Dante describe a man doing this.[18]
Secondly, his Roman authorities were as concerned as any later
Christian authors in explaining how man's freedom of will could set
him above the vagaries of Fortune. This is, in fact, what the *de
Consolatione* is about. It describes the Stoic good man who frees him-

self from Fortune by refusing to place his whole happiness in the transitory things over which she holds undisputed sway. The rewards open to such a man are the subject of the Proem of the *Parlement of Foules* – in contrast to the uncertain good of even natural love, working towards the preservation of the species.

The man who fixes his heart on a love which belongs exclusively to the sublunary world of change cannot expect permanence. There is, however, a love which is not under the government of the moon, and this love is not subject to loss or change. This is the 'celestial' love which Pandarus specifically rejects as unlikely to appeal to Criseyde:

> For this have I herd seyd of wyse lered,
> Was nevere man or womman yet bigete
> That was unapt to suffren loves hete,
> Celestial, or elles love of kynde . . .
> It sit hire naught to ben celestial
> As yet . . .
>
> (I, 976–84)

It is noteworthy that Pandarus calls both these loves 'natural'. St Bernard does the same:

> Excellit in naturae donis affectio haec amoris.
> (Of all the sentiments of nature this of love is the most excellent.)
> (*In Cantica Canticorum*, vii, 2)

and he adds 'praesertim cum ad suum recurrit principium, quod est Deus', a remark more in keeping with the attitude expressed in the epilogue than with Pandarus's. There is still another way in which love can achieve at least an affinity with permanence. This is through the marriage bond – the 'chaste love' of which Boethius writes and which Chaucer calls 'O parfit joye, lastynge everemo' in the *Knight's Tale*, where it provides an antidote to the sorrows of the earlier part of the poem.[19]

Troilus's love is no more 'celestial' than Criseyde's; and, since there is no possibility of its issue in marriage, Chaucer depicts it as an essentially and inevitably tragic love. This is not to say that he also depicts it as necessarily wrong or evil in itself. Its illicit nature, in being outside marriage, is certainly indicated; but, unlike many of his critics, Chaucer does not go out of his way to link it to Christian doctrine in the body of the work. Even in the epilogue, as we shall see, the implications are more complex than has sometimes been claimed.[20] Rather than explore the explicitly Christian moral and doctrinal implications of his love story, Chaucer prefers to present it as a most complete and perfect example of its kind, without at any point forgetting that its kind is not lasting. This means that the love of Troilus for Criseyde is subjected to a kind of double heightening which, on the one hand, makes their tragedy the most complete and impressive example which it would be possible to imagine and, on the other, makes their successful love as perfect and as noble (Chaucer is fond of applying the epithet 'worthy' to the lovers) as possible. This is very much in the medieval manner, which prefers to take an extreme as a typical case, where the modern mind believes that truth is better served by the average. It is this process of intensification which accounts for many of Chaucer's alterations.

In the first place, and much of this is already in Boccaccio, the story is presented in such a way that it would be hard to think of a love affair so circumstanced that it would be less likely to achieve permanence. The scene is set within the tragedy of the siege of Troy. It is near the end. It is already certain that Troy will fall and that the Greeks will destroy it utterly. Calkas knows this, and it is his knowledge which precipitates the denouement. Troilus is in daily danger of death and, in fact, is killed in the ordinary course of war, in a way which has nothing to do with his love. Criseyde must either be burnt to ashes with Troy or leave the city. All this is not a hopeful background.

Further than this, Troilus's love is secret and illicit. Criseyde will not consider remarriage; and, indeed, none of the three main characters takes the idea seriously. This subjects the lovers to uncertainty and delay as to their meetings, and to all the difficulty and inconvenience of a secrecy which is essential to preserve Criseyde's good name. This need for secrecy is one of the chief reasons for Troilus's failure to prevent her leaving Troy. Even the semi-permanence and open enjoyment of marriage is denied them.

Moreover, of the three main characters, two openly think of love as impermanent. Pandarus repeatedly reminds Troilus of its inevitably transitory nature; and, indeed, advises him to console himself by changing, in his turn, when Criseyde is lost to him (it is true that Chaucer apologizes for him). He suggests that sorrow is unnecessary:

'Syn thi desir al holly hastow had,
So that, by right, it oughte ynough suffise, . . .'
(IV, 395–6)

and that:

'This town is ful of ladys al aboute, . . .'
(401)

is certainly uncourtly; and Chaucer assures us that:

Thise wordes seyde he for the nones alle,
To help his frend, lest he for sorwe deyde;
For douteles, to don his wo to falle,
He roughte nought what unthrift that he seyde.
(IV, 428–31)

Troilus's reaction to the heresy does not have to be given us, since the
words go in at one ear and out at the other (434). Such a speech, in
fact, has no meaning in terms of Troilus's attitude to love; but, in
spite of the apology, it has all too much in relation to Pandarus's and
is entirely in keeping with his attitude throughout the poem, in its
clearsighted, unswerving attachment to expediency and its equally
clearsighted recognition of the kind of natural process he is dealing
with:

'Swich fir, by proces, shal of kynde colde;
For syn it is but casuel plesaunce,
Som cas shal putte it out of remembraunce.

For also seur as day comth after nyght,
The newe love, labour, or oother wo,
Or elles selde seynge of a wight,
Don olde affecciouns alle over-go.'
(IV, 418–24)

This 'casual' love is, like the natural cycles typified by day and night,
bound by its very nature to suffer change. Criseyde herself, of course,
sufficiently demonstrates the truth of Pandarus's statement.

Both Pandarus and Criseyde take up similar attitudes towards the
end. Criseyde closes her farewell to Troilus with the words:

'But al shal passe; and thus take I my leve'.
(V, 1085)

and Pandarus comments thus on Troilus's unquenchable hope that
she may yet return:

'Ye, fare wel al the snow of ferne yere!'
(V, 1176)

The narrator's own comment towards the end of Book V drives home
the point:

Gret was the sorwe and pleynte of Troilus;
But forth hire cours Fortune ay gan to holde . . .
Swich is this world, whoso it kan byholde;
In ech estat is litel hertes reste.

(V, 1744–9)

Pandarus uses the argument of love's impermanence to persuade
Criseyde to love in the first place. This is an argument which
Boccaccio's Criseida uses on herself – but with a difference. She
simply asks, and answers, herself:

'Chi me vorrà se io invecchio mai?
Certo nessuno'.

('Who will ever desire me if I grow old?
Certainly no one')
(II, 71)

Pandarus, on the other hand, states a general law, in which Troilus
is also involved:

'Thenk ek how elde wasteth every houre
In ech of yow a partie of beautee;
And therfore, er that age the devoure,
Go love; for old, ther wol no wight of the.'
(II, 393–6)

In his inability to change and his demand for permanence from
something which, on every count, could never last, Troilus is
certainly set for tragedy.

But Troilus's love is not only presented in its nature, and through all its attendant circumstances, as a love unlikely to last for ever in happiness; it is also given the highest possible value in our eyes, so that, as we are made to feel that his highest point of fortune was indeed high, so we feel that his fall is a great one. Chaucer achieves this in a variety of ways. In the first place, he devotes considerable space to the praise of love itself. It is everything that is good, except permanent. Early in the first book he establishes the universal, inescapable power of love:

> For evere it was, and evere it shal byfalle,
> That Love is he that alle thing may bynde,
> For may no man fordon the lawe of kynde.
> (I, 236–8)

There is, it is true, warning here, as well as praise. The law of Nature, which, through love, ensures the continuity of the world and its multifarious species, is, as we have seen, however noble and ultimately beneficient in itself, not a law which ensures the temporal preservation of the individual. Nevertheless, Chaucer emphasizes that it can only be seen as a power for good:

> Now sith it may nat goodly ben withstonde,
> And is a thing so vertuous in kynde,
> Refuseth nat to Love for to ben bonde,
> Syn, as hymselven liste, he may yow bynde.
> (I, 253–6)

If there is irony here and in the coincidental meeting with Criseyde (shortly to be described) which brings Troilus into the power of this great natural force, it is an irony inherent in the life of man, seen from a limited and temporal viewpoint, and not a cheap joke of the poet against the folly of lovers.

The first stanza of Troilus's song elaborates the idea of love as a great force whose ultimate goodness is not necessarily clearly demonstrated in individual instances of its power – Chaucer, and Dante before him, both following Boethius, took the same view of Fortune:[21]

If no love is, O God, what fele I so?
And if love is, what thing and which is he?
If love be good, from whennes cometh my woo?
If it be wikke, a wonder thynketh me,
When every torment and adversite
That cometh of hym, may to me savory thinke,
For ay thurst I, the more that ich it drynke.

(I, 400–6)

At the end of Book I the effect of this power on Troilus is shown as an influence for good:

And in the town his manere tho forth ay
Soo goodly was, and gat hym so in grace,
That ecch hym loved that loked on his face.

For he bicom the frendlieste wight,
The gentilest, and ek the mooste fre,
The thriftiest and oon the beste knyght,
That in his tyme was or myghte be.

(I, 1076–82)

These ideas are taken up again in the central third book, which celebrates Troilus's happiness. First, comes the very beautiful proem in invocation of Venus:

O blisful light, of which the bemes clere
Adorneth al the thridde heven faire!

(III, 1–2)

This is, of course, based on Troilo's song in *Il Filostrato*. Both versions deal with love from the philosophical and cosmological viewpoint, as a force concerned in the creation and maintenance of the universe. In Chaucer's version:[22]

In hevene and helle, in erthe and salte see
Is felt thi myght, if that I wel descerne;
As man, brid, best, fissh, herbe, and grene tree
Thee fele in tymes with vapour eterne.
God loveth, and to love wol nought werne;
And in this world no lyves creature
Withouten love is worth, or may endure.

> Ye Joves first to thilke effectes glade,
> Thorugh which that thynges lyven alle and be,
> Comeveden, and amorous him made
> On mortal thyng . . .
>
> (III, 8–18)

The effects of love on the individual are described in much the same terms as were used of Troilus himself:

> And as yow list, ye maken hertes digne;
> Algates hem that ye wol sette a-fyre,
> They dreden shame, and vices they resygne;
> Ye do hem corteys be, fresshe and benigne.
>
> (23–6)

Troilus's song – based on the *de Consolatione*, (II, m. 8) – 'Love, that of erthe and se hath governaunce' (III, 1744 ff.) – also deals with a cosmic and philosophically conceived love; and the book finally ends with a further assurance of the ennobling power love exerts on Troilus:

> Benigne he was to ech in general,
> For which he gat hym thank in every place.
> Thus wolde Love, yheried be his grace,
> That Pride, Envye, and Ire, and Avarice,
> He gan to fle, and everich other vice.
>
> (III, 1802–6)

It is obvious that these passages in Book III, the book which hymns the consummation of Troilus's love and presents it to us, in some of the most beautiful love poetry in the language, as of great nobility and worth, are crucial to our understanding of the poem, and that we must give them full weight when we come to consider Chaucer's viewpoint in the epilogue. For the moment, however, this problem must be set aside while we examine the whole organization of the material of Book III. It may be, indeed, that the beauty of much of the writing in praise and description of successful love blinds us a little to the purpose of this section within the work as a whole. As the first stanza of Book I makes clear – to say nothing of the epilogue – the *Troilus* is not primarily intended to set forth and praise the joys of

97

love. It is a tragedy. And the brief period when the lovers are 'in lust and in quiete' (III, 1819) is a part of the tragic pattern; it is, in fact, the fatal period when Fortune is most to be feared.

Chaucer does not really leave us in any doubt of his ultimate purpose in Book III. His account of the union of the lovers is shot through with foreboding – a foreboding which, as we have seen, is actually built into his conception of love as a part of nature. It is in Book III that Pandarus makes his serious speech in justification of his own actions:

> 'For the have I bigonne a gamen pleye,
> Which that I nevere do shal eft for other,
> Although he were a thousand fold my brother.
>
> That is to seye, for the am I bicomen,
> Bitwixen game and ernest, swich a meene
> As maken wommen unto men to comen; . . .'
>
> (III, 250–5)

His argument is an uneasy one. He can only entreat Troilus to be discreet, and plead that what he has done was done for love and not for money. Nor can we claim, with C. S. Lewis, that Pandarus operates on a different plane to Troilus, in that he stands outside the charmed circle within which the lovers have their being. Troilus's response is to offer to become a procurer in his turn:

> 'I have my faire suster Polixene,
> Cassandre, Eleyne, or any of the frape,
> Be she nevere so fair or wel yshape,
> Telle me which thow wilt of everychone,
> To han for thyn, and lat me thanne allone.'
>
> (III, 409–13)

It is clear that Pandarus, with his usual ability to see, but not necessarily to comprehend, has uncovered something fundamental, and threatening, to the love story. The ugly moment should prepare us for the language of the epilogue; and, indeed, it represents a basic conflict of values which Chaucer displays, but does not resolve.

Book III also contains Criseyde's speech on false felicity, which foreshadows so many of the phrases of the epilogue:

'O God!' quod she, 'so worldly selynesse,
Which clerkes callen fals felicitee,
Imedled is with many a bitternesse!
Ful angwissous than is, God woot,' quod she,
'Condicioun of veyn prosperitee; . . .
O brotel wele of mannes joie unstable! . . .
Wherfore I wol diffyne in this matere,
That trewely, for aught I kan espie,
Ther is no verray weele in this world heere.'

(III, 813–36)

Ironically enough, this long speech is called forth by a false accusation of unfaithfulness – part of Pandarus's manœuvring. The irony, however, does not end there, and the speech makes its effect as an ominous prelude to the felicity the lovers are about to experience. We are reminded of it at the end of the book, when, in his attempt to describe their joy, Chaucer echoes Criseyde's words:

Felicite, which that thise clerkes wise
Comenden so, ne may nought here suffise;
This joie ne may nought writen be with inke!

(1691–3)

We have read the earlier speech, and we know that wise clerks write of false felicity as well as true.

In Book III, too, Pandarus speaks of Fortune in terms necessary to the development of the tragic theme, but somewhat incongruous to his moment of success, when all his scheming has at last brought about the desired result:

'For of fortunes sharpe adversitee
The worste kynde of infortune is this,
A man to han ben in prosperitee,
And it remembren, whan it passed is.
Th'art wis ynough, forthi do nat amys;
Be naught to rakel, theigh thow sitte warme;
For if thow be, certeyn, it wol the harme.

99

> Thow art at ese, and hold the wel therinne;
> For also seur as reed is every fir,
> As gret a craft is kepe wel as wynne.
> Bridle alwey wel thi speche and thi desir,
> For worldly joie halt nought but by a wir.
> That preveth wel it brest al day so ofte;
> Forthi nede is to werken with it softe.'
>
> (III, 1625–38)

The ostensible purpose of the speech is to exhort Troilus to secrecy and discretion; but, in its references to Fortune and to the transitory nature of worldly joy – Criseyde's false felicity – it actually goes a good deal further; and by setting forth the Stoic view of moderation and mistrust of the unreliable pleasures of the world, a view not normally held by Pandarus, it casts a coldly ominous light on the transports of the lovers. Chaucer, in his own comment on this part of the action, once more brings together the key words 'Fortune' and 'joy' (by now firmly established in our minds as transitory):

> And thus Fortune a tyme ledde in joie
> Criseyde, and ek this kynges sone of Troie.
>
> (III, 1714–15)

A couplet which also suggests, aptly enough, the standard definition of tragedy.

Surrounded as it is by doubts and dangers, we are yet convinced of the value, in its kind, of the love of Troilus and Criseyde. But, more than this, Chaucer is at pains to convince us also of the personal value and excellence of the lovers. We have already seen that Troilus is conceived as one of the great heroes of Troy, second only to Hector. He is possessed of all the princely virtues, and they are even, as we have seen, increased by love. He is capable, too, of putting the commonweal before his private passion, and of refraining from the attempt to prevent Criseyde from leaving Troy when the country's good requires her exchange for Antenor. It is true that later he seems more ready to entertain the idea of keeping her by force, but his reason still holds him back in the fear that harm might come to her person and her honour if he indulged the impulse to violent action. Criseyde continually expresses her appreciation of his 'worthiness' –

which is also constantly praised by Pandarus[23] – and she esteems him, too, for his 'moral vertu':

> 'For trusteth wel, that youre estat roial,
> Ne veyn delit, nor only worthinesse
> Of yow in werre or torney marcial,
> Ne pompe, array, nobleye, or ek richesse
> Ne made me to rewe on youre destresse;
> But moral vertu, grounded upon trouthe,
> That was the cause I first hadde on yow routhe!'
>
> (IV, 1667–73)

We need not doubt either Criseyde's or Chaucer's sincerity: Chaucer uses similar terms of his hero in the epilogue:

> Swich fyn hath, lo, this Troilus for love!
> Swich fyn hath al his grete worthynesse!
> Swich fyn hath his estat real above,
> Swich fyn his lust, swich fyn hath his noblesse!
> Swych fyn hath false worldes brotelnesse!
>
> (V, 1828–32)

The point of both love story and tragedy is that they involve a man of the highest excellence.

The description of the way in which Troilus first feels love is organized, I think, so as to enhance this effect. He meets Criseyde by chance, and he succumbs to the direct stroke of the jealous God of Love. Moreover Chaucer emphasizes the naturalness of love and the inevitability that one of his age and condition should sooner or later feel it. When it is established, his love is frequently spoken of in terms of illness and, indeed, produces the physical symptoms of illness. Troilus disguises the cause of his weakness at the house of Deiphebus, but we are expressly told that he did not have to pretend as to his physical state (II, 1527 ff.). He suffers, in fact, from love at its most violent and devouring, and is left with very little ability either to help himself towards its consummation or to cure himself when he has lost Criseyde. Thus, on the one hand, seen as one of the ways in which nature operates in the world for good, love expresses itself through, and even enhances, the nobility of a noble nature; on the other, it can also be thought of as a great natural calamity – an irresistible force like flood or earthquake, which brings destruction with it. As far as Troilus is concerned, love always has this double aspect, and, as we shall presently see, this quality is established from the early part of Book I and runs consistently through the poem.

The presentation of Criseyde's character is profoundly affected by Chaucer's conception of the importance of Troilus's love. He emphasizes her corresponding worthiness, and also her sincerity – at least at the moment. But he is not as lavish in her praise as he is in Troilus's and thus leaves the way open for future cause for blame. In the first description of her, for example, only her beauty is mentioned, and even this only as an appearance: it is so great that she *seemed* 'As doth an hevenyssh perfit creature' (I, 103–4). She is praised for her popularity and good reputation in Troy (I, 130–1), that is, again, for what she *seemed* to onlookers to be. The ironic possibilities are even greater when Pandarus praises her for freedom from vice after he has corrupted her, in a speech which leaves no room for doubt that he regards his act as corruption (III, 257). The poem is not, however, so ordered at these points that we can understand these passages as clearly satirical. It is, surely, rather that they contain latent ironies and ambiguities. Criseyde is good enough, but not for the demands of Troilus's love, in the situation in which she is placed – and Chaucer's praise of her never implies that she is.

The long second book is devoted to her gradual conversion to the idea of love by a combination of the influence of Pandarus and of circumstances. It is here that Chaucer diverges most widely from Boccaccio. He gives us fair warning, when he explains that her love was not 'sodeyn':

> For I sey nought that she so sodeynly
> Yaf hym hire love, but that she gan enclyne
> To like hym first, and I have told yow whi;
> And after that, his manhod and his pyne
> Made love withinne hire herte for to myne,
> For which, by proces and by good servyse,
> He gat hire love, and in no sodeyn wyse.
>
> (II, 673–9)

The gradualness of her conversion and the difficulty and length of the process are the material of all Book II, and a great part of Book III, and this detailed treatment can only add to the impression that there is nothing light or wanton about her, and that she is, in fact, a worthy object of love for this 'Ector the secounde'. Nevertheless, with all her worth, she does, in the end, betray Troilus; and Chaucer uses Books II to III with great subtlety, not only to build her up as a sympathetic and admirable character, but also to show how her mind is open to be worked on. The conclusion is unavoidable: the woman who can be influenced once can be influenced again – and more quickly.

Only a line-by-line analysis of these parts of the poem could show just how all this is achieved. Here it will be enough to give some examples of the way in which Chaucer shows us how a combination of skilful persuasion and the force of circumstances brings about the desired results in a not unwilling subject. Pandarus's first suggestion, an oblique and cautious introduction to the theme of love, that Criseyde should set aside her widow's weeds, is received with horror:

> 'I? God forbede!' quod she, 'be ye mad?
> Is that a widewes lif, so God yow save?
> By God, ye maken me ryght soore adrad!
> Ye ben so wylde, it semeth as ye rave.
> It sate me wel bet ay in a cave
> To bidde and rede on holy seyntes lyves;
> Lat maydens gon to daunce, and yonge wyves.'
>
> (II, 113–19)

Not only is her reaction an exaggerated one (Pandarus is not really either mad or raving), but her picture of herself as a penitent saint in a cave (she has in mind the typical figure of the penitent Magdalen)[24] is hardly appropriate: as she says herself in a moment of franker self-assessment, ' "What, par dieux! I am naught religious" ' (II, 759). It is not, therefore, altogether surprising when a repetition of the suggestion is much more mildly received. Pandarus has contrived to fill her mind with curiosity concerning the news he has for her, and she has no thought for anything else:

> Quod Pandarus, 'Now is it tyme I wende.
> But yet, I say, ariseth, lat us daunce,
> And cast youre widewes habit to mischaunce!
> What list yow thus youreself to disfigure,
> Sith yow is tid thus fair an aventure?'

'A! Wel bithought! for love of God,' quod she,
'Shal I nat witen what ye meene of this?'
(220–6)

Pandarus uses the same tactics when he puts forward his more
startling suggestion that she should give her love to Troilus. This is
first received with tears and cries of dismay:

And she began to breste a-wepe anoon,
And seyde, 'Allas, for wo! Why nere I deed?
For of this world the feyth is al agoon.
Allas! what sholden straunge to me doon,
When he, that for my beste frend I wende,
Ret me to love, and sholde it me defende?'
(408–13)

and she continues in this vein for two stanzas more. By the end of the
long argument her response is much milder. When Pandarus finally
insinuates:

'Ther were nevere two so wel ymet,
Whan ye ben his al hool, as he is youre;
Ther myghty God yet graunte us see that houre!'
(586–8)

she reproves him sharply, but there are no tears, and she is easily
pacified:

'Nay, therof spak I nought, ha, ha!' quod she;
'As helpe me God, ye shenden every deel!'
'O, mercy dere nece,' anon quod he,
'What so I spak, I mente naught but wel,
By Mars, the god that helmed is of steel!
Now beth naught wroth, my blood, my nece dere.'
'Now wel,' quod she, 'foryeven be it here.'
(589–95)

Her private thoughts on the subject, as Chaucer gives them, for
example at 600 ff. and 694 ff., are expressed in sober language: she
does not make any virtuous outcry when there is no one to hear it;
she is concerned, rather, to weigh chances and contingencies:

And, Lord! so she gan in hire thought argue
In this matere of which I have yow told,
And what to doone best were, and what eschue,
That plited she ful ofte in many fold.
Now was hire herte warm, now was it cold.

(694–8)

We can see the same hidden receptiveness to an idea – the same ability to let it work on her mind even while she protests against it – in Criseyde's answer to Diomede in Book V, 956 ff., where every statement is qualified and her thoughts always seem to run ahead of her words: the Greeks are noble, but so are the Trojans (967–8); I know that you (Diomede) are expert in love, but I cannot consider such a subject, and yet I know that you are nobly born (972–80); I can have nothing to do with love (it would suit me better to live in wo and lamentation until I die), but of course I can't say what I shall do after that, and at any rate I cannot think of such things yet (983–7); perhaps much later, if things go in a way that I don't expect – if the town is won, if I see things I never thought to see – and, anyway, let me speak to you again tomorrow, but not of love (990–6); and I will at least say that you are the only Greek that I could think of in this light; and I do not say that I will love you (but then I do not say that I won't); and I can only say, in conclusion, that I mean well! (998–1004).

There is high comedy in the vagaries of Criseyde's mind, and the speech has behind it the weight of all that we have seen and learnt about her. With one final stroke, indeed, Chaucer places her reaction to Diomede within the context of her whole experience of life as he has shown it to us; he is not merely poking fun at the illogicality of the feminine mind, he is demonstrating to us what the world looks like, and indeed is, to Criseyde. She turns her thoughts towards Troy and uses a phrase which echoes one used of the lovers' time of bliss in Book III (1819), when Troilus was 'in lust and in quiete':

'O Troie town,
Yet bidde I God, *in quiete and in reste*
I may yow sen, or do myn herte breste.'

(V, 1006–8)

'But, in effect . . .', Chaucer continues, she actually stays and listens to Diomede. For Criseyde it is the security of her world, as it presents itself to her at any given moment, that matters and that turns her towards the known safety of Diomede and away from the risk of returning to Troy. Troilus saw love otherwise.

Criseyde's mind is as receptive to the pressure of circumstances as to Pandarus's suggestions. In Book II, Chaucer shows her responding, with increasing effect, to the coincidental happenings which bring the idea of love and of Troilus constantly before her. First, when he rides past her window from the battlefield:

> So fressh, so yong, so weldy semed he,
> It was an heven upon hym for to see.
>   (II, 636–7)

she responds with a directness which cuts cleanly through Pandarus's manœuvring and reminds us that her love is, in its way, as spontaneous and sincere as Troilus's:

> Criseÿda gan al his chere aspien,
> And leet it so softe in hire herte synke,
> That to hireself she seyde, 'Who yaf me drynke?'
>   (II, 649–51)

When Criseyde is debating with herself whether or not to accept Troilus's love (II, 771 ff.), she hears Antigone sing a Trojan love song (827 ff.), and responds at once to the suggestion contained in it. The song of the nightingale in her garden (II, 918 ff.) reinforces this effect; and finally, she is visited by a dream in which an eagle takes her heart from her breast (925 ff.); that is, the preoccupations of her own mind show her the matter under debate as already decided.[25] She is presented as readily susceptible to the pressure of all these circumstances; but she is, emphatically, not presented as forced by them into the position of acting against her inclinations or without consideration for the probable consequences. Even when Pandarus is at his busiest, in the organization of her meeting with Troilus at his house, when Chaucer the narrator has most to say about the influence on the affair of the stars and of destiny, we can, if we read carefully, see that Criseyde is very far from being the passive victim of contrivance.

Before the episode begins Chaucer makes it clear that the relation-

ship of Troilus and Criseyde has progressed to the point which makes
such a meeting likely. Troilus:

> so ful stood in his lady grace
> That twenty thousand tymes, er she lette,
> She thonked God that evere she with hym mette.
>
> (III, 472–4)

The impression is, once more, of a frank, wholehearted response on
Criseyde's part, which leaves little for scheming to do; although we
are assured that Pandarus left nothing undone:

> For he with gret deliberacioun
> Hadde every thyng that herto myght availle
> Forncast and put in execucioun,
> And neither left for cost ne for travaile.
> Come *if hem list*, hem sholde no thyng faille.
>
> (519–23)

The lovers must still complete his preparations by playing their
voluntary part.

Now, the main part of Pandarus's preparation is simple observation of the probabilities of the weather. It is 'upon the chaungynge of
the moone', and it looks like rain (549–51). Any English countryman
today would agree with Pandarus that a change of moon is likely to
bring change of weather, and that, if it has been dry, it will then be
wet; and, if 'auctorite' is needed, Macrobius says so too. Criseyde,
presumably, could have made the same prediction. In fact, she does
not have to do so because, when the invitation is given, the rain has
actually begun:

> she lough, and gan hire faste excuse,
> And seyde, 'It reyneth; lo, how sholde I gon?'
>
> (561–2)

Pandarus insists, as usual trading on their friendly relationship – he
will never see her again if she fails him (566–8). She then asks him, in
a whisper, whether Troilus would be there. He swears that he is out
of town; but, Chaucer says:

> Nought list myn auctour fully to declare
> What that she thoughte whan he seyde so –
>
> (575–6)

and, indeed, Pandarus is careful to prepare her mind for Troilus's presence:

> 'Nece, I pose that he were;
> Yow thurste nevere han the more fere.'
>
> (571–2)

Her plea for discretion in lines 582–8 shows that she is pretty certain that Troilus will, in fact, be there; if he were not, there would be no need 'For to ben war of goosish peoples speche', for an ordinary dinner-party at her uncle's ought not to give rise to gossip. Her final, resigned comment is, to say the least of it, ambiguous:

> 'Em, syn I most on yow triste,
> Loke al be wel, and do now as yow liste.'
>
> (587–8)

Criseyde, then, sets out, in the rain, prepared for what she is to find. The rain duly gets worse, and it is here that Chaucer invokes Fortune, destiny and the planetary aspects which are the physical causes of the weather:

> But O Fortune, executrice of wyrdes,
> O influences of thise hevenes hye!
> Soth is, that under God ye ben oure hierdes,
> Though to us bestes ben the causes wrie.
> This mene I now, for she gan homward hye,
> But execut was al bisyde hire leve
> The goddes wil; for which she moste bleve.
>
> (617–23)

And it is at this point that he describes not merely the changing moon – enough in itself to ensure the probability of rain – but a conjunction of planets which he may well have observed during the exceptionally rainy year of 1385, as J. D. North explains.[26] Once more the fullest possible pressure of circumstances is brought to bear on Criseyde's inclinations. Owing to the operation of forces beyond her control, she cannot *now* go home without serious inconvenience. 'Now were it tyme a lady to gon henne!' as Pandarus says. Criseyde, indeed, shares with her women 'a verray feere' of the smoky rain. She has not been presented to us as a character at all likely to resort to heroic means to protect her honour. She is no Constance or Lucrece to risk even wet feet to ensure her safety from Troilus. Indeed, as her inclination is wholly on his side, she does not even fall back on the more simple expedient of saying no, when she finds herself in the position which all the probabilities of the case have lead her and the reader to expect.

Why, then, does Chaucer insert the passage on Fortune, 'executrice of wyrdes'? It is, in the first place, part of a whole system of references to the gods and to the planetary influences which runs through the poem, especially in Troilus's various appeals and prayers. These have been collected and analysed by Curry;[27] and we must leave the consideration of their significance in the poem as a whole until we come to examine the epilogue and its relation to the themes and ideas of the main part of the *Troilus*. In the context, however, after the delicate comedy of an exchange in which both Pandarus and Criseyde have much to conceal, and in which each is manœuvring for position, it seems fair to ask whether we can take this rather elaborate intervention of the narrator wholly seriously. It is, I think, more reasonable to read it as a part of the whole serio-comic development of the scene between uncle and niece. It is not altogether safe to argue from one work to another, where the poet's total purpose may be quite different, but we can compare another solemn appeal to the ineluctable power of destiny, at a point where Chaucer has been at some pains to show the comic development as the result of the sheer folly of his character; this is in the *Nun's Priest's Tale*. Here, when the cock has got his well-earned reward (and his responsibility for his own foolishness is pointed up through the fun poked at learned arguments concerning necessity and free will in lines 3234 ff.), Chaucer exclaims: 'O destinee that mayst nat been eschewed!' (*CT* VII, 3338). It is true that the *Nun's Priest's Tale* is wholly comic,[28] while the *Troilus* is not; nevertheless, if we look closely at the context of the invocation in the *Troilus* we can, I think, see that, far from being the expression of determinism, it constitutes an ironic comment on Criseyde's conduct and situation.

In the first place, there is a distinction between *God* and *the goddes*.

Fortune and the planetary influences operate on mankind under the
control of God; they cannot, therefore, be thought of as so disposed
as to compel Criseyde to an act which she thinks of as wrong,
against her will. Since, as Chaucer has shown us, her will is by no
means in wholehearted opposition to that of Pandarus and Troilus,
it is not surprising that, since she has placed herself in a position in
which the operation of Fortune and the planets with regard to the
weather can affect the issue – giving her her choice between being
placed in an equivocal position or wetting her feet – the *goddes* will
is actually carried out, i.e., she does allow her conduct to be influenced by the weather; she does stay, and she does find herself in bed
with Troilus. Secondly, Chaucer uses a phrase which, if we are to
judge from his use of it elsewhere, has very definite implications for
him. He speaks of mankind, under the influence of Fortune and the
stars, as 'us bestes'. Now, in *Truth* he speaks of the man who falls
under the influence of Fortune, and all the chances and changes of
this transitory world, as a 'beast', with the exhortation:

> Forth, beste, out of thy stal!
> Know thy contree, look up, thank God of al.
> > (*Truth*, 18–19)

The good man is *not* to be, like a beast, at the mercy of chance, but is
to use his freedom of will to undertake a pilgrimage to his true home.
The same terms are used in Palamoun's falacious argument that
mankind is like the helpless beasts before the power of the uncaring
gods:

> 'O crueel goddes that governe
> This world with byndyng of youre word eterne,
> And writen in the table of atthamaunt
> Youre parlement and youre eterne graunt,
> What is mankynde moore unto you holde
> Than is the sheep that rouketh in the folde?
> For slayn is man right as another beest.'
> > (*CT* I, 1303–9)

If we take Palamoun's argument in the context of the *Knight's Tale* as
a whole, there is, I think, no doubt that his acceptance of the position
of a helpless beast under the power of the gods (plural; i.e., the

planetary influences) is a tacit criticism of his conduct from the narrator's viewpoint.[29] We could, perhaps, find one more indication that the invocation in the *Troilus* has an ironical function in the similarity of its somewhat grandiose style to that of the opening of the *Envoy to Scogan*: 'Tobroken been the statutz hye in hevene'. Again, the purpose of the whole poem is quite different, but we could with justification conclude that Chaucer associated a certain grandiose way of writing with a shifting off of human responsibility on to planetary machinery, with an ironical or even (in the *Nun's Priest's Tale*) frankly comic approach to his subject matter.

It is certain, at any rate, that, like the cock in the *Nun's Priest's Tale*, Criseyde is caught:

> What myghte or may the sely larke seye,
> Whan that the sperhauk hath it in his foot?
> (III, 1191–2)

and the metaphor is emphasized by being carried over into Troilus's speech:

> 'O swete, as evere mot I gon,
> Now be ye kaught, now is ther but we tweyne!
> Now yeldeth yow, for other bote is non!'
> (III, 1206–8)

But, unlike Chauntecleer, Criseyde negates this effect of the helpless victim of circumstances by honestly admitting her own responsibility and, incidentally, at the same time allowing us to put a higher value on her love:

> To that Criseyde answerde thus anon,
> 'Ne hadde I er now, my swete herte deere,
> Ben yold, ywis, I were now nought heere!'
> (III, 1209–11)

In the whole scene, with its complex ironies, Chaucer has given us something which has nothing to do with either determinism or Christian didacticism, but which belongs to the highest realm of human comedy.

It is, probably, in the case of Pandarus that we are most tempted to detect a 'character study' in the modern sense, that is, a self-contained, self-regulating entity shown as affecting the development of the story in certain ways precisely because it is a being of a certain sort. In a sense, too, this is what Chaucer achieves, since Pandarus is, in the main, naturalistically presented; but to put the emphasis in the *Troilus*, or in any medieval work, on the integrity of character rather than on the integrity of the story and of the thematic material is, surely, to get it wrong.

Considered in relation to the structure of the poem as a whole, Pandarus's function is complex. He provides a fixed point of reference for the whole action, and also for the other two main figures, who are very largely presented through his eyes and his speeches; he is used, in part, as an observer of an action in which he himself is also involved – a role Theseus plays (with a difference) in the *Knight's Tale*. He helps to develop the major themes, in that, as we have seen, much of the material concerning the natural brevity and changeability of love is contained in his speeches, so that he stands beside Troilus somewhat in the manner of a character in a morality, urging him to action likely to prove ultimately destructive but, at the same time, showing awareness both of his own place in the scheme of things and of the true consequences of the actions he recommends. So a 'Pride of Life', or a 'Riches', can utter a self-analysing speech which shows full awareness of its true nature and position in the overall moral scheme. 'Goodes', for example, is just as ready to tell Everyman of his true nature as Pandarus or Criseyde are to tell Troilus of the true nature of love: on the one hand, Goodes says:[30]

> 'Syr, and ye in the worlde haue sorowe or aduersyte
> That can I helpe you to remedy shortly.'
>
> (401–2)

on the other:

> 'I am to brytell, I may not endure.
> I wyll folowe no man one fote, be ye sure.'
>
> (425–6)

The morality character exists to give expression to the logic of circumstances, and there are moments when Pandarus and Criseyde do the same: Pandarus, for example, in the speech in which he attempts to console Troilus by explaining the very temporary nature of earthly love (IV, 380 ff.); and Criseyde in her farewell at the end of her letter to Troilus, when she seems to leave the stage with the finality of a morality personification, whose essential nature makes it necessary for it to step out of an action which has moved beyond it:

> 'And, gilteles, I woot wel, I yow leve.
> But al shal passe; and thus take I my leve.'
>
> (V, 1084–5)

So Beauty takes leave of *Everyman*:

> 'Adewe, by Saynt Johan!
> I take my tappe in my lappe, and am gon!'
>
> (800–1)

Unlike such a personification, however, Criseyde still lingers to produce the inconsistencies and hesitations of her final letter (V, 1590 ff.).

The morality personification remains inhuman and is apt to take a brutal view – so Goodes says, logically but not kindly:

> 'Mary, thou brought thy selfe in care,
> Wherof I am gladde.
> I must nedes laugh; I can not be sadde.'
>
> (454–6)

In the same way the personifications of the Vision of Fortune in *Piers Plowman* do not go out of their allegorical definition, but cheerfully fail their victim when his actions have brought their logical result.[31] Criseyde and Pandarus, however, are tender-hearted, although Criseyde's tenderness does not stretch to a subject not actually before her eyes. Pandarus's sympathy and the pain that Troilus's sufferings cause him are continually emphasized;[32] and Criseyde, with some prompting from Pandarus, and with her own safety at the back of her mind, does, in fact, show an earnest desire to 'quenchen al this sorwe' in the scene at Pandarus's house (III, 1100 ff.). But the poem is organized from the point of view of Troilus – it is *his* double tragedy. In the end, therefore, the other two main figures drop away and we are left, in the description of his death and in the epilogue, with Troilus alone. Nevertheless, Pandarus and Criseyde are not abstractions derived from him: they do not represent his vices or attributes, although they are so handled by the poet that they show us the working out of his, and only his, destiny. There is no reason for us to hear of the final fate of either Pandarus or Criseyde. Their function in the poem is over when their contribution to Troilus's story is complete. In this sense they do play a part similar to that of the morality personifications; but Troilus's destiny is shown as working itself out in the external world, naturalistically conceived, and not in an internal retrospect, as in *Everyman*, or through the externalization of an internal conflict, which is the subject of many allegories. Pandarus and Criseyde therefore have a separate existence as 'characters' of a kind that the personifications could never have.

Moreover, it is in relation to this external 'real' world, in which Troilus's experience takes place, that Pandarus plays his most important part. He is the link between the two lovers and the medium through which their union is shown as the result, not of an instantaneous and self-contained marriage of true minds, but of an interplay of forces and circumstances arising from their whole background and setting within the world of besieged Troy. This is, of course, especially clear in the way in which Pandarus brings pressure to bear on Criseyde. As we have seen, he exploits the relationship, with its peculiar intimacy, which exists between them, and also makes full use of the hopes and fears which arise from her situation: her prospects of safety in Troy in the state in which she finds herself; her fears for what other people think; her practical difficulties in managing her affairs, when he pretends that she is threatened with legal action, and so lures her to the house of Deiphebus. All the scenes which develop the social background of life in Troy depend on Pandarus's presence. The description of Criseyde's paved parlour, where she reads with her maidens, and of her house with its different rooms,[33] exists as a part of the exposition of her intimacy with him. An overwhelming passion does not require an elaborate backcloth for its representation, but the greater complexities of the kind of intimacy which exists between Criseyde and Pandarus does. So, in the course of Pandarus's busy activity, we find that we need a description of Deiphebus's house and garden, and of the details of Pandarus's own house and the entertainment offered there. It is in relation to Pandarus that we hear of ordinary day-to-day pastimes: reading, singing, dancing, story-telling, amusing talk.[34] The only social contact of Criseyde's in which he does not play a part is the occasion when she is visited by the ladies of Troy to condole with her on her departure, and we have a view of some of the people whose opinion she is always thinking of, besides an indication of the extent to which they bore her.[35] It is, in the main, through Pandarus that we hear of all the other people of Troy who impinge on the story for a moment, usually by his contrivance. Thus, Hector, Deiphebus, Helen, are brought into Criseyde's range through his devices; it is through him that we hear of 'false Poliphete', with whom Criseyde has had dealings before – 'What is he more aboute, me to drecche' (II, 1471) – and who is supported by Antenor and Eneas (II, 1474).

Troilus, too, is drawn within the circle of these people by Pandarus. It is through Pandarus's intervention that he is brought to the house of the 'brother that thow lovest best', and that he is there the subject of the sympathy in his illness of both this brother and 'the faire queene Eleyne' (II, 1571 ff.). It is in this scene, too, that we have the little sub-scene in which Deiphebus and Eleyne pore over a letter sent by Hector on behalf of someone condemned to death – a passage which is solidly convincing as to their ordinary, friendly relationship, as well as to the existence of a busy and complicated world of affairs extending beyond the confines of the love story:

> Deiphebus gan this lettre for t'onfolde
> In ernest greet; so did Eleyne the queene;
> And romyng outward, faste it gonne byholde,
> Downward a steire, into an herber greene.
> This ilke thing they redden hem bitwene,
> And largely, the mountance of an houre,
> Thei gonne on it to reden and to poure.
>
> (II, 1702–8)

In the careful presentation of the details of Pandarus's house, as they affect his contrivance for the lovers' meeting, Chaucer uses a technique reminiscent of that of the *fabliau* in its concentration on particular objects and details of the setting in their relation to the twists and turns of the plot.[36] Troilus is hidden away where he can look through 'a litel wyndow in a stewe' (III, 601). Criseyde is placed in Pandarus's 'litel closet', while her women are 'in this myddel chaumbre that ye se', and Pandarus is to sleep in 'that outer hous allone'. There is reference to the closet door, to the unpinning of the door of the 'stew' – of the 'secre trappe-dore' (759) to which Pandarus leads Troilus 'in by the lappe', so that he is, as he tells

Criseyde, 'thorugh a goter, by a pryve wente, / Into my chaumbre come in al this reyn' (787–8). There are references to 'this furred cloke upon thy sherte' (738), to the bed and the 'beddes syde' on which Troilus sits and from which Pandarus withdraws with 'an old romaunce' and a light (976, 989–90) – the same light which he finally takes back to the chimney (1141) – to the cushion for which he runs (964), and to the 'bare sherte' to which he strips Troilus (1099). In fact, there are probably more references to details of objects and background in this passage than anywhere else in the work. The effect is at once to emphasize the thoroughgoing nature of Pandarus's contrivance and to place the consummation of the love of Troilus and Criseyde within a setting which we feel as extending in its solidity of detail from their centre of ideal bliss back into a wider world of ordinary life – in this case that of Troy with its ominous problems.

The same technique is used, again through the medium of Pandarus, when Troilus's sorrow is also placed against the same solid background, although the detail is less striking. Troilus and Pandarus are on 'the walles of the town' (V, 1112) to see if they can see Criseyde coming. This location of the scene is carefully kept before us: Troilus says 'I wole unto the yate go. . . . I wol don hem holden up the yate' (1138–40). In his efforts to see 'fer his hed over the wal he leyde' (1145); the gates in the wall are mentioned again and a little scene is sketched:

> The warden of the yates gan to calle
> The folk which that withoute the yates were,
> And bad hem dryven in hire bestes alle,
> Or al the nyght they moste bleven there.
> (1177–80)

It is not only that the wall and its gates are kept before us: what Troilus sees from them is also indicated, briefly and lightly, but naturalistically, as it would in fact have been seen by anyone in such a position. Every figure seen in the distance raises his hopes until it comes near enough to be recognized:

> Tyl it was noon, they stoden for to se
> Who that ther come; and every maner wight
> That com fro fer, they seyden it was she,
> Til that thei koude knowen hym aright.
> (1114–17)

In the same way, an object glimpsed in the distance raises hopes, only to be recognized as it comes nearer:

> 'Have here my trouthe, I se hire! Yond she is!
> Heve up thyn eyen, man! maistow nat se!'
> Pandare answerede, 'Nay, so mote I the!
> Al wrong, by God! What saistow, man, where arte?
> That I se yond nys but a fare-carte.'
>
> (1158–62)

The same sense of perspective is observed – though, again, only lightly indicated – in Troilus's desperate survey of the ground:

> He loketh forth by hegge, by tre, by greve,
> And fer his hed over the wal he leyde.
>
> (1144–5)

Time, as well as space, is carefully marked out. Troilus sends for Pandarus at daybreak, after a sleepless night (1105 ff.). They wait until noon, when Troilus finds excuses for Criseyde: she would not come in the forenoon (1114 ff.). They dine and come again in the afternoon (1130 ff.). 'The day goth faste, and after that com eve' (1142), and more excuses are made (1147 ff.): she will come at night – 'And, deere brother, thynk not longe t'abide. / We han naught elles for to don, ywis.' (1155–6). Finally, the gates are shut, and anyone caught outside will have to stay there – 'And fer withinne the nyght, with many a teere / This Troilus gan homward for to ride' (1181–2). The details of place and the continual references to the wearing out of the long, anxious day contribute to build up the strongest impression of Troilus's feelings as he watches.

Again, in an earlier scene in Book V, when Troilus goes with Pandarus to look at Criseyde's empty house, besides his elaborate address to it as 'O paleys desolat', we have such concrete and naturalistic detail as:

> How shet was every wyndow of the place
>
> (534)

or the precision of

'And at that corner, in the yonder hous,
Herde I myn alderlevest lady deere
So wommanly, with vois melodious,
Syngen . . .'

(575–8)

Pandarus, as we have said, is not a mere static figure out of a morality. Chaucer shows him not only manipulating the affairs of the lovers, but reacting strongly to them. He loves Troilus wholeheartedly and wishes him well. He shows both tact and sensibility in his dealings with Criseyde. His business, the zeal with which he drives his niece like a deer to Troilus's net, may at times appal us, but we cannot deny that the total effect is of a figure for whom we feel liking and that his charm and tact reflect a pleasant light on the other two main figures – to have provoked such zeal and such devotion is an added worthiness. It is not Pandarus alone who has this positive effect. The whole social world of Troy – to which, as we have seen, Chaucer links the lovers – is conceived in terms which help to create the conviction that we are dealing with people of the highest excellence. Hector, the greatest of the heroes of Troy, is kind and courteous to Criseyde; Helen is gracious and sympathetic and shows responsibility in her attention to the demands of Hector's letter. Deiphebus, Troilus's favourite brother, shows the same qualities. Hospitality is always ready and good manners and consideration for guests are unfailing in the houses of Criseyde, of Deiphebus and of Pandarus. Unfortunately, all these people, together with Troy itself, are at the mercy of forces which have little regard for excellence; the bright feathers of Troy are plucked away; Hector, who was so kind to Criseyde, is dead before the poem ends; Troilus also falls a victim to the war as well as to love; the Trojans are to be defeated and their town burnt. Like Troilus's love for Criseyde, the whole gracious world of Troy is not built to last.

The love story, indeed, not doctrine, is the heart of the poem, and Chaucer has done with it what he was never to do again – exposed his reader directly, with only the slightest intervention on the part of the narrator, to the full impact of the action and the actors, that is, to 'love in dede' with all its inherent, painful and irresolvable contradictions. The naturalism with which the events and characters are presented in the *Troilus* is, certainly, repeated again and again in the *Canterbury Tales*, but never again at such close quarters without the intervention of the device of the frame and of a narrator who is clearly differentiated from his narration. The narrator, certainly, is present in the *Troilus*, but present as a familiar of the reader, addressing him quietly and intimately, in a way which is a continuation of the technique of the minor poems. It is this intimacy with the reader which makes possible a subtlety of detailed treatment which would be out of place in the longer perspective of the *Canterbury Tales*. The variations in feeling, the precise indications of what is held back, as well as what is openly said, in scenes, for example, like that in which Pandarus gives and Criseyde accepts the invitation to dinner, or the consummation scene itself, in which the lovers' moment of bliss flowers brilliantly out of the equally brilliant web of intrigue and cross-purposes; these are like nothing that we know of in any medieval literature, and they were not to find any parallel for a long time. Chaucer, at any rate, never exactly reproduced the manner or the achievement of the *Troilus*.

4

The *Knight's Tale*

In the *Complaint of Mars*, Chaucer built up a short *divertissement* around the idea of the planetary gods and, as we have seen, used this framework to introduce the themes of both love and philosophy. In the *Knight's Tale*, an incomparably more ambitious work, he once again put the planets in the forefront of the action, in a symmetrical arrangement in which each planet-god is linked to a figure in the human story. Once again the main themes are love and a philosophical system which embraces love as one of its leading ideas. The result is a poem which, in itself, without taking its context within the *Canterbury Tales* into account, is one of Chaucer's most important works. It is also, at the same time, a work which is very fully integrated into the scheme of the *Canterbury Tales*. We know – for example, from his use of it in the *Troilus* – that Chaucer must have been working on the *Teseida* of Boccaccio, his main source in the *Knight's Tale*, before he devised the plan of the *Canterbury Tales*;[1] but, nevertheless, the version we know as the *Knight's Tale* is thoroughly adapted to the character of the Knight, and, moreover, the intrusion of the teller in his tale is made an important structural device in a way which we must presently examine.

The *Knight's Tale* is an Italian-Latin derived romance – if we are justified in calling it a romance at all, and I think that there is, in fact, something to be gained by using for it a term that would never fit the *Troilus*. Chaucer, of course, knew that the actual story is not to be found in the *Thebaid*; but he would also have recognized that, whatever was the source of Boccaccio's story, the Italian poet drew heavily on this work.[2] Chaucer's own treatment of the story and his very extensive alterations of the *Teseida* have, I believe, two main impulses behind them. In the first place, he shortens and tautens because, no doubt, he prefers a tighter narrative structure, and also because the length of his original would be too great even for the freedom which he allows himself as to size in the *Canterbury Tales*. But he also tightens up the narrative because he is not, like Boccaccio, primarily interested in presenting the episodes of an episodic story. His interest, it is evident, is rather to use the story to develop certain themes, and these are of a philosophical kind. It is also true, I think, that many of his alterations are designed to turn the work away from the world and outlook of the Italian poet and back to those of Statius; Chaucer's more elaborate treatment of the gods, in the course of which he especially develops the figure of Saturn, who plays no part in Boccaccio's poem, points in this direction.[3]

To see how this comes about it will be necessary to look closely at the actual material which Chaucer handles in the tale; and first, at the risk of appearing paradoxical, it must be emphasized that for Chaucer, whatever it may have been for Boccaccio, the story is not primarily one of love in the normal sense of the word. It is, of course, the love story which provides the outline of the plot, but we have only to think of the very different way in which Chaucer approaches both plot and characters in the *Troilus*, where the love story *is* the main interest, to see that something else is in question in the *Knight's Tale*. A good deal is said about love, it is true, but there are no paeans in its praise, and the lovers are comparatively flat, undifferentiated figures,[4] while their lady is notoriously unresponsive to them and remains uninterested in love until the final moment, when at Theseus's bidding she, happily, becomes a perfect wife. While in the *Troilus*, in fact, Chaucer gives us a philosophical treatment of a love story, in the *Knight's Tale* a love story forms the pretext for a philosophical poem. This is, perhaps, one reason for the difficulty, and even the feeling of repulsion, with which this poem is sometimes approached by modern readers. The philosophical ideas are unfamiliar and sometimes misunderstood; and the apparently familiar ground of the love story does not fulfil expectations. To appreciate the poem, and to see what Chaucer is really doing, we must, I think, approach it from the right viewpoint.

I have already indicated something of this viewpoint in speaking of the epilogue to the *Troilus*.[4a] There, I have suggested, Chaucer develops a view of the gods, very like that which he would have found in Statius, as, on the one hand, the instruments of a benevolent providence and, on the other, as forces affecting the lives of men in an apparently random and usually unfortunate way – operating, that is (from the Boethian point of view), at the level of fortune and chance, and involving the cooperation of the irrational passions. We have also considered the place of human free will within this scheme. In the *Knight's Tale*, we have the same view of the gods and the same fundamental problem of human responsibility and free will. But, with the much flatter and less detailed presentation of the human protagonists, and the more elaborate presentation of the gods (who do not make a personal appearance in the *Troilus*), the emphasis shifts, from a demonstration of the human problem, primarily through human actions and reactions, to a much more theoretical type of treatment, in which the solution – and indeed all the turns of the plot – is seen rather as the result of the nature of the system within which human beings (free will and all) operate than as deriving directly from individual traits and acts. In fact, to put it shortly, the *Knight's Tale* generalizes where the *Troilus* particularizes; and, in place of the individual, even idiosyncratic, dilemma of the persons in the *Troilus*, we have something much nearer the type-situation of, for example, the morality play, which is devised to set forth general principles in a general way, not to show their particular application.

The formality of the scheme by which human and divine protagonists are coupled suits this purpose but would, obviously, be out of place in a more naturalistically conceived plot. The arrangement is as follows: Theseus corresponds to Jupiter, both as the king whose commands are obeyed by the other characters and as the beneficent force which brings order out of disorder. Egeus, his father, corresponds to the father of the king of the gods, Saturn. The function of Saturn, in the narrative, and his characteristics are somewhat complicated, and we must leave their definition until later.[5] Palamoun corresponds to Venus, who represents love seen first as a destructive force and later as a uniting and saving principle.[6] Arcite corresponds to Mars. Emily corresponds to Diana, the moon, who governs change. Four of these five gods have, further, a special astrological relation to each other. Jupiter and Saturn are, respectively, *Fortuna Major* and *Infortuna Major*, the greatest of the fortunate and unfortunate planets, and Jupiter is, therefore, the only planet which can 'master' Saturn. Venus and Mars have the same relationship, to a lesser degree; they are *Fortuna Minor* and *Infortuna Minor*. Venus, like

Jupiter in relation to Saturn, can overcome the bad influence of her partner in the scheme. Chaucer has thus, through the introduction of Saturn, gained a very simple, clearcut plan of planetary forces.

No such scheme is to be found in the *Teseida*, although the gods are, of course, mentioned by Boccaccio and do, as in the *Knight's Tale*, take part in the denouement. Nor would Chaucer have found it in the *Thebaid*. There, the gods act in parallel to the actions of men – for example, the activities of Jupiter and Juno, Venus and Mars, precede, and cause, the outbreak of war, although this is amply motivated by the human conduct of affairs; but they are not consistently associated with particular individuals. For the actual coupling of human figures with those of the gods, however, Chaucer would only need to turn to the *Aeneid*, where, for example, the affairs of Aeneas and Dido develop as they do because behind each human actor stands the figure of its corresponding goddess – Venus acts for Aeneas, Juno for Dido.[7] Chaucer has only elaborated this scheme to include more characters and to accommodate a more complicated and double-edged view of the gods, which derives in part from Statius and in part, especially in the case of Saturn, from medieval developments in the astrological conception of the planet-deities.

In his analysis of the astrological material of the *Knight's Tale*,[8] Curry states that for Chaucer the motivating force of the story is the 'formative and impelling influence of stars in which his age believed'; that, 'in order to furnish such a motivating force for the final stages of the action, (Chaucer) has skilfully gone about transferring the power of the ancient gods of his sources to the astrological planets of the same name; that the real conflict behind the surface action of the story is a conflict between the planets Saturn and Mars'.[9] These claims, it seems to me, need modifying in two ways. In the first place, as we have seen, the relation of the planets to the individuals is not as simple as Curry here suggests, and, in the second, we cannot so lightly assume a general acceptance of astrological lore. Nor, of course (as Curry himself points out, pp. 149 ff.), can we credit Chaucer with the whole change of gods to planets. This association goes back to the late Classical period – indeed, as we have seen, there are already signs of it in Statius. For Curry, the apparently random and cruel acts of the planetary gods are brought within a more comprehensive philosophical system by Theseus's final speeches and actions, although he considers that the poem offers no final resolution of the philosophical problem. But this resolution is, in fact, implied not only by the philosophical arguments of Theseus's great speech on the First Mover, but by the whole treatment of the gods throughout the poem, which shows them not merely as destinal forces, but also as aspects of the behaviour of the human beings to whom they are so closely linked. Just as, in the *Thebaid*, the infernal deities do not cast a *new* blight on the house of Oedipus, but merely emphasize 'it's *usual* gloom',[10] so Mars does not alter Arcite's character and the actions which spring from it, but merely illustrates and sums up these aspects of his personality – and the same is true of the other human-planet pairs. It is tempting, here, to compare a later, typically Renaissance, formulation of the relationship of human beings to the stars. In the *de Vita Triplici*, Ficino wrote:[11]

> Always remember that already by the inclinations and desires
> of our mind and by the mere capacity of our *spiritus* we can
> come easily and rapidly under the influence of those stars
> which denote these inclinations, desires and capacities.

In fact, it does not seem to me that, in the *Knight's Tale*, we are dealing so much with a study based on the Boethian world-picture, in which the main problem is expressed in terms of the power and influence of destiny and fortune (since this is not necessarily the major implication of the planetary machinery of the poem), as with a development of the theme of the effects on human life of disorder and unreason opposed to an order which extends from the most minor aspects of life up to that unmoved first mover on whom the very principle and idea of order depends.[12] Chaucer, as usual, is unwilling to indulge in didactic comment, which could only appear heavy-handed in a work of this kind; but he does, I think, assume that he shares with his audience a standpoint from which the problems besetting his characters are seen to be capable of solution and, moreover, so organizes the work that it is consistently viewed by the audience from this standpoint. How this is achieved, however, can only be shown by a detailed reading of the poem.

It is obvious that the whole structure of the *Knight's Tale* is built round two focal points within the narrative: these are the pair of lovers (as we have said, distinct, but not strikingly differentiated) and the figure of Theseus. It is also obvious that, if anything in the poem stands consistently for the principle of order, it is Theseus. From the beginning, he is represented as in the fullest possible control of his circumstances and his world. He is lord, governor, conqueror – these terms are constantly used and repeated in the opening lines of the poem. For the Middle Ages, the ruler was invariably seen as, above all, the ultimate source of law and order in the state.[13] There are, I think, signs that the term 'conqueror' had a special sense and was also related in a particular way to the achievement of order. In *Piers Plowman*, Christ is both king and conqueror, and it is explained that it is the function of a conqueror to bring benefits to his people:[14]

> It bicometh to a kynge to kepe and to defende,
> And conquerour of conquest, his lawes and his large.
>
> (B, XIX, 42–3)

In Christ's case:

> And sith he ȝaf largely alle his lele lyges
> Places in paradys at her partynge hennes,
> He may wel be called 'conquerour'.
>
> (56–8)

The same idea, that the conqueror is responsible for bringing benefits not destruction, seems still to be implied in Donne's use of the term in 'The Prohibition':

> But thou wilt lose the stile of conqueror
> If I, thy conquest, perish by thy hate.

Theseus's most recent conquest conforms to these ideas, since it is peculiarly well designed to serve the cause of order, and since he engages on it in a way which is clearly thought of as good:

> What with his wysdom and his chivalrie,
> He conquered al the regne of Femenye.
>
> (865–6)

Without necessarily going as far as D. W. Robertson, who sees in this the conquest of sensuality by reason,[15] it is evident that a realm consisting only of 'Femenye' is incomplete, and so lacking in order. Moreover, Theseus's conquest is so happily concluded that he brings back a bride from the campaign; and this is a further assertion of order, since for Chaucer, as for other medieval authors, marriage stands for order and harmony in human life in a fundamental way, both literally and figuratively – a point to which we must return.

It is in the course of this happy and ceremonial return – 'with muchel glorie and greet solempnytee' (870) – that Theseus encounters the lamenting widows of Thebes, who represent the reverse of his own marriage party and who are the victims of 'Fortune and hire false wheel' (925). They are suffering from the tyranny of a very different conqueror, Creon, 'fulfild of ire and iniquitee', who, far from restoring a happy state of order to the realm by his conquest, has so far insisted on disorder as to have even forbidden the decent burial of the corpses of his victims. The patterning which is so characteristic of the *Knight's Tale* is thus apparent from the beginning – we have the wedding and the widows: the true and the false conquerors bringing, respectively, order and disorder, happiness and misery – a pattern which is carried through to the end, when the funeral is followed by the wedding. In Boccaccio's much longer and more diffuse treatment this symmetrical arrangement does not emerge as significant.

Theseus is moved by this tragic reversal of fortune:

> Hym thoughte that his herte wolde breke,
> Whan he saugh hem so pitous and so maat
> That whilom weren of so greet estaat;
>
> (954–6)

and he loses no time in remedying the situation. He conquers Thebes, kills the false tyrant and gives back to the ladies what is left of their husbands 'to doon obsequies, as was tho the gyse'.

Order and decency are thus restored, but the battle gives rise to a new situation. After it – and we perhaps hear a note of grim professionalism from the Knight – things take their usual course:[16]

> To ransake in the taas of bodyes dede,
> Hem for to strepe of harneys and of wede,
> The pilours diden bisynesse and cure.
>
> (1005–7)

In such a heap of dead bodies are found, still breathing, Palamoun and Arcite. They are brought to Theseus, who, acting with apparent arbitrariness, consigns them to prison forever, without hope of ransom. This act is perhaps more intelligible when we remember that they are Theban princes, a part of the guilty tale of Thebes, a prime instance of wickedness and disorder among gods and men. Theseus here, as at other key-points in the action, is intent on settling the political problem of Thebes – a purpose good in itself and conducive to order, but unfortunate in its effects in the particular case of the Theban princes. There is, too, a sense of fundamental difference between the two princes and Theseus, which goes deeper than the mere ability of the latter to enforce an arbitrary decision. When we read the following lines, we are aware of a basic difference in the destiny of the two parties:

> But by hir cote-armures and by hir gere
> The heraudes knewe hem best in special
> As they that weren of the blood roial
> Of Thebes, and of sustren two yborn.
> Out of the taas the pilours han hem torn,
> And han hem caried softe unto the tente
> Of Theseus; and he ful soone hem sente
> To Atthenes, to dwellen in prisoun
> Perpetuelly, – he nolde no raunsoun.
> And whan this worthy duc hath thus ydon,
> He took his hoost, and hoom he rit anon
> With laurer crowned as a conquerour;
> And ther he lyveth in joye and in honour
> Terme of his lyf; what nedeth wordes mo?
> And in a tour, in angwissh and in wo,
> This Palamon and his felawe Arcite
> For everemoore; ther may no gold hem quite.
>
> (1016–32)

Palamoun and Arcite are to be imprisoned 'perpetuelly': Theseus, who has only acted in accordance with his function of a worthy conqueror, is to live in joy and honour 'terme of his lyf'. There is nothing to be done about either destiny. In Theseus's case, 'what nedeth wordes mo'; in that of the princes 'ther may no gold hem quite'.

In bringing about the event which starts the story, Theseus acts, then, in an arbitrary way, but in accordance with his essentially benevolent function of conqueror. His action is like those acts of Jupiter which express an ultimately benevolent providence: although they may not be easily understood or immediately pleasing, they are yet part of the total divine scheme. When we come, however, to the catastrophic love which overwhelms Palamoun and Arcite, the emphasis shifts to the lower and more random influences on human life. In lines 1086–91, Arcite blames their imprisonment, not on providence, but on Fortune, working through Saturn and through their personal horoscope at birth:

> 'Fortune hath yeven us this adversitee.
> Som wikke aspect or disposicioun
> Of Saturne, by som constellacioun,
> Hath yeven us this, although we hadde it sworn;
> So stood the hevene whan that we were born.
> We moste endure it; this is the short and playn.'

Palamoun expresses similar ideas in his despairing speech on the 'crueel goddes' (1303 ff.). Now, these are ideas and beliefs which, as we have seen, Chaucer elsewhere condemns as 'filth' and 'ordure', which are contrary to the nobility of man in his possession of free will.[17] These speeches, therefore, are an important part of the statement of the argument of the poem and serve to develop the contrast between Theseus, associated with Jupiter and acting like a beneficent providence, who, as we have seen in the case of the unfortunate Theban ladies, is not in the power of fortune but is able to reverse its bad effects, and the two princes, who are ranged with the lesser, fully planetized gods and who submit themselves, like the beast in the stall in *Fortune*, to their influence. Since, as we have again already seen, it is the passions which are peculiarly subject to the influence of the stars, it is in keeping that the love which comes to the two princes is described mainly in terms of its unbridled, unreasoning and disruptive effect:

> 'Wostow nat wel the olde clerkes sawe,
> That "who shal yeve a lovere any lawe?"
> Love is a gretter lawe, by my pan,
> Than may be yeve to any erthely man;

And therefore positif lawe and swich decree
Is broken al day for love in ech degree,
A man moot nedes love, maugree his heed.
He may nat fleen it, thogh he sholde be deed.'
(1163–70)

So Arcite, using with unconscious irony terms so ambiguous as to be almost riddling. Love seen as the greatest, overriding law, more important than *lex positiva* – law which, in contrast to natural law, depends on human decrees – points forward to the love described by Theseus as the great chain which holds the universe in its place. On the other hand, as Arcite sees it, the love he describes is the cause of a disruption – breaking of the law – which extends through all the orders of society – 'in ech degree'.[18] The image which he uses to bring home his point, of the quarrelling dogs robbed of their bone by the kite (1177–80), reinforces the impression of disorder, and the conclusion he draws is in keeping:

'And therfore, at the kynges court, my brother,
Ech man for hymself, ther is noon oother.'
(1181–2)

It is not only that this describes a state of disorder, but that it places it at the heart of human affairs and human relationships. The king's court ought to be the source of order in human society, and the ties of friendship and brotherhood – Palamoun and Arcite stand in the important relationship of sworn, blood-brothers – ought not to be so easily broken, nor the human 'brothers' so easily debased to the conduct of the wrangling dog and kite.

When Arcite is freed and finds himself in a worse prison than before, since he is even further from his lady, it is Fortune that he blames:

'O deere cosyn Palamon,' quod he,
'Thyn is the victorie of this aventure . . .
Wel hath Fortune yturned thee the dys,
That hast the sighte of hire and I th'absence.
For possible is, syn thou hast hire presence,
And art a knyght, a worthy and an able,
That by som cas, syn Fortune is chaungeable,

Thow maist to thy desir somtyme atteyne.
But I, that am exiled and bareyne
Of alle grace, and in so greet dispeir,
That ther nys erthe, water, fir, ne eir,
Ne creature that of hem maked is,
That may me helpe or doon confort in this,
Wel oughte I sterve in wanhope and distresse.
Farwel my lif, my lust, and my gladnesse!'
(1234–50)

The reference to the four elements and the creatures made of them is significant. This is, precisely, the realm over which love as a universal force has power, as we know from the *Troilus* and are to learn from Theseus's great speech. Arcite, in fact, looks to changeable Fortune, which has power over a love as temporary and changeable as herself, instead of to the stable forces which, under providence, hold all Nature together. This is underlined by the reference to divine 'purveiaunce' which immediately follows. It is a reminder to the reader that Fortune is not all-powerful, although Arcite himself makes no distinction:

'Allas, why pleynen folk so in commune
On purveiaunce of God, or of Fortune?'
(1251–2)

The passage in Boethius's *de Consolatione Philosophiae* which Chaucer is using does make a distinction. This comes in prosa vi of Book IV, and, in the first place, Philosophy points out the difference between Providence and *Fata* (here equivalent to destiny):

'And thilke devyne thought that is iset and put in the tour (*that is to seyn, in the heighte*) of the simplicite of God, stablissith many maner gises to thinges that ben to done; the whiche manere whan that men looken it in thilke pure clennesse of the devyne intelligence, it is ycleped purveaunce; but whanne thilke manere is referred by men to thinges that it moeveth and disponyth, than of olde men it was clepyd destyne. . . . For purveaunce is thilke devyne resoun that is establissed in the sovereyn prince of thinges, the whiche purveaunce disponith alle thinges; but, certes, destyne is the disposicioun and ordenance clyvyng to moevable thinges.'
(IV, pr. vi, 47–65).

Secondly, neither Boethius nor any other Stoic-inspired philosopher ever suggested that the kind of goods which Arcite enumerates as deceiving – riches, material freedom – were anything else. Moreover, the reference to the man who 'dronke is as a mous' relates to a passage of Boethius which is about something quite different. The drunkenness which Boethius laments is that which makes man's quest for the sovereign good uncertain,[19] not the search, which Arcite has in mind, for the 'felicitee' which is situated 'in this world'. The passage, in fact, is so framed that it gives a clear picture of Arcite's wrong-headed point of view, and yet ensures that a reader familiar with the philosophical background is all the time clearly signposted to the opposite one.

This speech is balanced by one made by Palamoun, which, again, is based on a passage in Boethius, this time on metre v in Book I. This metre is spoken by Boethius in his own person, lamenting his cruel fate, and to understand its significance we have to read on to Philosophy's reply in the prosa which follows. Arcite's speech is built up from scraps from several different parts of the *de Consolatione*, used in an altered sense, but in Palamoun's speech Chaucer is able to use a consecutive passage, because in this metre Boethius expresses a mistaken and wrong-headed view set up only to be knocked down by Philosophy, who comments dryly:

'Whan I saugh the,' quod sche, 'sorwful and wepynge, I wiste anoon that thow were a wrecche and exiled; but I wyste nevere how fer thyn exil was yif thy tale ne hadde schewid it me . . . thow hast fayled of thi weye and gon amys.'

(I, pr. v, 4–11).

Even here, Chaucer has modified his source and has worked in other material. The first part of the speech is closest to Boethius.[20]

Thanne seyde he, 'O crueel goddes that governe
This world with byndyng of youre word eterne,
And writen in the table of atthamaunt
Youre parlement and youre eterne graunt,
What is mankynde moore unto you holde
Than is the sheep that rouketh in the folde?
For slayn is man right as another beest,
And dwelleth eek in prison and arreest,

> And hath siknesse and greet adversitee,
> And ofte tymes giltelees, pardee.
> What governance is in this prescience,
> That giltelees tormenteth innocence?'
> (1303–14)

The alterations, however, are almost as striking as the likenesses. In the first place, the Creator of the Heavens, the Governor of all things, becomes the 'crueel goddes' in the plural, and the emphasis shifts from the question of guilt and innocence to a comparison of mankind with the beasts. Secondly, Chaucer does not here use the long passage which describes the cycle of time and the seasons. This, as he must have been well aware, in fact belongs to the argument in favour of the goodness of Providence, as is made clear in metre vi, where Philosophy says:

> Signat tempora propriis
> Aptans officiis deus.
>
> (God every several time
> With proper grace hath crowned.)
> (Loeb trans.)

In fact, Chaucer restricts the speech to the manifestations of the stars and of Fortune and does not make Palamoun, like Boethius, call in question the whole operation of God's providence in the natural world. He thus makes the argument a more trivial one than Boethius's, more obviously aimed at forces far below providence in the Boethian scheme.

He then introduces the image of the slaughtered beast, which has no parallel in Boethius, but which, as we have seen, is used elsewhere by Chaucer as a part of the argument in favour of man's free will and independence of Fortune. This image is carried over into the next part of the speech:

> 'And yet encresseth this al my penaunce
> That man is bounden to his observaunce,
> For Goddes sake, to letten of his wille,
> Ther as a beest may al his lust fulfille.
> And whan a beest is deed he hath no peyne;
> But man after his deeth moot wepe and pleyne,
> Though in this world he have care and wo.'
> (1315–21)

Here, Chaucer has moved on to Book III, prosa vii, of the *de Consolatione*, in which Philosophy argues that if physical pleasure were man's only good, the beasts ought to be called blessed, since they certainly have no other goal:

> And yif thilke delices mowen maken folk blisful, thanne by the same cause moten thise beestis ben cleped blisful, of whiche beestes al the entencioun hasteth to fulfille here bodily jolyte.

At the beginning of prosa viii, Philosophy concludes that:

> Now is it no doute thanne that thise weyes ne ben a maner mysledynges to blisfulnesse, ne that they ne mowen nat leden folk thider as thei byheten to leden hem.

If Palamoun had understood where true pleasure lay, he would not have envied the beasts. That he does so shows the depth of his error.

To end the speech, Chaucer returns briefly to Boethius for the contrast of the treatment meted out in the world to guilt and innocence, and concludes with Palamoun's application of his arguments to his own circumstances, in which he blames his fate wholly on the activities of the gods – Juno, who is at the bottom of all the troubles of Thebes; Saturn and Venus, who are responsible, on the one hand, for his imprisonment and, on the other, for his painful love (a love which has plunged him in 'jalousie and fere') and who are to be seen acting in concert later in the poem. The whole speech, therefore, illustrates Palamoun's complete submission to Fortune and to the influences of the gods who help to bring about particular events within the transitory world. The arguments are familiar ones, which, in their usual context, either carry the reverse meaning or are only used to be contradicted. As in the case of Arcite's earlier speech, the reader who is familiar with material of this kind will have no great difficulty in seeing what the poet is aiming at and in taking up the position which he is intended to occupy. As we have seen from the treatment of such material in the short poems, there seems no reason to doubt that Chaucer's audience shared with him a knowledge of, and interest in, philosophizing of this type.

This, then, is the situation – the philosophical groundplan – as it is laid out in part i. The end of this part brings us the first of the prosaic, semi-ironical comments which remind us vividly of the presence of the Knight as story-teller and, at the same time, set us at a little distance from the story itself, allowing us the space to look at it dispassionately. As we have seen, the actual style of these comments, like that of many of Theseus's speeches, is in accordance with the methods of earlier romance. Chaucer's innovation lies in the subtlety with which he uses such methods. The Knight puts his question:

> Yow loveres axe I now this questioun:
> Who hath the worse, Arcite or Palamoun?
> That oon may seen his lady day by day,
> But in prison he moot dwelle alway;
> That oother wher hym list may ride or go,
> But seen his lady shal he nevere mo.
> Now demeth as yow liste, ye that kan,
> For I wol telle forth as I bigan.
>
> (1347–54)

We are not only disengaged for a moment from the story. By the posing of the conventional *problème d'amour*, we are also disengaged from any tendency to take too high a philosophical flight. The problems which have been raised are serious ones. The themes of determinism and free will and of order and disorder are fundamental to human life and to human happiness; but, nevertheless, Chaucer has chosen to make them the themes of a tale told for entertainment as well as profit, and therefore demanding more frequent and complex modulations than would be possible, or necessary, in a more single-minded treatise on philosophy. The love story, as has been said, may not be the main purpose of the work, but it is not to be set aside as a mere artificial pretext for the philosophy. The immediate source of disorder in the poem is the disastrous love which falls upon the two princes, and it is in order to ponder the significance of all their frenzied acts and speeches that we need, at times, to set them at a distance. We are not, in this tale, to be too closely involved with what Henry James likes to refer to as the victims bleeding in the arena – towards whom, too, he has much of Chaucer's attitude of compassionate, occasionally half-exasperated irony, and whom he also likes to view through the eyes of an observer only partially involved in the struggle. Chaucer arranges his distancing partly through such an observing figure – that of the Knight – and partly through the figure, to some extent a duplicate of the Knight, of

Theseus, who is not only the observer of the lovers' activities but also the kingly ruler in whom is to be found the ultimate earthly source of order in their world. His down-to-earth comments, therefore, although they may seem intrusive, or even flippant, to some readers, help to indicate a change of focus and to reinforce the effect of the careful organization of the philosophical arguments. They help, in fact, to show the difference between the state of disorder in which the lovers suffer and struggle and that of order within which Theseus operates, and which, though with some loss, he is finally able to impose on the situation.

Part i, then, sets the scene and establishes the basic themes and patterns. Part ii carries on the story and develops the contrast between the lovers and Theseus. This part opens with a description of the 'loveris maladye of Hereos' which afflicts Arcite, and to which is added symptoms pointing to 'manye / engendred of humour malencolik'. Boccaccio also describes Arcite's frantic sorrow and changed appearance,[21] but the medical treatment of the subject is wholly Chaucer's. 'Heroical love' (Burton's term for it) was a well-recognized illness, which was discussed in numerous medieval medical treatises.[22] It was likely, in itself, to lead to madness, but Chaucer suggests that Arcite's mania derives rather from melancholy. This, too, was for the Middle Ages not merely a frame of mind, but a serious medical problem.[23] Melancholy is invariably associated with the influence and characteristics of Saturn, so that, through this description, Chaucer not only establishes the extreme seriousness of Arcite's morbid state, but places it within the pattern of links between the planet-gods and men which is so important in the poem. Arcite shows associations with Saturn in this illness and also in the final one which ends his life, although he dies after expressing his devotion to Mars and placing himself under his protection, and it is to Mars that he corresponds in the arrangement of gods and human beings round which the poem is built. Arcite's association with both the unfortunate planets is important, since it places him in the position, not only of great personal danger, but also of assisting in the ultimate solution. This is because, although the immediate effects of Saturn's power are invariably unpleasant, he is, as we shall see, ultimately, and in his wider operations, a force on the side of order.

At the end of the description, Chaucer emphasizes the results of such an illness, which are to bring disorder to the sufferer's whole nature and constitution:

> And shortly, turned was al up so doun
> Bothe habit and eek disposicioun.
>
> (1377–8)

In the same way the injuries which cause his death bring about a state of affairs in which 'Nature hath now no dominacioun' (2758). Arcite dies, as he had lived, a victim to a state of disorder which is typical of the evil influence of the planets on the natural world and on the physical nature of a man who, through failure to rule his passions, lays himself open to their power.

Part ii also contains several references to the capriciousness and arbitrary character of the activities of the gods. We hear in line 1536 of 'geery Venus', who can overcast the hearts of lovers 'in hir queynte geres' (1531); of Juno (1542) and her ancient enmity towards Thebes. Just as Troy forms a background, of which we are constantly reminded, to the story of Troilus, so in the *Knight's Tale* the background is not Athens, which remains a shadowy city in spite of the fact that almost all the action takes place there, but Thebes and all its evil history. Again, in line 1623, we have the telling paradoxical conceit of 'Cupide, out of alle charitee', as the source, not of love, but of a jealousy which brings about the near mortal combat between Palamoun and Arcite.

The fight between the lovers is described not only in terms of the utmost violence – 'up to the ancle foghte they in hir blod' (1660) – but also with a cluster of the wild beast similes of which Statius is so fond:

> Thou myghtest wene that this Palamon
> In his fightyng were a wood leon,
> And as a crueel tigre was Arcite;
> As wilde bores gonne they to smyte,
> That frothen whit as foom for ire wood.
>
> (1655–9)

Not only are the sworn brothers, like Cupid, out of charity, they are also reduced to the level of savage animals. Nevertheless, although love has brought them to this paradoxical state, they have not lost all their noble and chivalric characteristics. Arcite provides food and arms for Palamoun and is willing to give him the best weapons and take the worst for himself (1614). Chaucer is careful to show that, while the two lovers become the apparently helpless victims of their unrestrained passions, their essential nature is still not necessarily debased.

Theseus appears on the scene in time to stop the fight; he acts, in fact, as Reason to bring under control this particular burst of Sensuality. That Chaucer sees him, however, as something more than Reason is shown by the passage which introduces him. This is the passage on destiny spoken by the narrator, which provides for Theseus the same kind of anchorage in the philosophical ideas of the poem as their earlier speeches do for Palamoun and Arcite. The narrator says 'And forth I wole of Theseus yow telle' and then continues:

> The destinee, ministre general,
> That executeth in the world over al
> The purveiaunce that God hath seyn biforn,
> So strong it is that, though the world had sworn
> The contrarie of a thyng by ye or nay,
> Yet somtyme it shal fallen on a day
> That falleth nat eft withinne a thousand yeer.
> For certeinly, oure appetites heer,
> Be it of werre, or pees, or hate, or love,
> Al is this reuled by the sighte above.
> This mene I now by myghty Theseus . . .
>
> (1663-72)

What is said of destiny is thus linked to Theseus both at the beginning and at the end. He acts to stop the unbridled savagery of the lovers; and rules their passions, just as destiny, the power nearest to God in the chain of influences through which His providence is enacted in the world,[24] rules all human appetites. But, and this must be emphasized, Theseus is not destiny itself, still less providence. He is a man who is able to act because of a chance encounter, not through any share in divine 'purveiaunce', the knowledge which God alone possesses. Since, however, unlike the lovers, he acts in accordance with reason, he naturally has a closer affinity to providence than they can have. Chaucer ensures that the action, in spite of the omnipresent gods, is played out in human terms.

At first sight, with its insistence on the inescapable nature of destiny, this passage bears a resemblance to Palamoun's on the 'eterne graunt', but the likeness is superficial. Instead of the lower, and more random, forces of Fortune or chance governing the accidents of human existence – sickness, adversity, imprisonment – we have a power which, coming nearer to God, has a more profound influence – that is, it operates, in a comprehensive way, on the whole of human feeling and activity. We are, in fact, in the presence of a system, not, as in Palamoun's speech, of a series of random observations. Moreover 'purveiaunce', 'providence', is now in question. The word was not used by Palamoun who only speaks of 'prescience'.[25] This latter, too, belongs to the gods in the plural; it can be thought of in connection with the planetary dispositions, while 'purveiaunce' belongs to God in the singular, who, far from being cruel and regardless of His creatures here below, operates for their good to prevent violence and restore the state of order.

Theseus shows himself as a king both in power – he stops the fight with a word – and in the possession of the kingly virtues. He is merciful and magnanimous, wise and just. More than this, in his long speech on the nature of love, he does two things: he shows us the disruptive and destructive power of love and its lack of sense, or obedience to reason, and he also, through his humorous, matter-of-fact style, helps to reinforce the distancing effect which we have already seen induced by the narrator's comments. It is not only the fight that stops when Theseus calls 'Ho!' The reader, too, pauses to look at the story from a different angle. Theseus thus emphasizes the paradoxical situation to which love has reduced the princes:

> 'Lo heere this Arcite and this Palamoun,
> That quitly weren out of my prisoun,
> And myghte han lyved in Thebes roially,
> And witen I am hir mortal enemy,
> And that hir deth lith in my myght also;
> And yet hath love, maugree hir eyen two,
> Broght hem hyder bothe for to dye.
> Now looketh, is nat that an heigh folye?
> Who may been a fool, but if he love?
> Bihoold, for Goddes sake that sit above,
> Se how they blede! be they noght wel arrayed?
> Thus hath hir lord, the god of love, ypayed

Hir wages and hir fees for hir servyse!
And yet they wenen for to been ful wyse
That serven love, for aught that may bifalle.' . . .
(1791–1805)

But these reversals of the probable and normal order of things are not all. The crowning piece of unreason is that the lovers' passions are operating in a vacuum. This is not yet a mutual love, leading to a union in which both parties cooperate to produce a new order and a new wholeness:

'But this is yet the beste game of alle,
That she for whom they han this jolitee
Kan hem therfore as muche thank as me.
She woot namoore of al this hoote fare,
By God, than woot a cokkow or an hare!'
(1806–10)

This sums up what has already been implied concerning love of this kind; and, at the same time and with a vengeance, it cuts the lovers and their problems down to size. We are dealing with serious problems and with important topics, but neither in the heroic nor in the romantic manner.

Theseus's common sense is not harsh, nor yet wholly unsympathetic. He too, in his time, has been a servant of love, and therefore, with royal magnanimity, he offers the lovers pardon, provided that they swear friendship to him and:

'That nevere mo ye shal my contree dere,
Ne make werre upon me nyght ne day.'
(1822–3)

Theseus's concern, in fact, is to use this disorderly, individualistic love to further the establishment of a general state of peace and order: he is, once more, primarily concerned with the political problem of Thebes. He also offers to take their individual problem in hand. Their position is, as he points out, a fundamentally unreasonable one:

'Ye woot yourself she may nat wedden two
Atones, though ye fighten everemo.
That oon of you, al be hym looth or lief,
He moot go pipen in an yvy leef;
That is to seyn, she may nat now han bothe.'

(1835–9)

He proposes to resolve this dilemma by arranging matters so that:
'ech of yow shal have his destynee / As hym is shape' (1842–3). There
is, in fact, nothing to be done but to submit to the 'ministre general'
of God and to await the outcome of divine 'purveiaunce'. Theseus is
not, it must be emphasized, removing or affecting their freedom of
will. Each remains at liberty to withdraw and to cede Emely to the
other, now or at any time in the story.

Theseus makes a somewhat subtle distinction between this general
submission to destiny and the operation of Fortune in the tournament
which, he proposes, is to settle the matter. He undertakes to give
Emely 'to whom that Fortune yeveth so fair a grace' as to gain the
victory. In this he speaks accurately, since at the level of the tournament, the destinal decree will be worked out through the apparently
random operation of Fortune. This also prepares the way for the part
played *in propria persona* in the tournament by the capricious planet-
gods, who, as in Arcite's speech (1086 ff.), are, in certain respects,
hardly distinguished from Fortune.

Part iii is largely taken up by the development of the theme of the
gods, through the long descriptions of their temples and the prayers
offered there. But, just as the gods (whether they are thought of as
pagan deities or planets) act under the ultimate control of Provi-
dence-Jupiter, so the whole elaborate setting of their temples is
shown to be part of Theseus's ordering of the situation and arises
through his plan to resolve the lovers' problem.

The temples form part of the edifice constructed to hold the lists
for the tournament, and the whole structure is presented to us as an
expression of Theseus's ability to achieve a perfectly ordered arrangement. Chaucer introduces the description as a matter of importance:

I trowe men wolde deme it necligence
If I foryete to tellen the dispence

> Of Theseus, that gooth so bisily
> To maken up the lystes roially,
> That swich a noble theatre as it was,
> I dar wel seyen in this world ther nas.
>
> (1881-6)

The adverb 'roially' and the epithet 'noble' – a word, as we have seen, which carries important connotations for Chaucer – imply an activity which is both serious and typical of Theseus's kingly nature. This 'noble theatre' is circular:

> The circuit a myle was aboute,
> Walled of stoon, and dyched al withoute.
> Round was the shap, in manere of compas,
> Ful of degrees, the heighte of sixty pas,
> That whan a man was set on o degree,
> He letted nat his felawe for to see.
>
> (1887-92)

The actual lists, which Chaucer does not describe in detail, would be marked off by barriers and would run across the circle, as we presently learn, from west to east. Chaucer has departed from Boccaccio in causing Theseus to build the theatre specially for this occasion. In the *Teseida*, the theatre is already in existence, and in describing it, with its marble walls, seating formed from stone steps and two gates, Boccaccio probably had an actual Roman amphitheatre in mind. He certainly does not, as Chaucer does, depart from the Classical model by incorporating temples in the structure.[26] By these two innovations – the description of the actual erection of the theatre and the incorporation of the temples – Chaucer, as we shall see, alters the meaning of the whole episode and uses it not only to provide a brilliant description of an artifact, very much in the traditional manner of romance, but also to further the exposition of his plan of linked planet-gods and human protagonists.

There are few medieval romances, either in French or English, which lack a passage of description of some splendid building or work of art in which the writer dwells on all the details of ornamentation.[27] Chaucer, therefore, in bringing together in one splendid passage the temple descriptions and that of the theatre, was no doubt catering for this taste. He was also writing for an audience which, in the London of the second half of the fourteenth century, could actually see buildings of unsurpassed splendour and workmanship around them.[28] His approach to his description, with its emphasis on method and good workmanship, is appropriate enough to a Clerk of the Works, but it also recalls that of Chrétien de Troyes in *Cligès*, a romance which makes exceptional use of architectural description. Chaucer mentions the craftsmen who work on the theatre in the following order: men 'that geometrie or ars-metrike kan', that is the architects responsible for the plan and basic structure;[29] 'portre-yours', painters; and 'kerveres of ymages', sculptors. The whole passage is one of hyperbole – no man skilled in these ways was absent from the building. Chaucer may, in writing in these terms, be think-ing of the actual assembling of a swarm of workmen on one of the great building projects of his own day. The romances, less realistic-ally, tend to concentrate these three essential functions in one man. Thus Cligès's servant John is famous 'for the works which he has made and carved and painted',[30] but even in real life the range of the medieval architect tended to be greater than his modern counterpart. Villard de Honnecourt, for example, made architectural, decorative and sculptural working drawings, and painting and sculpture were often practised by the same man.[31] The formula of praise which Chaucer uses to sum up the excellence of his theatre is a traditional one, used of John's work in *Cligès*. Chaucer says:

> And shortly to concluden, swich a place
> Was noon in erthe, as in so litel space,
> (1895–6)

and of John it is said 'there is no land where he is not known . . . there are no arts however diverse, in which anyone can vie with him'.[32] Once again, this formula could also be used of real-life artists. Froissart used it of André Beauneveu, who was employed by the Duc de Berri; and Thomas Walsingham, a monk of St Albans, used it of Matthew Paris.[33]

Chaucer thus prepares his audience for a description in the best of taste, in terms of both romance and real life. But, in so far as we have seen Theseus enacting a providential rôle on earth, parallel to that of Jupiter in heaven, it seems likely that there are other and wider implications to a building activity which unifies the conflicting planetary powers within an all-embracing circular scheme. The same division of the work of building into architectural and decorative is used in accounts of the activities of the divine Architect in the creation of the world. This plan is followed, for example, in the very influential *Hexameron* of St Ambrose. Here the work of creation is divided into two on the basis of Genesis 1:1–2: 'In the beginning God created heaven and earth. And the earth was void and empty', and Genesis 2:1: 'So the heavens and the earth were finished, and all the furniture of them' ('et omnis ornatus eorum'). These two passages gave St Ambrose the formula 'to create, and afterwards to beautify', which enabled him to compare God to the good architect who 'lays the foundation first, and afterwards, when the foundation has been laid, plots the various parts of the building, one after the other, and then adds thereto the ornamentation'.[34] That the created universe was circular, like Theseus's theatre, or rather formed a perfect sphere, hardly needs illustration. The whole principle of the concentric spheres leading up to the *primum mobile* depends on this idea, which was an important part of the cosmology of both Plato and Aristotle. The idea of God as an arithmetician and geometrician derives from Wisdom, 11:21: 'thou hast ordered all things in measure, and number, and weight'. This leads to the familiar motif of visual art of the creative hand of God holding the compasses – the tool also used to identify human architects in painting and sculpture.

The order which Theseus imposes through the circle within which he brings the temples of the gods, even though it may be comparable to that imposed on the universe by its divine Architect, remains, it is clear, of a strictly subordinate kind. The immediate purpose of the building is conflict, although it is hoped that a solution will arise from the meeting of the lovers in the lists. Moreover, in the descriptions of the temple decorations, the sinister, adverse and apparently discordant activities of the planet-gods are stressed. Theseus's achievement, by means of which the planets can work towards a final solution, is, clearly, essentially an earthly one in its limitations and its need to accept all the anomalies which belong to the world of change: once more he is like, but not identical with, providence. Nor is the element of discord absent from the world of the planet-gods: the conflict in the lists only echoes the conflict between Venus and Mars, while the impression that the cruel and irrational attributes of the gods actually belong to them, and are not merely due to the human viewpoint, is confirmed by the effect of Saturn's speech, in which he characterizes himself in terms similar to those of the temple paintings (the work of human hands). Order is finally achieved only when the different planes of disorder, among gods and men, are brought under the influence of something which transcends both – when, in fact, the ultimate ordering force exemplified by the chain of love in Theseus's speech in part iv, is brought to bear.

The three temples – of Mars, Venus and Diana – are brought, as we have said, within Theseus's circular scheme. Saturn and Jupiter are not included, although Saturn is given a self-descriptive speech which runs parallel to the descriptive decorations of the temples. In so far as Jupiter is identified with a providential power above the minor gods, with which Theseus and his architecture are also associated, he is as much outside the scheme as Theseus himself. In so far as he is a planet-god, his function, as we shall see, is closely linked to, and even overshadowed by, that of Saturn. Theseus, we are told at line 1902, built the temples 'for to doon his ryte and sacrifise', but in point of fact we do not see him using them. It is only the lovers and their lady who each offer up prayers at the appropriate altar. The tournament is not initiated by any general ceremonial directed towards the gods. The day before, it is true, is spent by the whole company 'in Venus heigh servyse' (2487) – but this is a somewhat ambiguous activity.

In his descriptions of the decoration of the three temples and in Saturn's self-characterizing speech, Chaucer utilizes the tradition known as 'the Children of the Planets'. This takes the form, in visual art, of a representation of the planet-deity, at the top of the picture, presiding over a crowded composite scene below, in which all the various human accidents and occupations that can be ascribed to the influence of the planet in question are depicted.[35] It is, obviously, from such sources that the unheroic element comes in, for example, the list of catastrophes caused by Mars – the cook scalding himself with his own ladle, the baby eaten by the sow and, possibly, the carter run over by his own cart.[36] Chaucer, however, blends the Children of the Planets scheme with another. The fact that he is describing actual temples demands that the gods should be shown not as inhabiting the heavens, but as presiding over their altars. Thus, Venus and Diana appear in typical scenes: Venus rising out of the water[37] and Diana equipped for hunting and standing on a crescent moon, like the Lady of the Apocalypse. Mars is actually given a temple within a temple, because here Chaucer follows, in part, the long description of Mercury's arrival at the house of Mars in the *Thebaid*, VII, 40 ff. Chaucer thus preserves the ambiguity of his lesser gods, who remain part planet, part deity, although in other respects in these passages he tends to heighten the impression that we are dealing with astrological forces.[38]

The effect of the Children of the Planets material is to emphasize the way in which the gods are implicated in the details of human life, down to the most trivial and unpleasant accidents. This is, of course, not incompatible with the view that their influence stops short of the soul; it does, however, significantly link the providential scheme to the apparently random operation of chance in the world, just as lines 1663 ff. link Theseus and his chance appearance in the grove to 'the purveiaunce that God hath seyn biforn'. It is, too, this kind of random, undeserved and apparently malicious operation of chance which gives rise to the darker view of life expressed in the lovers' speeches. The descriptions of the planetary activities and influences do much to reinforce, and even to justify, their point of view, and thus play an important part in the overall balance of the poem: we are not, in fact, to see Arcite's tragedy as in any sense unreal. On the other hand, a more complete and unbiased view of the planets sees them working towards joy as well as woe, while an even more profound and philosophical perception places them as a part of the whole providential design for good. The parts of the descriptions which are more appropriate to the temples as Chaucer found them in his Italian or Classical sources, on the other hand, work in a grander manner to support the more heroic elements in the narrative. In these passages, in fact, as everywhere in the *Knight's Tale*, Chaucer is careful to modify a romantic-epic set piece by bringing it into relation with the actual and everyday, without, however, allowing the epic character to be entirely lost.

In the case of Venus, it is hardly possible to give her much variety in the events she controls or to distinguish the more commonplace, everyday ones, but her activities are brought within the scope of Theseus's humorous, deflating comments on the love story by the narrator's summing up:

> Lo, alle thise folk so caught were in hir las,
> Til they for wo ful ofte seyde 'allas!'

Suffiseth heere ensamples oon or two,
And though I koude rekene a thousand mo.
(1951–4)

Mars, as we have seen, has his curiously unheroic accidents, and Diana has the lifelike representation of a woman in childbirth before her:

But for hir child so longe was unborn,
Ful pitously 'Lucyna' gan she calle.
(2084–5)

Saturn's influence is as wide as his course: he causes unromantic and unheroic stranglings and hangings,[39] revolts on the part of the peasants,[40] treasons and secret poisonings,[41] and diseases and pestilence of all kinds;[42] the unfortunate miner and carpenter are coupled with 'Sampsoun shakynge the piler'.

The influence of the four gods is described in every case, as unfortunate. In the case of Mars and his 'sory place', there are no mitigating circumstances, unless we can take the phrase 'the infortune of Marte' (2021) as suggesting that the planet could have another more fortunate aspect. In fact, this could be brought about, and is, as the story develops, by conjunction with Venus. As Saturn says:

'Though Mars shal helpe his knyght, yet nathelees
Bitwixe yow ther moot be som tyme pees.'
(2473–4)

That Chaucer sees the denouement in terms of a conjunction of Mars and Venus is shown by the concluding lines of part iii:

Now wol I stynten of the goddes above,
Of Mars and of Venus, goddesse of Love.
(2479–80)

Venus is shown surrounded by unhappy lovers, as is the Venus of the *Parlement of Foules*. The emphasis is all on

The broken slepes, and the sikes colde,
The sacred teeris and the waymentynge,
The firy strokes of the desirynge
That loves servantz in this lyf enduren.
(1920–3)

There is no indication that she can also stand as Venus-Cytheria, as a force tending to peace and harmony. She seems entirely in keeping with the view of love as a destructive force on the side of disorder which is emphasized throughout the early parts of the *Knight's Tale*. It is only when we come to Theseus's speech that we realize that Venus can have a more fortunate aspect and can see love as a principle or order, working to bring about a new unity in which the problems of the poem are resolved in the final marriage of Palamoun and Emely.

Diana is the moon and the avenger of unchastity, but she has a wider function too. She is triple Hecate:

Hir eyen caste she ful lowe adoun,
Ther Pluto hath his derke regioun
(2081–2)

and Emely speaks of 'tho thre formes that thou hast in thee' (2313). Moreover, she is also Lucina, who presides over childbirth, which prepares us for her rejection of Emely's plea 'noght to ben a wyf and be with childe' (2310). It is significant that in the *Paradiso* the sphere of the moon is occupied by the blessed souls of those who have had, for good reason, to break vows of chastity, not by those who pre-served them.

Saturn is Chaucer's addition to the company of the gods – a fact which suggests that he regarded him as of particular importance in his conception of the story. The series of misfortunes over which he has rule are unmitigatedly sinister. Nevertheless, 'al be it that it is agayn his kynde', he is finally seen as a supreme force working towards order and unity, when he intervenes after such serious con-flict has broken out between Venus and Mars that Jupiter is unable to compose it:

Til that the pale Saturnus the colde,
That knew so manye of aventures olde,

Foond in his olde experience an art
That he ful soone hath plesed every part.
As sooth is seyd, elde hath greet avantage;
In elde is bothe wysdom and usage;
Men may the olde atrenne, and noght atrede.
Saturne anon, to stynten strif and drede,
Al be it that it is agayn his kynde.
Of al this strif he gan remedie fynde.

(2443–52)

The list of typical Saturnian accidents which follows shows that
Saturn's means to this end are unlikely to be pleasant and may
indeed seem as blindly cruel and capricious as the acts attributed to
the gods by Palamoun. Nevertheless, it is clear that, seen on a higher
level, his action is designed to bring order out of disorder. We may be
reminded of the dual aspect of Fortune explained by Philosophy in
Boethius's *de Consolatione*[43] and hymed by Dante in the *Inferno*:

Vostro saver non ha contasto a lei:
        questa provede, giudica, e persegue
        suo regno come il loro li altri dei. . . .
Quest' è colei ch' è tanto posta in croce
        pur da color che dovrìen dar lode,
        dandole biasmo a torto e mala voce;
Ma ella s'è beata e ciò non ode;
        con l'altre prime creature lieta
        volve sua spera e beata si gode.

(She is past your wit to understand; but she
Provideth, judgeth, governeth her own,
As the other Gods do theirs in their degree . . .
This is she who is cursed without a cause,
And even from those hath maledictions got,
Unjustly, of whom she should have won applause.
But she is in her bliss, and hears them not.
In chime with the other primal creatures glad,
She turns her sphere and tastes her blissful lot.)

(VII, 85–96; Binyon trans.)

It would, I think, be possible to account for Chaucer's treatment of
Saturn as a force for ultimate good on this basis – simply as an

instrument of a benevolent providence. But the way in which he introduces the god, with the emphasis on age and wisdom, shows that there is rather more to it than that. Chaucer, in fact, appears to know the tradition of Saturn as wisdom and also as Chronos, time. The idea of a good Saturn, and indeed the idea that all the planets were essentially good, since they were part of a descending scheme originating in the divine source of all goodness, is ultimately neo-Platonic. It was elaborated, in slightly different ways, by Plotinus and Proclus.[44] Transmission of these ideas to the later Middle Ages is mainly through a source well known to Chaucer: Macrobius in the *Saturnalia* and the *Somnium Scipionis*. Macrobius treated the gods as names for the planets – that is, as fully and unambiguously astrologized. Although this process had begun with the neo-Platonic writers, especially with Proclus, their main interest was in the formulation of a philosophical system rather than a cosmological one. Chaucer, therefore, in retaining (in part from his immediate source, the *Teseida*) so many of the characteristics of the gods as against the planets, is actually, though no doubt unwittingly, going back to a stage which lies behind Macrobius.

The relevant passages on Saturn from Macrobius are from:
1. The *Saturnalia*, I, xxii:[45]

Saturnus ipse, qui auctor est temporum et ideo a Graecis inmutata littera Κρόνος quasi Χρόνος vocatur, quid aliud nisi sol intelligendus est, cum tradatur ordo elementorum, temporum numerositate distinctus, luce patefactus, nexus aeternitate conductus?

(Saturn, who is the author of time and is therefore called Kronos by the Greeks, that is, with a change of letter, Chronos (time) – how else is he to be understood but as the sun, through which the ordering of the elements is brought about, separated by appropriate numerical intervals, and made manifest by light, a bond made fast to eternity.)

Elsewhere, in the *Somnium Scipionis*, Macrobius refers to the 'unbreakable chain' ('mutuatus insolubili inter se vinculo elementa devinxit', I, vi, 24) by which the elements are bound and which, according to the *Timaeus*, depends on the numbers three and four. This is the chain which Chaucer attributes to love in Theseus's speech and to Nature in the *Parlement of Foules*.[46] For Macrobius, the bond of the elements is especially associated with the planetary movements and spheres, a fact which may throw some light on the transition in the *Knight's Tale* from the planet-gods as prime movers in the love story in parts i–iii to, in part iv, the Aristotelian unmoved first mover which initiates their, and all other, movement and which is also the '*amor che muove il sole e l'altre stelle*'.

2. The *Somnium Scipionis* which also has an important passage on the planets, including Saturn:

> Hoc ergo primo pondere de zodiaco et lacteo ad subiectas usque sphaeras anima delapsa, dum et per illas labitur, in singulis non solum, ut iam diximus, luminosi corporis amictitur accessu, sed et singulos motus, quos in exercitio est habitura, producit: in Saturni ratiocinationem et intelligentiam, quod λογιστικόν et θεωρετικόν vocant; in Iovis vim agendi, quod πρακτικόν vocant; in Martis animositatis ardorem, quod θυμικόν nuncupatur; . . . desiderii vero motum, quod ἐπιθυμητικόν vocatur, in Veneris; . . . φυτικόν vero, id est naturam plantandi et augendi corpora, in ingressu globi lunaris exercet.

> (By the impulse of the first weight, the soul, having started on its downward course from the intersection of the zodiac and the Milky Way to the successive spheres lying beneath, as it passes through these spheres, not only takes on the aforementioned envelopment in each sphere, but also acquires each of the attributes which, by approaching a luminous body, it will exercise later. In the sphere of Saturn it obtains reason and understanding, called *logistikon* and *theoretikon*; in Jupiter's sphere, the power to act, called *praktikon*; in Mars' sphere, a bold spirit or *thymikon*; . . . in Venus's sphere, the impulse of passion, *epithymetikon*; . . . and in the lunar sphere, the function of molding and increasing bodies, *phytikon*.)

$$(\text{I, xii, 13–14})$$

This passage describes a neo-Platonic descent of the soul through the spheres, acquiring, as it becomes further and further separated from the divine, characteristics in each, ending with the one which, Macrobius says, is furthest removed from the gods, since it relates to the bodies which are the prisons of souls on earth.[47] Chaucer certainly makes no explicit use of this journey through the spheres, though he does use the idea of descent (and ascent) in Theseus's

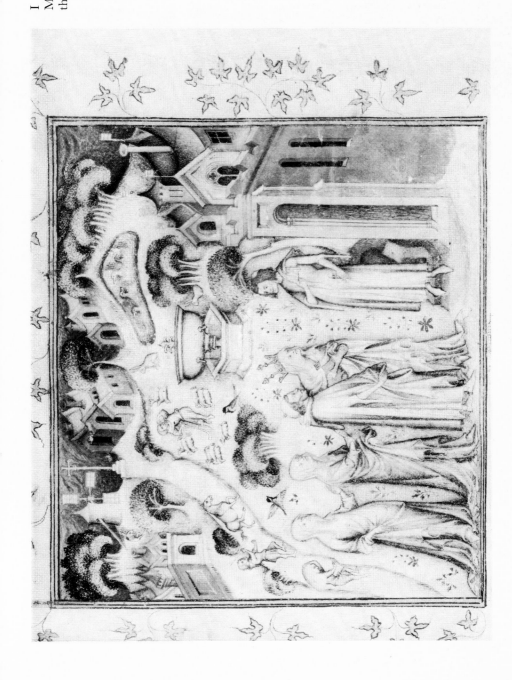

II   The Gods at the Fall of Troy

speech on the Prime Mover (2987 ff.). Nevertheless, as we shall see, he certainly presents us in this poem with a Saturn and Jupiter who represent theory and practice and with a Venus who, clearly, stands for the impulse of passionate love, which, with the cooperation of a Diana who presides over childbirth, can find issue in marriage and, presumably, the increase of mankind. Macrobius's description of the activities proper to the lunar sphere are very suggestive of Nature's labour in her forge in the *Roman de la Rose*, where she propagates all natural beings including man – a similarity which is unlikely to have escaped Chaucer. The characteristics gained in each sphere are certainly also the leading ones of each human character. Egeus shows theoretical wisdom, and Theseus the power to act successfully. The lovers' fates are determined on the one hand by the passion which leads Palamoun to pray to Venus, on the other by the warlike courage which causes Arcite to put his faith in Mars. Emely, as the virgin follower of Diana who is converted to marriage, lends herself at last to the φυτικόν, which she at first repudiates when she prays 'noght to ben a wyf and be with childe'.

Macrobius, as a neo-Platonist influenced by Stoic ideas, does not regard the planets as in any way evil. How ideas derived from him could be combined with the idea of Saturn as an influence producing evils in the world – fraud, deceit, melancholy, for example – is shown by a writer like William of Auvergne in the thirteenth century, who argues for the fundamental goodness of the planet, as accomplishing the divine will, and places the blame for any evil results on the misuse of its gifts by mankind.[48] Another thirteenth-century writer who takes an optimistic view of the planets is Alexander Neckham. He equates them with the seven gifts of the Holy Spirit, and his description of Saturn is very close to Chaucer's:[49]

Sapientia vero quae superiorem videtur tenere locum inter dona, sicut Saturnus inter planetas, maturitatem generat ex se sicut Saturnus in cursu peragendo longum tempus sibi vendicat. Nec sine causa fingitur a philosophis quod Saturnus sit senex, maturi enim pectoris senes esse consueverunt.

(Wisdom, which occupies the highest place among the gifts, as Saturn does among the planets, is generated by maturity from itself, just as Saturn takes a long time to complete his course. And Saturn is rightly described as an old man by the philosophers, because old men are of mature judgement.)

The existence of such well known authorities (although we cannot say precisely which Chaucer might have read) justifies the supposition that he knew of a Saturn who, though he may be associated with disagreeable accidents, is still fundamentally beneficent, is wise with the experience of old age and, if we follow out the hint given by Macrobius, is associated with the order and stability of the universe in a way which gives him (together with the whole planetary system) something of the function which Chaucer elsewhere attributes to Nature as God's Vicaire on earth or to Love as the force which holds the warring elements together. He would certainly have found this idea reinforced by his reading of Boccaccio's *de Genealogia Deorum*, where the old etymology *sacer nus*, that is, the neo-Platonic universal spirit which made everything, is given as an explanation of the name Saturn (VIII, 1),[50] and where Saturn is a god of sowing, that is, natural increase, as well as time. His scythe is explained as denoting agriculture in this chapter, and Ceres is one of his daughters. Boccaccio, too, has the peculiar blend of Classical myth and astrological lore which is so typical of Chaucer's treatment of the gods in the *Knight's Tale*, and especially of Saturn;[51] and, through his genealogical method of organizing his material, he naturally gives Saturn the supreme place above his descendant gods (see Plate I).

It is, I think, this activity of Saturn as a composer of strife and a bringer of order out of disorder, achieved in combination with Jupiter – *vis agendi* to Saturn's *theoretikon* – which is the 'grete effect' which Chaucer announces as the subject of the poem as a whole – 'for which that I bygan' – and of the fourth part in particular. It is not, I think, likely that he would use these words merely of the tournament, which is no more spectacular as a set piece, and no more important to the unfolding of the story, than the great descriptive passages of part iii. We must rather take them as an indication of a single, overriding purpose towards which the whole narrative is tending, and this, clearly, is the final solution, not any one incident on the way towards it.

The relation of Saturn and Jupiter may seem puzzling to the modern reader. On the one hand, Saturn acts here to bring about the denouement, as he says, in the cause of peace and the restoration of order. On the other, it is Jupiter who is the supreme ruler of the gods, who corresponds to divine providence and who is invoked as the ultimate source of order in Theseus's speech. The reason for this is that in a moral-philosophical view of the gods, of the kind that

Chaucer would find indicated in the *Thebaid* and, at times, in Macrobius and other sources of the same type, it is Jupiter who rules the world and who exists on a different plane to the lesser gods, who are equated with Fortune. But in a purely astrological system, the fact that Saturn, according to ancient and medieval knowledge of the planets, is the highest planet, with the widest course, tends, at any rate for those who reflect neo-Platonic ideas about the planets, to put him in the supreme place. We can see too, from Macrobius, that if Saturn (who significantly heads his list, coming before Jupiter since it is a list of planets not of gods) is theory, while Jupiter is practice, they form a natural and, even necessary, pair and can, indeed, be regarded as different aspects of one whole. In the same way, Venus as passion and Luna as increase could be regarded, especially by a reader of the *Roman de la Rose*, as two aspects of the natural order of the propagation of the species.

On the human plane, the third part of the *Knight's Tale* continues the development of the theme of order and disorder in various ways. The orderliness of Theseus's dispositions is shown in other ways besides the architecture of the theatre. For example, in line 2190, he treats his guests to an ideal hospitality which fulfils all the requirements of social order – each man is lodged 'at his degree' (2192) and the festivities are so well organized

> That yet men wenen that no mannes wit
> Of noon estaat ne koude amenden it.
>
> (2195–6)

In contrast, the lovers remain in a state of disorder. Just as, in part i, love was said to bring physical disruption to Arcite, now Palamoun laments his state of mental confusion:

> 'Allas! I ne have no langage to telle
> Th' effectes ne the tormentz of myn helle;
> Myn herte may myne harmes nat biwreye;
> I am so confus that I kan noght seye
> But, "Mercy, lady bright, that knowest weele
> My thought, and seest what harmes that I feele!"'
>
> (2227–32)

The motif of the wild beasts, which was used of the savagery of the quarrel between the sworn brothers earlier in the poem, is used again in the description of their chief supporters, Lygurge, King of Thrace, who is compared to a griffon and accompanied by huge white hounds, and Emetreus, King of Inde, who is compared to a lion and accompanied by a tame eagle and by lions and leopards. As Curry points out, these two are probably also to be understood as easily recognizable types of the Martian and the Saturnian man,[52] and are thus a further reminder of the vulnerability of the unbridled passions to the influence of the planets in its, apparently, most capricious and dangerous form.

Part iv of the *Knight's Tale* is dedicated, as we have said, to the 'grete effect' towards which the whole work is designed. It is, of course, dominated by the ordering figure of Theseus, although it also contains the final, and fatal, development of disorder in the overthrow and death of Arcite. Since, however, this is brought about by Saturn, it is also part of his intervention to resolve the problem. As we have seen, Arcite's subjection to Saturn, although fatal to him, is a necessary part of the final solution.

This part begins with Theseus's just and merciful rules for the conduct of the tournament, intended to prevent needless slaughter. The people applaud him, crying 'God save swich a lord, that is so good' (2563). Theseus here, in fact, exercises an important function of the medieval good king, who was particularly required to protect his subjects by preventing needless warfare.[53] The lists are now put to use, and the fight itself is described with great technical relish by the Knight, of whose professional expertise we are once more reminded. There is a return to the motif of the savage beasts when the prowess of Palamoun and Arcite is in question:

> Ther nas no tygre in the vale of Galgopheye,
> Whan that hir whelp is stole whan it is lite,
> So crueel on the hunte as is Arcite
> For jelous herte upon this Palamon.
> Ne in Belmarye ther nys so fel leon,
> That hunted is, or for his hunger wood,
> Ne of his praye desireth so the blood,
> As Palamon to sleen his foo Arcite.
>
> (2626–33)

As in the case of the fight in the grove, described with similes of the same kind, Theseus puts a stop to this savagery and, unlike the cruel gods as they were conceived by the lovers, promises to be 'trewe juge, and no partie' (2657).

His verdict, however, leaves room for a further turn to the story. He had decreed that the lovers must experience their destiny if they both persist in the pursuit of Emely and, in the actual lists, must put their fortune to the test. Now he says:

> 'Arcite of Thebes shal have Emelie
> That by his fortune hath hire faire ywonne.'
>
> (2658–9)

Fortune, or Mars, has given Arcite the immediate victory; but destiny has not finished working itself out. Saturn, to help Venus, brings about just such a tragic accident as we hear about in his list of evil influences. He causes a fury to start out of the ground; Arcite's horse stumbles, and he receives a fatal injury and dies in a manner which is, as Curry has shown, peculiarly Saturnian.[54]

Yet the description of his death, with all its harrowing and accurate medical detail, is set within a further exposition of the theme of order. Theseus takes all proper action for the due care of Arcite and all the other wounded. He makes special provision against 'disconfytinge' (2716 f.), that is, he sees to it that no further quarrels break out as a result of the tournament. And, more important still, Arcite dies reconciled to Palamoun, with his 'manie' apparently cured. His speech in lines 2783 ff. is significant:

> 'I have heer with my cosyn Palamon
> Had strif and rancour many a day agon
> For love of yow, and for my jalousye.
> And Juppiter so wys my soule gye,
> To speken of a servaunt proprely,
> With alle circumstances trewely –
> That is to seyen, trouthe, honour, knyghthede,
> Wysdom, humblesse, estaat, and heigh kynrede,
> Fredom, and al that longeth to that art –
> So Juppiter have of my soule part,
> As in this world right now ne knowe I non
> So worthy to ben loved as Palamon,

> That serveth yow, and wol doon al his lyf.
> And if that evere ye shul ben a wyf,
> Foryet nat Palamon, the gentil man.'
>
> (2783–97)

For the first time he recognizes with regret that his love has broken his friendship with Palamoun, a friendship, as we have seen, of a particularly serious and important kind; and he now calls not on Mars, but on Jupiter, as he urges Emely to provide a final solution to the conflict, and places Palamoun before her, and before us, in a light which, for the first time, allows us to see a lover not as brought to the level of the wild beasts by his passion, but, as Troilus was, ennobled by it. It is, of course, essential that our view of love, and of at least one of the lovers, should undergo this shift, since the solution depends on our recognition of the other, uniting aspect of the ambivalent love which brought Arcite to dissolution. This speech is thus an important structural device, and it is important too in that it prepares the way, through the appeal to Jupiter, for Theseus's speech, in which, since the ideas it expresses are philosophical not astrological, the emphasis shifts once more from Saturn to Jove.

Arcite dies with reconciliation in his heart and a proposal for a solution. Chaucer, however, leaves him at this point:

> His spirit chaunged hous and wente ther,
> As I cam nevere, I kan nat tellen wher.
> Therfore I stynte, I nam no divinistre;
> Of soules fynde I nat in this registre,
> Ne me ne list thilke opinions to telle
> Of hem, though that they writen wher they dwelle.
> Arcite is coold, ther Mars his soule gye!
> Now wol I speken forth of Emelye.
>
> (2809–16)

The opinion which he does not wish to reproduce is that of Boccaccio in the *Teseida*, who had described the flight of Arcite's soul under the guidance of Mercury. There are practical reasons for Chaucer's omission of this. For one thing, he had used it in the *Troilus* – if we accept that this poem probably preceded the final version of the *Knight's Tale* – for another, the introduction of Mercury here would have upset the symmetry of his arrangement of gods and human protagonists. It is more appropriate to leave Arcite to the care of Mars, from whom he got the warlike courage which gives him success in the lists, but not in love. A celestial flight would, also, be even more inappropriate in his case than in that of Troilus – where, as we have seen, Chaucer encounters some difficulty – since it would mean sending to the spheres and the blissful realm the soul of one who actually dies (as Troilus does not) through his indulgence of 'the blinde lust'. Such an ending, too, would have spoilt the uncompromising naturalism with which Chaucer has depicted Arcite's plight. He does not, in the *Knight's Tale*, give us a happy ending which is an easy or sentimental solution of the human problem. Arcite's death, like all individual deaths, is a part of the cycle of change which leads to true stability; but, as an individual case it loses none of its painfulness through serving as part of a process which leads to happier things. Arcite's last despairing protest is so poignant, and so convincing, that some critics have even been tempted to see in it the main theme of the poem. Such a view, however, disrupts the work and puts it out of period. When Chaucer makes Arcite ask:

> 'What is this world? what asketh men to have?
> Now with his love, now in his colde grave
> Allone, withouten any compaignye.'
>
> (2777–9)

he is only giving us a peculiarly forceful repetition of the lovers' earlier speeches. He is also providing support for the development of the theme of the cruel gods in the temple descriptions. From the viewpoint of the philosophical ideas which inform the *Knight's Tale*, this, as we have seen, is only part of a whole which, seen whole, has a very different significance. But it is, nevertheless, one of the emotional mainsprings of the poem, not only in the sense that it accounts, naturalistically, for the part Arcite plays, but also in its inevitable effect on the reader. These passages work together to build up the tension which it is the function of the 'grete effect' to resolve.

The resolution is prepared in the second half of Arcite's speech through his concern for his soul's fate at the hands of Jupiter – a reminder of the source of providential order which he has up to now forgotten. Egeus and Theseus, in their key speeches, provide in full the theoretical basis for the solution, which is acted out in practical terms by Palamoun and Emely at the end of the poem. This, however, is to anticipate.

The natural and violent outburst of sorrow which follows Arcite's death is checked and brought to order by the speech of Egeus:

> No man myghte gladen Theseus,
> Savynge his olde fader Egeus,
> That knew this worldes transmutacioun,
> As he hadde seyn it chaunge bothe up and doun,
> Joye after wo, and wo after gladness,
> And shewed hem ensamples and liknesse.
> 'Right as ther dyed nevere man,' quod he
> 'That he ne lyvede in erthe in some degree,
> Right so ther lyvede never man,' he seyde,
> 'In al this world, that som tyme he ne deyde.
> This world nys but a thurghfare ful of wo,
> And we been pilgrymes, passynge to and fro.
> Deeth is an ende of every worldly soore.'
> And over al this yet seyde he muchel moore
> To this effect, ful wisely to enhorte
> The peple that they sholde hem reconforte.
>
>   (2837–52)

This speech has been criticized as trite, or even as the utterance of a dotard; but this, I think, is to read too hastily and to be misled by two devices which Chaucer employs seriously. One is the circular form of statement within the speech, which is used not because Egeus is represented as repeating himself, but because he is describing the movement of a cyclic process; and the other is the assurance that he said much more, which is, surely, intended to indicate the extent of his wisdom and to emphasize that he made an important contribution, not to suggest that he was a long-winded bore. We need, rather, to ask why Chaucer should bring Egeus forward at this important moment as the poem moves towards its conclusion – and here only. The reason, I think, is obvious if we pay due attention to the introduction to his speech. Arcite's tragic death has threatened to throw everything into confusion, since its immediate effect is grief and dismay, and it can only help towards the solution when it has been understood and, through the proper exercise of reason, brought within the scheme of order. Theseus is as grief-stricken as anyone else and unable to see any way to proceed, now that his practical scheme of the tournament has, apparently, failed. We thus have the counterpart to the situation among the gods at the end of part iii, when Jupiter was unable to compose their strife, but a way was found when Saturn came forward with the theoretical wisdom to guide Jupiter's *vis agendi* into a profitable channel. Now, in part iv, Jupiter's human counterpart, Theseus, is similarly helpless until Egeus, described in terms which echo those applied to Saturn at the end of part iii, provides the necessary *logistikon* and *theoretikon*. As soon as he has done this, Theseus is able to embark on the series of practical measures, the first of which is the provision of appropriate funeral rites, which lead to the ultimate solution. We can now see why a speech which Boccaccio could give to Theseus is no longer appropriate to him, although it perfectly suits Egeus as the human counterpart of Saturn.

Egeus, like Saturn, is old. Like Saturn, too, with his 'olde experience', Egeus knows 'this worldes transmutacioun / As he hadde seyn it chaunge bothe up and doun'. If we are to judge from the opening of the *Fortune*:

> This wreched worldes transmutacioun . . .
> Governed is by Fortunes errour –

Chaucer uses the word 'transmutacioun' to mean change, not merely from one thing to another, but from one thing to its opposite (since the change of fortune is in the form of a wheel, and anything fastened to it must eventually pass opposite points). Such pairs of opposites form a totality of which the wheel is, of course, the figure. There may also be a hint of another meaning in 'transmutacioun', since it is a meaning well established in the fourteenth century,[55] that of what we should call 'chemical change', that is, change which brings into being something new. Egeus restricts his consideration of such changes – at any rate in the quotation Chaucer gives from what he tells us was a longer speech – to the cycle of life and death, a pair of opposites making up the totality of human earthly existence, whose 'transmutacioun' is a new and different state of being. This new state is suggested by the image of the pilgrim. This image is, of course, a predominantly Christian one – it is used in unequivocally Christian terms in the *Parson's Tale* – but, as we have already seen in the case of *Truth*, it lends itself to combination with a philosophical viewpoint

compatible with Christian thought without necessarily being
explicitly Christian, and therefore does nothing to disrupt the epic-
pagan tone which the use of the figures of the gods, whether astrological or philosophical, helps to sustain in the *Knight's Tale*.[56]

Egeus's speech is thus an important one and occupies an important
position in the scheme of parallel gods and men. It releases Theseus
from his momentary inactivation, and he proceeds with the funeral
rites. A proper period of mourning follows, and it is only 'By processe
and by lengthe of certeyn yeres' – a state of affairs which, again,
suggests both due decorum and the working out of a natural cycle[57]
– that we arrive at a point at which it is proper for the development of
the action to continue to its end. In this final development, Theseus
is the dominant figure – Egeus-Saturn does not reappear – and
Theseus acts as an ideal ruler who brings about the solution to the
dilemma of the love story only as part of a wider scheme for the
common profit. He acts, at last, because it becomes politically
desirable

> To have with certein contrees alliaunce
> And have fully of Thebans obeisaunce.
>
> (2973–4)

The old, evil problem of Thebes is to be dealt with; high policy is to
be served; and, at the same time, but not necessarily as the primary
purpose, the love story is to be brought to a happy conclusion. This
final scheme of order is prefaced by the long and famous speech in
which Theseus is at his most kingly, and the poem at its most
philosophical. Since this speech is an important part of the 'grete
effect' which Chaucer tells us is the subject of part iv (and, so that
there is no mistake, he repeats the phrase in line 2989), we must
pause over its content.

Chaucer's problem, in writing Theseus's speech is, it is obvious, to
provide something which will be worthy not only of a major character who has been built up in an extremely impressive way, but also
of the climax of an extremely ambitious work. To do this he needs
to draw on philosophical material which would be reasonably well
known to his audience and, therefore, calculable in its effect – and

material, moreover, which would have its full share of what Lovejoy has aptly called 'philosophical pathos', that is, which involves ideas with the power, within a given period, to exert a strong emotional effect on the audience. It is, I think, true to say that, in his handling of philosophical matter, it is always considerations of this kind which concern Chaucer: his aim is always to make structural use within his poem of the ideas he takes from the philosophers, not to explore and develop their meaning for its own sake. The latter course, indeed, is apt to be a dangerous one for poets, as we can see from the way in which Langland's grim struggle to follow out all the implications of an idea can, on occasion, disrupt his poem. If we try to trace out the different threads which Chaucer twists together in the speech, we shall see that he achieves his purpose in a way which shows full knowledge and mastery of the various arguments involved and, incidentally, the use of considerably more than an amalgam of phrases and ideas from Boethius.[58] Much, certainly, does come from the *de Consolatione*, but combined with material from other sources and arguments.

Theseus's argument is built up in the following way:

1. He takes as his premise the idea of God as both first mover and first efficient cause, Who begins the work of creation, that is, of outflowing love, by binding together the elements in such a way that they cannot fly apart and return created matter to its original state of chaos (2987–93). The ideas involved in the chain, or bond, of the elements and the various sources Chaucer used have already been discussed at length.[59] Here, two aspects are of importance: first, the idea of an order which is at the same time a limitation – 'In certeyn boundes, that they may nat flee' – and, secondly, the idea of a stability which is brought about by cyclic change. In the case of the elements this is the perpetual transmutation of one to another described, for example, by Cicero in the *de Natura Deorum*, II, xxxiii.[60] This second idea is present by implication in the chain-image, but only comes to the fore in the application of the argument to 'speces of thynges' in lines 3013 ff.

2. The argument now turns from the elements, matter itself, to the actual kinds of things which are produced from it in the world. All these are subject to time – 'certeyne dayes and duracioun' – and, therefore, the limitation which is part of the creative order is, in their case, primarily a temporal one – they have a limited period of existence:

Over the whiche day they may nat pace,
Al mowe they yet tho dayes wel abregge.
(2998–9)

This is proved (3000 ff.) by experience, not 'auctoritee' (written evidence), because it is sufficiently obvious, and also because the unfolding of a process in time can only be comprehended by an observer who lives through it – just so in the *Wanderer*, the old English poet, who also utilizes philosophical commonplaces concerning the nature of the world's existence, remarks that a man cannot become wise until he has spent time in the world; that is, not that age is automatically wise, but that process, unlike state, in the nature of the physical world, requires time for its apprehension.[61]

3. In lines 3003 ff. Chaucer returns to the idea of order and takes the presence of order in the world as proof of the stability and eternity of God. This is because the part must resemble the whole from which it derives. The orderliness of the world implies the perfection of God, its stability within time His eternity. This is the argument for the existence of God from observation of the world which is to be found, for example, in Cicero's *de Natura Deorum*, where, after describing, as an instance of the natural order, the progression of the seasons, he concludes:[62]

Haec ita fieri omnibus inter se concinentibus mundi partibus profecto non possent nisi ea uno divino et continuato spiritu continerentur.

(These processes and this musical harmony of all the parts of the world assuredly could not go on were they not maintained in unison by a single divine and all-pervading spirit.)

(II, vii)

4. From this idea, Chaucer passes at once to another: that of the actual way in which the parts, which together make up the natural world, derive from the divine whole. Here he uses the idea of the Scale of Creatures – the Homeric chain which Macrobius describes in the *Somnium Scipionis*.[63] This scale of descent is also referred to by Boethius in the *de Consolatione*, Book III, prosa x, in a passage which Chaucer follows here:

For the nature of thinges ne took nat hir begynnynge of thinges amenused and inparfit, but it procedith of thinges that ben alle hole and absolut, and descendith so doun into uttereste thinges and into thinges empty and withouten fruyt.

(Chaucer trans.)

This corresponds to lines 3007–3010 of the *Knight's Tale*:

> For nature hath nat taken his bigynnyng
> Of no partie or cantel of a thyng
> But of a thyng that parfit is and stable,
> Descendynge so til it be corrumpable.

5. Boethius's argument in Book III, prosa x, is concerned with the contrast of the incorruptible 'one' and the degree of corruptibility which comes with multiplicity. This would not suit Chaucer's purpose, and the 'therefore' of line 3011 introduces a different conclusion. He returns to the idea of cyclic transmutation, and says that permanence in the world means

> That speces of thynges and progressiouns
> Shullen enduren by successiouns,
> And nat eterne.
>
> (3013–15)

Boethius, in Book IV, prosa vi, also has this idea:

Thilke ordenaunce moveth the hevene and the sterres, and atemprith the elementz togidre amonges hemself, and transformeth hem by entrechaungeable mutacioun. And thilke same ordre neweth ayein alle thinges growynge and fallynge adoun, by semblable progressions of sedes and of sexes.

(Chaucer trans.)

Lines 3017–33 support this argument by a series of instances drawn from the natural world. These are: (a) the growth and decay of the oak tree; (b) the wasting away of the rock; (c) the drying up of a broad river; (d) the rise and fall of a great town; (e) the inevitable progress towards death of human beings of all kinds. These are all 'preeved by experience', but, although 'Ther nedeth noon auctoritee t'allegge', it is likely that the list does, in fact, owe something to books.

.Lists of natural phenomena of this kind used to illustrate duration, change and succession as the order of nature are fairly common in works which have a philosophical tendency. Boethius, for example, has one, featuring living creatures with souls (i.e., human beings), trees and stones, in the *de Consolatione*, Book III, prosa xi. Here the examples are used to prove that all created things naturally try to ensure their continued duration and eschew corruption, and only fail of this end in so far as they are separated from the one and eternal. Ovid uses the argument at length in the *Metamorphoses*, XV, 175 ff. Here he marshals time and the seasons, the alternations of sea and land, and of mountain and plain, the growth and decay of animals, the fall of cities and nations and, finally, the life of individual men, in support of the thesis:

Cuncta fluunt, omnisque vagans formatur imago.

(All things are in a state of flux, and everything is brought into being with a changing nature.)

(XV, 178)

Jean de Meun uses a similar sequence in Nature's complaint, where the mutability of the species of things is made the basis of her plea for the reproduction of the human race, which is alone in disregarding this fundamental necessity. She cites the movements of the heavens (i.e., the seasons and weather); the sea; the plants, including trees; the beasts and man; in lines 18947 ff. The argument long remained a powerful one. Spenser used it in the *Mutabilitie Cantos*,[64] and Hakewell set it out at length in his *Power and Providence of God*.[65] The ultimate source of such lists is the argument in the *Meteorologica* of Aristotle for an eternal world of continual cyclic change. In Book I, 14, this is proved by the example of the interchange of water and dry land; rivers dry up, creating more land, only to reappear elsewhere, thus restoring the balance of land and water (351a). This process is compared to the length of human life and to the life of nations and cities (351b). The basic list is, thus, the water and the dry land ('stone', 'rock', 'mountain', which, for Aristotle, are particularly concerned in the making of rivers and lakes [see 352b]), the nation or city and the short-lived human being. The addition of the tree or plant and the beasts, which are not needed in Aristotle's original argument, seems natural enough.

In the *Meteorologica* these changes are, it is emphasized, (a) cyclic (see the summary in 358a) and (b) caused by the alteration of the humours, wet and dry, cold and warm. They are thus linked both to the transmutation and to the qualities of the elements and so, quite properly, belong within the sequence of ideas unfolded so far in Theseus's speech.

6. For Aristotle, the cyclic progressions of nature simply make a closed system in which the earth is eternally wasted and eternally renewed:

> 'All of these [he refers to the processes of change by evaporation] are in a constant state of change, but the form and quantity of each of them are fixed, just as they are in the case of a flowing river or a burning flame. The answer is clear, and there is no doubt that the same account holds good for all these things alike. They differ in that some of them change more rapidly or more slowly than others; and they are all involved in a process of perishing and becoming which yet affects them all in a regular course.'

(357b–58a)

For Boethius, in a famous passage wholly Platonic in tone, the case is different – and it is Boethius whom Chaucer follows in drawing a conclusion from the principle of cyclic change:

> Hic est cunctis communis amor
> Repetuntque boni fine teneri,
> Quia non aliter durare queant,
> Nisi conuerso rursus amore
> Refluant causae quae dedit esse.

(This is the comune love to alle thingis, and alle thinges axen to ben holden by the fyn of good. For elles ne myghten they nat lasten yif thei ne comen nat eftsones ayein, by love retorned, to the cause that hath yeven hem beinge (*that is to seyn, to God.*)
de Consolatione, IV, m. vi, Chaucer trans.)

In the *Knight's Tale* this becomes the assertion of an ascending, as well as a descending, sequence:

> What maketh this but Juppiter, the kyng,
> That is prince and cause of alle thyng,

Convertynge al unto his propre welle
From which it is dirryved, sooth to telle?
And heer-agayns no creature on lyve,
Of no degree, availleth for to stryve.

(3035–40)

With the last two lines, Chaucer links the argument from a cyclic system of change, which now includes a return to the unity and perfection of 'the Firste Moevere of the cause above', to the immediate problem of the death of an individual creature. To strive against the divine order is only to cling to imperfection and change and to refuse the perfect good, which, according to Boethius in the *de Consolatione*, III, prosa x, consists in union with the godhead.

From this point, the culmination of the philosophical argument, Chaucer turns back to the matter in hand, that is, to Arcite's death; and in the next few lines, he uses material typical of the *consolatio* – the topic of condolence addressed to the survivors that was developed so often by Seneca and by many medieval authors after him.[66] To this topic belong such arguments as the need to make virtue of necessity and that it is best for a man to die 'in his excellence and flour'. But Chaucer uses this passage in a way which has little to do with the conventional *consolatio*. In a manner which is very typical of his treatment of philosophical argument, he turns from general, abstract considerations to the particular and concrete and, in the process, develops the hint in line 3040 of a return from philosophical tranquillity to the mood of earlier passages. The suggestion in line 3040 that it will avail no creature to strive against the divine process, inevitably bringing the idea of conflict before us, is quite out of keeping with the noble detachment of the main part of the argument – a detachment like that of Boethius's Lady Philosophy, who speaks with magisterial certainty and feels none of the doubts and temptations of mortality. The idea of rebellion – that, even though death may bring the ultimate good, we may yet be perverse enough not to want to die – is developed in lines 3041 ff. with the idea of a forced submission to what cannot be avoided (3043); this is further emphasized by the repeated 'gruccheth' (3045) and 'grucchen' (3058) and in the use of terms like 'rebel' (3046) and 'wilfulnesse' (3057). In fact, Chaucer once more allows the painful, bewildered and fundamentally pessimistic viewpoint of the earlier parts of the poem, and of Arcite on his deathbed, to make its impact, with the result that, while in a sense

Philosophy speaks a tranquil last word, we are not allowed to forget the difficulty of applying her tenets in an actual world of contradictory and contradicting beings. In the same way the clearcut formulation of Nature's position in the *Parlement* was applied not by an ideal, submissive audience, but by a quarrelsome set of birds clinging determinedly to a variety of irreconcilable viewpoints.

Theseus's speech is thus, philosophically speaking, much more comprehensive and closely argued than has sometimes been allowed. It shows a free and flexible use of several well-known philosophical topics which range far beyond a mere rehash of disconnected passages of Boethius. But, typically with Chaucer, although it leads logically into the final solution of the poem, it is not allowed to stand as an unchallenged last word – any more, indeed, than any implied challenge to the solutions of philosophy contained in lines 3039 ff. is allowed to stand as final. Chaucer is not in the habit of speaking definitively or of giving us a final pontification.

The close of Theseus's speech, as we have said, reintroduces the specific instance of providential activity with which the poem is concerned, that is, Arcite's death. Reconciliation to the sorrow that this causes is certainly sought, but this is not the whole of the 'grete effect' which we have been promised. Something more is needed if the poem is to end with a satisfactory solution to all the problems it has raised. Theseus, in fact, has more to offer than the proposition 'after wo I rede us to be merye'. Even this means submission to, and cooperation with, the divine plan for the world; but his further proposal for the marriage of Palamoun and Emely goes beyond submission, to the enactment of something which parallels the creative union of the elements and brings the remaining characters within the links of the fair chain in a literal and practical sense. To see how this can be, we need to look closely at the way in which Chaucer uses the theme of marriage in this particular context.

What the marriage means is apparent from the terms which Chaucer causes Theseus to use of it:

> 'I rede that we make of sorwes two
> O parfit joye, lastynge everemo.'
>
> (3071–2)

It is to be a combination of two things, both sorrows, and both, therefore, painful and imperfect, and it is to produce unity and perfection ('O parfit joye') and duration ('lastynge everemo'). To achieve such a result, the two things combined must necessarily be opposites, as the two sorrows are, since they arise from love and death. Through the marriage, therefore, a true conjunction of opposites is achieved, just as it is in the reconciliation of the warring pairs of elements and in the 'marriage' of the masculine and feminine (odd and even) numbers. Moreover, love and death, which, according to Theseus's exposition, together represent the cyclic change in which the stability of the world resides, are here combined to produce an ascent towards the single, the perfect and the durable – the 'thyng that parfit is and stable' of line 3009 – which parallels the descent into the 'corrumpable' described in lines 3005 ff. Thus, all the implications of the poem's earlier references to the creative cycle and its relation to divine providence are developed and fulfilled in a conclusion which is, indeed, a 'grete effect'.

We are, it is obvious, dealing with marriage seen from a viewpoint which is, in part at least, symbolical or even archetypal. It is by no means the only possible point of view in the fourteenth century, as Chaucer himself shows us in the *Wife of Bath's Prologue* and *Tale* and elsewhere;[67] but it is, nevertheless, not an uncommon one. The idea of marriage as a state capable of showing a supreme perfection and unification of humanity is, in fact, rooted in Christian tradition, in spite of the influence of St Paul and of the monastic bias in favour of virginity.[68] This is largely due to the way in which the creation of man is described in Genesis, where the marriage of Adam and Eve and its issue is a part of man's perfection in paradise:

And God created man to his own image: to the image of God he created him. Male and female he created them. And God blessed them, saying: Increase and multiply, fill the earth and subdue it.

(1:27–8)

Thus, the *Parson's Tale* praises marriage because it was instituted by God in the Garden of Eden,[69] and Langland can even use it as a paradigm of the perfection of the Trinity:

Adam owre aller fader, Eue was of hym-selue,
And the issue that thei hadde, it was of hem bothe,
And either is otheres Ioye, in thre sondry persones,
And in heuene and here, one syngulere name;
And thus is mankynde or manhede, of matrimoigne yspronge,
And bitokneth the Trinite and trewe bileue.

(B, XVI, 205–10)

Although Langland is perhaps eccentric, it is easy to find patristic authority for an exalted view of marriage. Two citations from well-known and influential works will suffice. The first is from St Ambrose on the creation of Eve, in the *de Paradiso*:[70]

'And God cast Adam into a deep sleep, and he slept.' What does the phrase 'deep sleep' signify? Does it not mean that when we contemplate a conjugal union we seem to be turning our eyes gradually in the direction of God's kingdom? Do we not seem, as we enter into a vision of this world, to partake a little of things divine, while we find our repose in the midst of what is secular and mundane? Hence, after the statement, 'He cast Adam into a deep sleep and he slept', there follows: 'The rib which God took from Adam he built into a woman'. The word 'built' is well chosen in speaking of the creation of a woman because a household comprising man and wife seems to point towards a state of full perfection.

The second quotation is from St Augustine's treatise on *The Good of Marriage*.[71] The language is more restrained, but the basic viewpoint is the same:

The first natural tie of human society is man and wife. Even these God did not create separately and join them as if they were strangers, but he made the one from the other, indicating also the power of union in the side from which she was drawn and formed. They are joined to each other side by side who walk together and observe together where they are walking. A consequence is the union of society in the children who are the only worthy fruit, not of the joining of male and female, but of sexual intercourse.

The Parson's account of marriage, in his tale, has much in common with these authorities, although he draws on other sources as well:

Trewe effect of mariage clenseth fornicacioun and replenysseth hooly chirche of good lynage; for that is the ende of mariage; and it chaungeth deedly synne into venial synne bitwixe hem that been ywedded, and maketh the hertes al oon of hem that been ywedded, as wel as the bodies. / This is the verray mariage, that was establissed by God, er that synne bigan, when natureel lawe was in his right poynt in paradys.

(*CT* X, 919–20)

Moreover, there is a sense in which marriage belongs to those human goods which are not under the sway of fortune. Chaucer makes this point (in the context, with ironical effect) in the *Merchant's Tale*:

A wyf is Goddes yifte verraily;
Alle othere manere yiftes, hardily,
As londes, rentes, pasture, or commune,
Or moebles, alle been yiftes of Fortune.
(*CT* IV, 1311–14)

His immediate source here is Albertano of Brescia, *Liber de Amore Dei*, but the ultimate authority is Biblical – Prov. 19:14; 'a prudent wife is properly from the Lord.' A similar distinction between the love which is at the mercy of fortune and that which, because it is in accordance with reason, is not, is made by Jean de Meun. This passage is included in the Chaucerian translation, 5201 ff. Here, the love that is free of fortune is *amicitia*, which, as we shall see in the next chapter, plays an important part in Chaucer's conception of married love.

To the idea of marriage as a source of unity and perfection for humanity, Chaucer adds the idea of it as a source of unity and peace in the state. This, as we have said, is the real reason why Theseus, the ideal ruler, concerns himself with it. This conception of marriage, which, of course, arises from contemporary practice in royal marriages as well as from theory, is one that recurs in Chaucer's writings. It is important in the *Clerk's Tale* and also in the *Man of Law's Tale*, while we have seen that in the *Troilus* a marriage which would have dangerous political results is not considered possible for a member of the royal house.

The *Knight's Tale* ends with a description of the blissful state brought about through the 'bond' of matrimony, when this bond is seen as a repetition of the bond or chain which brings harmony to the discordant elements through a marriage of numbers. This state is, in every way, the opposite to that of unhappiness and disorder in which the lovers were formerly tormented. Fear, jealousy and all discord are banished:

> For now is Palamon in alle wele,
> Lyvynge in blisse, in richesse and in heele,
> And Emelye hym loveth so tendrely,
> And he hire serveth al so gentilly,
> That nevere was ther no word hem bitwene
> Of jalousie or any oother teene.
> Thus endeth Palamon and Emelye,
> And God save al this faire compaignye!
>
> (3101–8)

The 'grete effect' is now complete, and the influence which brings harmony out of the discordant elements of the universe proves itself capable of harmonizing the painful and discordant elements in human life into a new and creative unity. But just as, in the case of the elements, the fundamental discord is not eliminated, but remains as the basis of their cyclic transformation, so, as far as the poem is concerned, Arcite's death and all its painful associations remain an unaltered part of the process of transformation which culminates in the union of Palamoun and Emely. Chaucer makes no attempt to soften the facts. He merely exhibits to us what happens in a world controlled by a love which, as Boethius tells us, not only 'halt togidres peples joyned with an holy boond, and knytteth sacrement of mariages of chaste loves' (II, m. viii, 21), but which is also the cause of that 'attempraunce which hideth, and bynymeth and drencheth undir the laste deth, alle thinges iborn' (IV, m. vi, 34).

5

The *Canterbury Tales*: the problem of narrative structure

Most modern critics of Chaucer have, sooner or later, raised the question of the overall structure of the *Canterbury Tales*. It is a puzzling question, partly because the work is unfinished and partly because what is left suggests a unique combination of an extremely varied selection of tales, on the one hand, and, on the other, of a much fuller and more coherent development of the frame device than is usual.[1] Many of the tales are so closely interwoven with the frame, and consequently with each other, that we seem to glimpse a method by which their very diversity is made to serve a consistent purpose. The aim of this and the next two chapters is to explore the various ways in which this purpose manifests itself, principally through the very nature of Chaucerian comedy as it appears to us in the *Canterbury Tales*, but also through the use of complexes of tales and frame to develop certain major themes. First, however, since the most obvious and the most important fact about the *Canterbury Tales* is that it employs (with the exception of two tales) the medium of narrative poetry, it is essential to ask what this kind of writing meant to Chaucer – what, in fact, did he consider to be the purpose of narrative? How did he expect it to be read? And what kind of structural principles would he expect to govern it? These are not questions that can be answered either fully or confidently. They must be asked; but to answer them adequately would require a treatise on medieval aesthetics of a kind which can probably, in the absence of contemporary critical writing, never be written.[2] At any rate, only the briefest sketch can be attempted here.

There are two ways of approaching the problem – neither will give a complete answer, but both can provide useful indications. One is through Chaucer's own rare references to his art. These have little to do with the special problem of narrative, and indeed, in the main, concern only the common topic of the relation of art to nature. The other method is to look at the kinds of narrative with which Chaucer was familiar and to examine his use of earlier examples and his choice among them.

To take the latter first: in Chaucer's day the long narrative poem existed in a number of different forms, all worthy of imitation.[3] There was, first and most distinguished, the Classical epic of Virgil and Statius. In Ovid similar material could be found, but differently organized by being broken up into smaller units within the overall scheme of the *Heroides* and *Metamorphoses*. There was, secondly, the typically medieval form of romance in its various branches and types; and, thirdly, the kind of writing broadly covered by the term allegory, including as one branch the kind of visionary journey outside normal terrestrial places (whose greatest achievement was Dante's *Divina Commedia*) and, as another important branch, allegorical satire. Jean de Meun's section of the *Roman de la Rose* could be taken as the supreme achievement of this branch. In varying degrees, Langland, in England, and de Guilleville, in France, used similar methods. Works of this kind, however, tend to display great individuality. There are, for example, points of view from which Dante's work is not allegorical or Langland's satirical; all have, however, in common a narrative method which is fundamentally unlike that of all other narrative kinds – a point to which we must return.

Chaucer's attitude towards the great Classical narrative poems is not likely to have been a simple one. Much has already been said on the subject in relation to both the *Knight's Tale* and the *Troilus*. There is, I think, no doubt that he reacted in a straightforward, uncomplicated way to the sheer achievement in poetry of these Classical authors, and that, like any Renaissance poet, it is this he hopes to equal or at least approximate in the *Troilus*, with its final plea to be measured against the work of 'Vergile, Ovide, Omer, Lucan and Stace'.[4] But there are signs that he saw something more than a successful style to admire and imitate. We have seen his insistence on purpose of the *Knight's Tale* to unfold a 'grete effect', and it is likely that the phrase has the same meaning for him when he applies it to the *Aeneid* in the *Legend of Good Women*. The whole direct reference to Virgil, with which the 'Legend of Dido' begins, is worth quoting:

Glorye and honour, Virgil Mantoan,
Be to thy name! and I shal, as I can,
Folwe thy lanterne, as thow gost byforn,
How Eneas to Dido was forsworn.
In Naso and Eneydos wol I take
The tenor, and the grete effectes make.

(F, 924–9)

The 'tenor' is the meaning, the narrative content:[5] Chaucer under-takes, by translation (in fact, largely paraphrase), to follow the content of the story, using both Virgil and Ovid. This, indeed, implies the assumption that Classical subject-matter, as distinct from Classical narrative, has a kind of absolute existence in its own right. Thus, the story of Dido is something which exists and which finds special and particular expression in the version of Virgil or the version of Ovid. Either, or both, can be used to make a fresh version. This kind of approach to Classical story is implied, as we have seen, in the *House of Fame*, in which Dido's fame (insisted on by both Virgil and Ovid) is considered in relation to the 'facts' which give rise to it, as well as to the versions of the 'excusing' poets. Considered from this point of view, the Classical poets are repositories of material, in the form of stories, of which they give not the thing itself, but their own redactions.[6] This material can be used by later generations as they please, either to make new versions – Chaucer's usual purpose – or as repositories of useful information. That this latter was a common attitude to Classical writers during the Middle Ages is well known. It led to such later reworkings as Bersuire's *Ovide Moralisé* and to the collections and interpretations of classical material like Boccaccio's *de Genealogia Deorum* and Christine de Pisan's *Othéa*. In the last two, and in many other works, even the form of Classical poetry dis-appears, and the aim is a useful reorganization and interpretation of its basic material.

We have to distinguish here between two distinct tendencies. One is to what may roughly be called the allegorization of a Classical work, that is, the consistent reading of its situations and characters in a new sense, thought of as existing at the same time as, and parallel to, the literal one.[7] The second is the use of incidents, legends, tales, from the past for the practical information they supply about life or morals. The first method affects poetry, the second does not.

To use a story as a warning, or to extract a moral from it, has

nothing to do with allegory, nor does it involve any necessary alteration of the original writer's intention. Thus, Aeneas's behaviour as a
lover – left in a fascinatingly ambiguous state by Virgil – could be
held up as a warning to women not to trust to men's constancy or to
fear the results of irregular marriages; or the useful lesson could be
drawn that love and statesmanship can seldom be reconciled. None of
these applications would invalidate the story or involve any doubt
about Virgil's purpose. If, however, the story were to be read with
Dido standing consistently as Sensuality to Aeneas's equally consistent Reason – and this kind of interpretation was often proposed
in the Middle Ages[8] – we should constantly find ourselves running
counter to Virgil's obvious intention, as it is expressed in the structure
of his narrative. The storm and the scene in the cave, for example, as
they stand, are obvious and straightforward narrative devices, used
in order to place the two main characters in the appropriate position
at the appropriate moment. It is easy to see how, in a Spenserian
narrative, for example, they would feature quite differently, and how
the tumult and disturbance of the storm and the darkness of the cave
would be brought to bear on the story in a different way, so as to
emphasize what would, in such a context, be the real action in which
the protagonists were involved – that of virtue against vice.

Now, Chaucer promises us not only the story – the 'tenor' – which
could be used in various ways, but also that he will make the same
'grete effectes'. This means, I think, that his aim is to reproduce, as
we should say, 'the spirit' of Virgil's writing – or at any rate to try to
retell his story in a comparable way and with a comparable purpose.
That this is the meaning of the phrase 'grete effect' (and its precise
meaning was left somewhat in the air when we were considering the
Knight's Tale) is, I think, shown by Chaucer's use of it elsewhere.
In the two places in which he uses it in the *Knight's Tale*, it refers to a
creative purpose. First, to Chaucer's own, in the work he is writing –
'The grete effect for which that I bygan' (*CT* I, 2482) – and, secondly,
to the creative purpose of the First Mover in forming the chain of
love – 'Greet was th'effect, and heigh was his entente' (2989).[9]

For Chaucer, therefore, it is characteristic of the greatness of
Virgil's work (the whole tendency of the Dido introduction is towards
serious praise of an important poet) that it is conditioned and controlled by a high purpose; and this could, of course, well be an
allegorical one. It would, indeed, be quite possible that Chaucer misunderstood Virgil; but we are not now concerned with the correct-

ness or otherwise of his understanding, but only with the idea of narrative to which this understanding led him. Chaucer makes ample use of Classical material for the purpose of *exempla*, that is, he is always ready to use the moral-encyclopaedic method.[10] But, in his two retellings of the story of Dido, there is, I believe, no sign that he was concerned with anything but the face-value of the narrative and the reproduction of a clear and single narrative line without allegorical significance. His very manipulations of Virgil (and they are numerous) go to prove this. We have already discussed the special function of the story of Dido within the larger frame of the *House of Fame*. In the *Legend of Good Women* version, Chaucer makes two important changes, both of which have significance as a part of the organization of his version of the narrative, *qua* narrative, but which cannot be related to any interpretation of its meaning. First, he adds a passage clearly designed to support his view of the characters as peculiarly magnificent and princely:

> To daunsynge chaumberes ful of paramentes,
> Of riche beddes, and of ornementes,
> This Eneas is led, after the mete.
> And with the quene, whan that he hadde sete,
> And spices parted, and the wyn agon,
> Unto his chambres was he led anon
> To take his ese and for to have his reste,
> With al his folk, to don what so hem leste.
> There nas courser wel ybrydeled non,
> Ne stede, for the justing wel to gon,
> Ne large palfrey, esy for the nones,
> Ne jewel, fretted ful of ryche stones,
> Ne sakkes ful of gold, of large wyghte,
> Ne ruby non, that shynede by nyghte,
> Ne gentil hawtein faucoun heroner,
> Ne hound, for hert or wilde bor or der,
> Ne coupe of gold, with floreyns newe ybete,
> That in the land of Libie may be gete,
> That Dido ne hath it Eneas ysent;
> And al is payed, what that he hath spent.
> Thus can this quene honurable hire gestes calle,
> As she that can in fredom passen alle.
>
> (1106–27)

It is obvious that this passage is used not for any associations with Luxuria nor to strengthen the idea of the temptation of Aeneas by a Dido who has a more general application than that of the heroine of a particular story, but simply to make the narrative clearer and more easily understood. This is the nobility of a noble queen, and it helps to explain the strength of Aeneas's reaction and the proportionate strength of her despair. Both characters, however, remain parts of a straightforward action and have no resonance in a world of general ideas. That the passage also bends the Classical story in the direction of romance is another matter, to which we must presently return.

Another major change in this version is the elimination of the references to the gods and to the dubiousness of the validity of the marriage. This point had been retained in the *House of Fame* version. Now, probably with Ovid rather than Virgil in mind,[11] Chaucer places the responsibility on Aeneas alone and does not allow him the measure of excuse which the use of the figures of the gods provides. The result is, again, a strengthening of the purely narrative line. Chaucer would not, I think, have regarded himself as altering Virgil's intention. We have seen that his treatment of the Classical gods is always worked out in relation to free will and personal responsibility – so that in the *Knight's Tale*, for example, they become little more than extensions of the human actors – and that it is likely that he thought the same attitude was characteristic of the Classical poets.[12] What he has done here, therefore, is not to alter Virgil's intention, as it appeared to him, but merely to alter the pace of the story by removing a piece of machinery appropriate to a more leisurely and philosophical treatment of the narrative. In this he is only taking Ovid a little further, since Ovid eliminates most of the heavenly machinery and, accordingly, deals with the validity of the marriage in a less clearcut way than Virgil does.[13]

Chaucer's manipulation of the Classical story, therefore, in a context where it stands by itself, and is not subordinated to any wider purpose, is conditioned by purely narrative considerations, that is, his changes relate to motivation, to effective presentation of the main characters, to pace. There is no sign – even in the passage on the splendours with which Dido welcomes Aeneas, which could easily lend itself to such a purpose – of the manipulation of the material in order to extend the meaning beyond the face-value of the literal narrative. In fact, the 'grete effect' which he thinks Virgil is aiming at must be contained within the narrative, understood in the ordinary way as a sequence of events concerning the characters and consist, therefore, in a structural purpose – in the intention to shape an effective work of art, not to expound a serious moral – although we must allow that these two aims are not necessarily incompatible.

Since the 'Legend of Dido' is not, in fact, a particularly successful reworking of the Classical material,[14] we cannot use it with any confidence to show just where, in Chaucer's eyes, this structural greatness within the narrative lay. He has not, unfortunately, achieved any effects here, or carried out any purpose comparable to Virgil's. In the *Knight's Tale*, however, we have an example of Classical epic material – admittedly transmitted via Italian romantic-epic – which is superbly handled in such a way as to show us exactly what Chaucer meant. Here the 'grete effect' is carried out through the successful structuring of the narrative, a constant and deliberate patterning of incidents and characters, in such a way that everything contributes to the resolution of the conflicts which form the substance of the work. The pace is leisurely, but the narrative drive is unbroken; it does not, however, work itself out in purely naturalistic terms, as the 'Legend of Dido' does. Nevertheless, the method is the reverse of that used in the fully non-naturalistic form of allegory. All the elements of the work, the philosophical passages, the machinery of the gods, are brought to bear upon the particular problem of the protagonists. This, it is true, is, in its widest sense, seen as a problem which is common to mankind; but, nevertheless, the movement is always inwards – the wider applications only deepen our comprehension of the particular instance before our eyes. In allegory the reverse is true. We proceed from the particular of the story material outward, to its implications in ideas and concepts which are general.

It may be helpful here to pause for a moment over the question of the meaning for Chaucer, if we can establish it, of the relation of art and nature. Paradoxically, it is not likely that the conviction which he expresses in the *House of Fame* – that the great artists, among whom he certainly includes the Classical masters, imitate nature – would have led him in the direction of what we mean nowadays by naturalism in art. We tend to equate this with realism and mean by reality the external world as it actually presents itself to our perceptions. It then has the characteristic of lack of deliberate organization. Thus, nature is opposed to art as simpler, cruder or less selective and so more inclusive, but lacking in the planning of detail to make a significant pattern. From this idea, of course, it is possible to progress to something like its reverse: that nature, owing to its vast amorphousness, is actually more significant and meaningful than the particular patternings which can be arrived at by organized selection. Chaucer would certainly not have associated any of these ideas with nature. For him, and for his age, amorphousness and lack of organization were the well-known characteristics not of nature, but of nature's enemy and raw material, chaos. Nature's function is to create significant forms out of this shapelessness and to organize and maintain purposeful processes. For this reason, it is not really correct to speak of the discussion of the relation of art to nature in the Middle Ages. It is, rather, that the *artist* is compared to nature, because both use a creative, ordering process which results in the emergence of clearly defined and demarcated things. Thus, the usual illustration of the likeness (and unlikeness) of the artist to nature is that of Pygmalion.[15] Like nature he makes a form out of the formlessness of the unshaped stone; but, unlike nature, he cannot give it the special quality of life. Art, therefore, always falls short of nature, but it is an analogous activity.

Chaucer, as we can, I think, see from the *House of Fame*, is interested in the problem of the relation of the poet's narratives to actual events. There is no reason, however, to believe that he would have related the idea of 'truth to a particular actuality' to that of 'truth to nature' in the poet's work. Truth to nature would, rather, consist in the imitation of her ordering, organizing methods so as to produce significant forms; and, in the case of narrative this would necessarily mean the shaping of a story by a clearly apprehended purpose rather than any devotion to 'realism'. This is the kind of procedure we actually find, for example, in the *Knight's Tale*. In the case of Virgil's and Ovid's treatments of the story of Dido, it is likely that Chaucer saw the same kind of thematic structure, as the story unfolds in terms of a conflict of love and duty, in which the crucial question is (as he understood it) the personal responsibility of Aeneas for his own conduct.

If we turn from Classical, or Classical-derived, narrative to pure romance, we shall find Chaucer's attitude harder to define. On the one hand, he seems reluctant to use the form, or rather forms, and never does so in their own right. On the other, we can, I think, detect a kind of pull towards a way of ordering the narrative which is more characteristic of romance than of anything else, and this tendency crops up in surprising places.

There are, in fact, a number of puzzles involved in Chaucer's apparent attitude to romance. One would like to know why he shows so little interest in the greatest achievements of the French romance writers. It is possible that he knew the romances of Chrétien de Troyes and learnt, directly, from their technique,[16] but he shows no obvious sign of having done so and never attempts to write anything of the same kind. He shows no knowledge of or no interest in – we do not know which – the cyclic Arthurian romances: he does not appear to have been inspired by the possibilities of the allegorical treatment of romance themes or by the potentialities of *entrelacement*.[17] All this is surprising when we consider the very detailed way in which he utilizes possibilities and techniques derived from the *Roman de la Rose* and from later love visions. One would like to know whether he equated the long Classical-derived poems of Boccaccio with romance, or whether he regarded them as something new and different. Among all the uncertainties, one thing is abundantly and rather surprisingly clear: what actually ring in his ears are the phrases and rhythms not of sophisticated French romance, but of much less sophisticated English ones, and it is in the direction of these that he sometimes diverts the narrative method of a more sophisticated author, by using the moment-to-moment techniques of popular romance writers in order to move his story on from point to point in a particular way.

Chaucer showed in *Sir Thopas* a detailed knowledge of a number of more or less popular English romances, as Mrs Loomis's study of the poem has proved.[18] It has sometimes been assumed that this is the only place in which he draws on the English romances, and that his only interest in them was therefore to poke fun at them.[19] This, however, is clearly not the case. It is minstrel inconsequence and verbal incompetence that Chaucer laughs at in *Sir Thopas*. Elsewhere he shows that he can prefer the techniques of romances of this popular type to more sophisticated ones, and that he considers them compatible with writing of the highest kind. We have already seen that, in the 'Legend of Dido', for example, in his list of the splendid gifts given to Aeneas by Dido, he can write in a passage which is absolutely unclassical and, at the same time, absolutely typical of romance, and we have seen how this addition is made to serve the narrative development as Chaucer handles it. It is not possible to say whether this particular list derives from English or French romance, but it is typical of romance method and pace. The narrative method of the simple type of French romance, and the majority of English ones, is one of enumeration or, to put it another way, of coordination rather than subordination. In the smallest units, this appears as the list. In the larger units of the narrative, it can be seen as the presentation of the separate scenes or incidents as of equal value and perhaps duration. There is no attempt at an organization which subordinates one part of a narrative to another in such a way as to concentrate attention on certain aspects of its development rather than others. Even in a poem as highly organized as *Sir Gawain and the Green Knight*, the author keeps to this method, and the hunting scenes are laid out on exactly the same scale, with the same amount of detail, as the indoor scenes which develop the main plot-line. We can, if we choose, perform for ourselves the act of subordinating the hunting scenes to the main plot by regarding them as implied comments on it, but there is nothing in the author's actual treatment which compels us to do so.[20] In extreme cases, for example in that of *Guy of Warwick*, the succeeding incidents are never welded into a whole. In this romance the first part is devoted to the noble deeds by which Guy proves himself worthy of his love, Felice. In the second, having married her, he decides that his future adventures shall be in honour of God, and Felice plays little part in this section. This means that we have to take the love story as it stands and then transfer our attention completely from it to the quasi-religious story which follows. If we try to link the two into a coherent scheme, we cannot account for Guy's final lack of interest in his wife, so hard-won in the first part. The art of such narrative lies in the selection of episodes which are, in their own right, sufficiently interesting to engage the audience's whole attention for their duration, so that there is no room left for any sense of clashes and inconsistencies between them.

This episodic method of laying out the material in the romance leads to the development of various devices for making the transition from one self-contained unit to another. Thus, for example, the author of *Sir Gawain and the Green Knight* links the succeeding indoor and outdoor scenes by indicating their relative positions in time – while one set of characters does one thing, another does another.[21] Chaucer uses the same, somewhat sophisticated method in the *Knight's Tale* to mark off and interrelate the episodes in which the different characters offer their prayers in the temple. Palamoun goes to the Temple of Venus 'The Sonday nyght, er day bigan to sprynge' (2209); Emely starts for the Temple of Diana:

> The thridde houre inequal that Palamon
> Bigan to Venus temple for to gon.
>
> (2271–2)

Arcite goes to the Temple of Mars 'The nexte houre of Mars folwynge this' (2367). Here the device is useful not only as a framing one, to separate and keep distinct the three episodes involving the three characters, but also because the times are astrologically significant – the prayers are made in suitable 'hours' for appealing to the different planets.[22] Chaucer uses the same temporal device to describe the incidents which bring together the three characters – Arcite, Palamoun and Theseus – in the grove. Palamoun happens to make his escape 'of May / The thridde nyght' (1462–3). Arcite goes out because it is a fine May day 'for to doon his observaunce to May' (1500); and Theseus is also influenced by the time of year – 'That for to hunten is so desirus, / And namely at the grete hert in May' (1674–5).

A more usual framing method, common in both French and English romances, is the formula 'now we will leave A and turn to B'.[23] Chaucer uses this, in its simplest form, in the *Squire's Tale*, to end each part – indeed, he brings in the device so simply and blatantly that we cannot help wondering whether he is entirely serious. Thus, at the end of the second part, the Squire starts in the normal way 'Thus lete I Canacee hir hauk kepyng', but goes on not merely with the other half of the formula, but with a complete table of contents, combined with a description of his prospective method as a story-teller:

> I wol namoore as now speke of hir ryng,
> Til it come eft to purpos for to seyn
> How that this faucon gat hir love ageyn
> Repentant, as the storie telleth us,
> By mediacion of Cambalus,
> The kynges sone, of which that I you tolde.
> But hennesforth I wol my proces holde
> To speken of aventures and of batailles,
> That nevere yet was herd so grete mervailles.
>   First wol I telle yow of Cambyuskan
> That in his tyme many a citee wan;

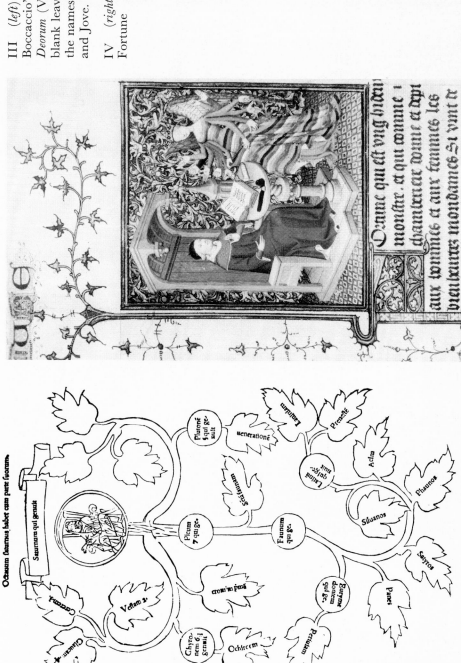

III (left) Saturn page of Boccaccio's *de Genealogia Deorum* (Venice, 1497). The blank leaves should contain the names of Juno, Neptune and Jove.

IV (right) The Poet and Fortune

V The Marriage of Adam and Eve

And after wol I speke of Algarsif,
How that he wan Theodora to his wif,
For whom, ful ofte in greet peril he was,
Ne hadde he ben holpen by the steede of bras;
And after wol I speke of Cambalo,
That faught in lystes with the bretheren two
For Canacee er that he myghte hire wynne.
And ther I lefte I wol ayeyn bigynne.

(652–70)

This suggests a composite romance of the scope of a *Faerie Queene*, and it is hard to believe that Chaucer ever seriously considered including anything on this scale in the *Canterbury Tales*.[24] It seems more likely that the exuberance of the project is intended to match the exuberance of the Squire's youth and inexperience. Nevertheless, whether seriously or not, Chaucer lays the ambitious plan out in relation to narrative construction; he does not merely give a list of adventures to be related. Thus, Canacee's ring will come in again when 'it come eft to purpos', that is, at the appropriate point in relation to other parts of the narrative. The Squire promises 'hennesforth I wol my proces holde'. 'Proces' could mean simply 'story' and refer to the adventures and battles – that is, this section will be a straightforward, unbroken account of the deeds of Cambyuskan, Algarsif and Cambalus, whose adventures will be given one after another ('And after wol I speke . . .' 663, 667) – or it could mean 'plan', 'constructive design'.[25] In either case, it implies a preoccupation with the shape of the narrative, which is further emphasized by the promise to pick up the story once more, when it is 'to purpos' again, where it left off at the end of part ii – 'And ther I lefte I wol ayeyn bigynne'. The joke, if there is a joke, is surely against the Squire's literary ambition. It is unlikely that Chaucer regarded the careful construction of a composite narrative as in itself a bad thing; although he does not himself attempt – or, if he meant the *Squire's Tale* to be taken seriously, complete – a romance of this kind. The passage does, however, show that, just as he had a reasonably clear idea of the characteristics of Classical epic narrative, so he was fully aware of the constructional problems of the long romance narrative. That the overall problem comes into his mind in connection with the framing device is also significant. It suggests that, whether with or without the added complexity of *entrelacement*, he considered this separation of the story into comparatively independent episodes to be typical of romance structure – as, indeed, it was.

In the *Knight's Tale*, Chaucer uses the same framing formula to effect transitions from one episode, and character, to another. Here, however, we can see even more clearly what he is aiming at, because he is working from a known source, and the introduction of this narrative device is a departure from it. The main differences between Chaucer's treatment of the story and Boccaccio's have already been discussed.[26] We can summarize the result by saying that Chaucer has made the story much tauter by cutting away material which, in Boccaccio's version, is not sharply focused on the main plot. He has also used the story to develop ideas and themes which are not present in the *Teseida*. In imposing this kind of thematic development on the Italian poem, he has, I think, gone back to the methods and purpose, according to his understanding of it, of Classical epic. Yet, paradoxically, in imposing this more coherent structure on the material, he makes use, as we have seen, of a technique which properly belongs to a more loosely constructed kind of narrative, that is, to the episodic romance. There are, I believe, two main reasons behind this paradox. In the first place, it would seem that Chaucer could rely on a very considerable familiarity with, and liking for, the older type of romance, whether in French or (more probably) in English, on the part of his audience – indeed, unless this were the case, *Sir Thopas* would have fallen very flat. To adjust the unfamiliar Italian type of narrative in this direction would, therefore, be to make it more immediately acceptable and comprehensible. It is notable that Chaucer, who clearly assumes intimate knowledge of French love vision – and, I would suggest, of English romance and lyric[27] – does not appear to assume that his audience had any knowledge of Italian literature. Here, he seems to work as a popularizer and transformer of essentially foreign material into something more suited to the taste of his own audience.

The use of the framing device is not the only means by which Chaucer suggests the style and approach of earlier romances in the *Knight's Tale*. He treats the description of the tournament in a way which, by its general method and also by its actual phraseology, suggests the use of several specific English romances known to us and may have suggested more to Chaucer's audience. The use of alliteration in the lines beginning 'Ther shyveren shaftes upon sheeldes thikke' (2605 ff.) has often been remarked on. If Chaucer has a specific model in mind here, he is probably drawing on either *Ipomedan* or *Partonope of Blois*.[28] It is significant, however, that other English romances use alliteration as an appropriate part of battle description. *Ywain and Gawain*, which is, of course, based on a French source, also slips into this peculiarly English way of writing on this subject.[29] The reason for Chaucer's use of it here is, therefore, probably not so much that the sound-effects of alliteration are appropriate to the noise and confusion of battle, but that it had become an accepted part of the romance writer's technique, no doubt in the first instance because of the superiority of alliterative romances in descriptions of this kind, but becoming equally appropriate to romances using the normal, non-alliterative style based on French. But it is not only through this momentary use of the technique of alliteration that Chaucer recalls the English romance type of battle description. The Italian provides a leisurely passage, employing similes; and, after a general description of the onslaught, first singles out Palemone and Arcita, then gives a long passage describing 'Come gli altri baron tutti s'afrontarono' (VIII, st. 18 ff.). Chaucer substitutes a general description of a quite different kind and cuts out all the references to the other knights. This general description, in contrast to the Italian, is of the enumerating kind common in English romances, laid out by weapons and not by heroes – it proceeds from spears and shields to swords and helmets and on to maces.[30] Further, Chaucer uses a device which helps to organize enumerations of this kind by dividing them into sections. This is the formula 'Ther seen men' introduced in line 2604, which is found, for example, in *Guy of Warwick* and in *Havelok*.[31] The chief organizing device, however, is the general 'he': 'He feeleth', 'He rolleth', 'he foyneth', etc. The whole passage (2600–51) should be compared with *Teseida*, VIII. The contrast between the knightly setting, which forms a fitting background for the deeds of Palemone and Arcita, and the destructive and impersonal violence of the weapons, which leads up to the even more violent encounter of Palamoun and Arcite, is very striking.

If we now return to the framing device and examine some of Chaucer's transitions in relation to his source, it will, I think, be possible to understand the paradox of this use of an episodic technique to promote an essentially closely constructed narrative.[32] Chaucer uses the device three times within 150 lines, at the end of part i and the beginning of part ii of the *Knight's Tale*. First:

> Now wol I stynte of Palamon a lite,
> And lete hym in his prisoun stille dwelle,
> And of Arcita forth I wol yow telle.
>
> (1334–6)

Secondly:

> And in this blisse lete I now Arcite,
> And speke I wole of Palamon a lite.
>
> (1449–50)

And thirdly:

> Now wol I turne to Arcite ageyn,
> That litel wiste how ny that was his care,
> Til that Fortune had broght him in the snare.
>
> (1488–90)

Even before this, Chaucer uses repetitive introductions to the passages in which the two lovers lament and make their philosophical speeches, which have a similar framing effect:

> How greet a sorwe suffreth now Arcite!
> The deeth he feeleth thurgh his herte smyte;
> He wepeth, wayleth, crieth pitously;
> To sleen hymself he waiteth prively.
> He seyde, 'Allas . . .'
>
> (1219–23)

> Upon that oother syde Palamon,
> Whan that he wiste Arcite was agon,
> Swich sorwe he maketh that the grete tour
> Resouneth of his youlyng and clamour,
> The pure fettres on his shynes grete,
> Weren of his bittre, salte teeres wete.
> 'Allas', quod he . . .
>
> (1275–81)

All these passages help to separate the two characters whose fate is in many ways so alike. Taken together, they emphasize the fact that

their love has a disruptive effect, breaking their friendship and part-
ing them. If we turn to the other framing passages in the poem, we
shall see that they serve a similar purpose. They all work to keep
characters, or groups of figures, separate from each other. Thus
Theseus, who acts on the basis of a different view of the world and a
different set of assumptions to those of the lovers, is introduced in
this way when he comes to interrupt the fight in the grove, in lines
1661–2; a similar formula emphasizes the separate plane of action
of the planet-gods and ends part iii (2479–82); and, finally, Chaucer
uses the same device to dismiss Arcite from the action and to bring
forward Emely, now at last an effective character, in the final section
of the poem (2815–16).[33]

In all these passages, the Italian treats the material quite differently. The enmity of the two lovers, and their philosophical speeches,
are changes made by Chaucer. In the *Teseida* there is no initial
quarrel and nothing to correspond to the bitter arraignments of fate
and the gods; the lovers part with embraces (at the end of Book III).
In the case of Theseus's sudden arrival to stop the fight, Boccaccio
seems to feel a difficulty. His solution is to emphasize this one abrupt
coincidence in his otherwise smooth, consecutive narrative by
excusing it as allowable:

> Ma come noi veggiam venire in ora
> Cosa che in mill' anni non avvenne,
> Cosi avvenne veramente allora
> che Teseo. . . .
>
> (V, st. 77)

Chaucer uses these lines; but not to help to smooth over an awkward
moment in the narrative. After the framing formula:

> And in this wise I lete hem fightyng dwelle,
> And forth I wole of Theseus yow telle,
>
> (1661–2)

he gives us a passage which, in its general, philosophical content,
corresponds, as has already been noted,[34] to the speeches of Palamoun and Arcite, and he puts Boccaccio's lines on coincidence into
the middle of this, thus making them refer to the general way in
which Theseus's actions correspond to destinal forces, rather than to

the immediate succession of events. Indeed, the generalization is taken even further, by linking the coincidence on the one hand to God's 'purveiaunce' and on the other to all human appetites:

> The purveiaunce that God hath seyn biforn,
> So strong it is that, though the world had sworn
> The contrarie of a thyng by ye or nay,
> Yet somtyme it shal fallen on a day
> That falleth nat eft withinne a thousand year.
> For certeinly, oure appetites heer,
> Be it of werre, or pees, or hate, or love,
> Al is this reuled by the sighte above.
>
> (1665–72)

The total impact of the passage, which has the effect of a digression, is, of course, to reinforce the reader's feeling of the separation of the characters and the incidents, by emphasizing the difference between the basis of Theseus's actions and that of the lovers.

Just as Palemone and Arcita are not treated primarily from the point of view of the disruption of their friendship by love in the *Teseida*, so the machinery of the gods is not given the same separate existence; Boccaccio, through the conceit of the flight to heaven of the prayers, incorporates the temple descriptions and the actions of the gods much more closely into the action of the three human characters and, in fact, never devotes a separate section to them. Thus, where Chaucer has a framing passage (2479–82) to end part iii and introduce part iv, Boccaccio merely describes Emilia's reactions to the doubtful reception of her prayer and goes straight on to the events of the next morning (VIII, st. 93–4). Lastly, Chaucer does everything possible to emphasize the finality of Arcite's end and his cutting off from the rest of the story. Thus, instead of finishing off his account of this major character by describing his soul's destination, as Boccaccio does, he repudiates any further knowledge of him:

> His spirit chaunged hous and wente ther,
> As I kam nevere, I kan nat tellen wher . . .
> Arcite is coold, ther Mars his soule gye!
> Now wol I speken forth of Emelye.
>
> (2809–16)

Boccaccio, apart from allowing Arcita a more gradual exit from the story by his description of his soul's flight, eases the transition to the lamentations which follow his death ('Shrighte Emelye and howleth Palamoun', 2817) by relating them specifically to his last words:

> A la voce d'Arcita dolorosa
> quanti v'eran gli orecchi alti levaro,
> aspettando che piú alcuna cosa
> dovesse dir; ma poi che rimiraro
> l'alma partita, con voce angosciosa
> pianse ciascuno e con dolore amaro;
> ma sopra tutti Emilia e Palemone,
> la qual cosí rispose a tal sermone. . . .
>
> (XI, st. 4)

In all these passages, where Boccaccio takes pains to ensure smooth transitions in a narrative which develops in a very leisurely, but a strictly consecutive way, Chaucer takes equal pains to introduce devices which break the narrative flow and ensure the effective separation of its episodes and, at the same time, its characters. This, it is obvious, helps to develop his very different conception of the main themes of his poem and, especially, of the theme of disorder *versus* order and of the disruptive nature of love.[35] Chaucer, therefore, uses a device, which was originally developed to help to make the necessary transitions in an episodic type of narrative, for the purpose of thematic development. He has thus, I believe, achieved a poem which has, on the one hand, a greater superficial similarity to a kind of romance which would be more familiar to his audience than his source, and, on the other, a method of handling the narrative entirely new to a work of this type. Both his purpose and the way he sets about achieving it show that he was fully aware of the problems of narrative structure and had a clear idea of certain ways in which they could be solved.

Chaucer uses different types of romance in the *Man of Law's Tale*, the *Franklin's Tale* and the *Wife of Bath's Tale*. The first of these belongs to the special category of the hagiographic romance and has also a special thematic relation to the *Knight's Tale* – in fact it plays such an important part in the exposition of the major themes of the *Canterbury Tales* that discussion of it must be held over to chapter 4. The other two are both short romances; one, the *Frank-lin's Tale*, belongs to a special category of shorter romances, the Breton lay.[36] The narrative form in short romances presents no problems – their very briefness compels a closer structure and allows of less diversity of episodes than is the case with the long romances. It may be significant, however, that the Franklin tells his tale out of compliment to the Squire, and that it is, at the same time, some-thing of the sort that the Squire has shown himself to like and also a marked contrast to the enormously complicated narrative on which he had embarked. It would be rash to conclude that it implies Chaucer's own preference for a more manageable type of narrative; but it is certainly one that is easier to finish. All three of these romances, as we shall see, play an important part in the develop-ment of certain themes which are of major importance in the *Canter-bury Tales* as a whole. In fact, apart from the doubtful case of the *Squire's Tale*, there is every sign that Chaucer found romance particularly suitable for thematic development, in spite of his recogni-tion of its episodic nature.

The third important type of narrative structure of which Chaucer would have known is the allegorical one. Its main characteristic, in sharp contrast to the other two we have been considering, is that it seldom aimed at a naturalistic method of developing the story, that is, the sequence of events and the behaviour of characters are not conditioned by the ordinary successions of cause and effect or of temporal development which typify ordinary experience and are therefore characteristic of realistic treatment.[37] Chaucer never attempted a complete narrative of this kind, but he does use some of its methods in his handling of certain comic characters – a tribute to the great importance in the Middle Ages of allegorical satire.[38] It seems likely that he would have understood – as we are now begin-ning to understand – a type of structure in a long narrative work which depended on the development of ideas and of themes, rather than on the devising of a plot with appropriate characters.[39] If so, this would have reinforced any feeling that narrative structure was dependent on a more total and intimate organization of the material than could be achieved by a construction which was based on the story line alone. This, I have suggested, seems to have been his view of epic and romance. It is possible, however, that we should include allegory not so much in the category of the individual narrative, as in that of the long work which included within its organization a number of separate narratives. The various devices of confession (Gower's *Confessio Amantis*);[40] a journey (Dante's *Divina Commedia* which, with a relation to the *Metamorphoses* probably more obvious to Dante and to Chaucer than to us, might well strike a medieval reader as a story collection within a frame); and pilgrimage or quest (*Piers Plowman* with its separate dreams and episodes; the two *Pèlerinages* of de Guilleville, and, most important of all, the *Roman de la Rose* with its diversity of material and its many stories and separable speeches) all lend themselves to the creation of works which can best be seen as large composite narrative structures. They have in common the inclusion of very diverse material within this structure, and this diversity is characteristic of the *Canterbury Tales*, in contrast to the collections of tales within a frame which are usually cited as Chaucer's models. These, no doubt, play their part, but they are not enough to account for the distance Chaucer has travelled in his conception of a tale collection.

The question of Chaucer's knowledge and use of collections of tales within a framing device is discussed at length in the contribution of R. A. Pratt and Karl Young to the *Sources and Analogues of the Canterbury Tales*.[41] Broadly speaking, these collections fall into two main groups. There are those held together by linking devices which merely provide a reason for bringing the tales together.[42] Secondly, there is the more didactic approach which makes the framing device determine the nature of the stories, by setting out a problem to be discussed or a subject to be elaborated, so that all the stories have some relation to a central theme.[43] This is the method used by Chaucer in his two unfinished series, the *Legend of Good Women* and the Monk's series of tragedies. He is, thus, well aware of the possibility of using the frame to ensure a kind of unity through the content of the tales in the series; and, if we are to judge from their unfinished state, he is also aware of the drawback, that is, of the difficulty of sustaining interest through a series of similar tales. In the *Canterbury Tales* the frame is, obviously, basically of the other kind, that is, it lends an air of probability and gives a solid background to the telling by different persons of a series of otherwise unconnected tales. The advantage of this method, of course, is that there is no reason why the tales should all be of the same kind, or why their content should relate to any one central subject. In choosing a pilgrimage, as has often been pointed out, Chaucer is able to bring together the widest possible variety of tellers and to exploit this fact to provide the widest possible variety of tales. In this, although the Italian collections of *novelle* may well have given him a hint,[44] he goes further than any other medieval user of the device. Nevertheless, with this very complete exploitation of the possibilities for variety and dissimilitude goes an obvious interest in certain major recurrent themes which are developed by means of both frame and tale. These will be discussed in detail in chapter 4. As far as the overall narrative structure of the *Canterbury Tales* is concerned, their presence suggests that Chaucer was ready to exploit the advantages of both types of story collections: the advantage of a connecting theme for unification and the achievement of coherence within the collection; and the advantage of the looser type of device, which made probable and acceptable the introduction of any type of tale, without necessary reference to the central purpose of the collection as a whole. Everything that we can tentatively conclude about Chaucer's understanding and use of narrative structure, in the long single narrative and in composite form, suggests, I believe, that he would have regarded it as something which, while it was certainly not obliged to serve the special purposes of allegory, yet owed its coherence and shape to the underlying ideas and themes which it expressed. It seems likely that, if the *Canterbury Tales* had ever been finished, it would have been possible to see some coherence of this kind within the variety of its parts, that is, a 'grete effect' carried through to the end, although it could hardly have been of the clearcut kind of the *Knight's Tale*.

It is necessary, in fact, to be very careful in defining exactly what is meant by thematic development in the *Canterbury Tales*. There is no doubt that, in his experimentation with and blending of different narrative techniques, Chaucer has achieved something that is substantially new, and a naïve attitude towards the way in which he manipulates his major themes could lead to serious misinterpretation. As we have said, for Chaucer, the successful artist imitates nature, not other works of art, and his success is measured by the degree to which his work approximates to its model. So much emerges, for example, from the *House of Fame*. The perfection of nature, as we learn from, *inter alia*, the *Parlement of Foules*, consists in the fulfilment of that infinite possibility for variety and completeness through which it expresses the infinitude and perfection of the One from which it has its source: this is 'God's plenty' as Dryden perceived it in Chaucer. If there is any work of Chaucer's which could, by any stretch of the imagination, be said to attempt to imitate this natural variety, it is, surely, the *Canterbury Tales*; and, if we try to isolate the special quality and achievement of this work, taken, as far as we can do so, in its unfinished state, as a whole, we cannot do better than to fix on the variety and inclusiveness which it achieves through its wide choice of subject-matter and kinds of writing. To look, except with extreme caution, for any more specific architectural principle is, in fact, to negate a good deal of Chaucer's achievement. If, for example, we think that he devised the series primarily to explore certain leading themes, then a number of the tales have to be dismissed as irrelevant to the main purpose or, alternatively, interpreted in a way which does violence to their author's obvious intention. Certain major themes do recur in the *Canterbury Tales*, and, as we shall see, we cannot fully appreciate the work without some understanding of them. But it is only to a very limited extent that they provide any obvious organizing principle. There is no indication that the *Canterbury Tales* would ever have become a work comparable to the *Confessio Amantis*, with its more or less clearcut exposition of love in relation to the vices and virtues; to the *Faerie Queene*, where the choice of the story material is determined by the ideas to be expressed; or even to Jean de Meun's part of the *Roman*, whose structure is conditioned by the need to work out a variety of ideas in their relation to love, rather than by any necessary, predetermined progression of the love story.

Similar difficulties arise from any such thesis as, for example, that the individual tales, and the characters who tell them, are designed as a series of *exempla* in illustration of the Christian moral system laid out in the *Parson's Tale*.[45] True, the Parson deals systematically with the deadly sins, and equally true that most of the characters of the tales, especially of the churls' tales, are busily engaged with one or other of them; but difficulties arise when we come to tales like the Knight's and the Franklin's. To fit this scheme these tales have to be shorn of a good deal of their subtlety. Tales of a more light-hearted kind, on the other hand, especially the *Nun's Priest's Tale* and *Sir Thopas*, have to be invested with so much subtlety that they become scarcely recognizable to the unprejudiced reader. Characters, too, have to be distorted – the Wife of Bath and the Prioress are obvious examples. The first has to be reduced to a schema and shorn of her humanity, the other built up so as to serve as a more serious warning against sin than Chaucer appears, at first sight, to have intended. In the same way, too earnest a concern with the souls and ultimate destinations of the *fabliau* characters introduces distortion into the churls' tales: we need to allow for a certain willing suspension of the moral faculty in this genre. Such a suspension is not total – the *fabliau* kind has a rough justice, based on the acceptable social norm, built securely into it; but to read the tales with too sensitive a moral awareness is surely to suffer an unnecessary degree of disquietude.

If, bearing all this in mind, we try to see what the completed series would have been like, we can, I think, only postulate more variety and, no doubt, more complexes of links and tales, more thematic interlacing of all kinds. But it seems clear that Chaucer would never have allowed the *Canterbury Tales* to develop the kind of schematization which is reached either by giving all the parts a uniformity which arises directly out of the nature of the frame or by a development of the frame which would render it completely independent of the tales and so allow complete freedom to introduce stories of any kind without any thematic interconnection. What he has arrived at, it seems to me, is a method by which frame and tales grow together, as the characters of the tellers reveal themselves increasingly through the frame and as the tales, in their turn, continue the revelation or arise naturally from one another, as Miller 'quites' Knight, or Clerk the Wife of Bath, or as Friar quarrels with Summoner. But with all this, there seems no reason to believe that Chaucer would have entirely given up the licence to introduce the occasional unconnected tale, as he does in the case of the Canon's Yeoman and of the saints' tales of the two Nuns. All these are linked into the frame by their appropriateness to their tellers but do not play an appreciable part in any thematic development between a group of tales. In thus extending the problem of narrative structure, solved so often and so brilliantly in so many individual tales, to that of a narrative complex, Chaucer seems, as far as we can judge his unfinished work, to have drawn on many different prototypes to produce something which would have been wholly new.

The *Canterbury Tales*:
Chaucerian comedy

It is obvious that the inclusiveness and variety of the *Canterbury Tales* help to provide ideal conditions for the exploitation of comedy to an extent which had not been practicable in Chaucer's early works. In these, indeed, comedy only enters in as an incidental.

In the love visions – the *Parlement of Foules* and the *House of Fame* – the only characters to emerge as clearly comic are birds – those of the lower classes in the *Parlement* and the pedagogic eagle in the *House of Fame*.[1] It is notable that, in the *Parlement*, Chaucer makes no attempt to treat the assembly of birds as a whole, or its purpose, in a comic spirit. He merely introduces the comic viewpoint through some individual members. This fact may perhaps give us a clue to one of the most characteristic aspects of Chaucerian comedy: that it arises out of the breadth and inclusiveness of his view of the world. Love is a serious subject and, as we have seen, has cosmological as well as individual implications. But the very fact that it is a fundamental and inescapable part of nature as a whole makes any consideration of it incomplete which does not extend through the whole of nature – and the whole of nature includes the vulgar-minded, but essentially useful and practical, duck. In the *Troilus*, the serious and beautiful description of the lovers' bliss when they are finally physically united grows out of a scene of comic intrigue, and this sudden emergence of seriousness out of comedy gives us a sense of completeness we could not otherwise feel. Elsewhere, the bedroom scene can have the reverse effect and becomes a kind of common denominator of humanity, which brings excessive dignity of rank or splendour, or even of sainthood, into a more comprehensive picture of mankind. The resulting sense of completeness is experienced by the reader through a momentary invasion of the comic spirit into a serious passage. Thus, for example, the high-flown description of the divine lovers Venus and Mars and their extremely overwrought emotional reactions ends in one blunt line:

> Ther is no more, but unto bed thei go.
>
> (73)

And, of the saintly Constance, Chaucer relates:

> They goon to bedde, as it was skile and right;
> For thogh that wyves be ful hooly thynges,
> They moste take in pacience at nyght
> Swiche manere necessaries as been plesynges
> To folk that han ywedded hem with rynges,
> And leye a lite hir hoolynesse aside,
> As for the tyme, – it may no bet bitide.
>
> (*CT* II, 708–14)

It is notable that in one of the rare cases where exclusion, not inclusion, is his aim, in the *Clerk's Tale*,[2] he is careful to avoid this modulation. There is no description of the marriage bed of Walter and Griselda. At the two points where it would naturally come (*CT* IV, 392 and 422), Chaucer breaks off and substitutes praise of Griselda's virtue.

In the two instances just quoted, we have only a moment which we feel is in any sense comic, and the structure of the narrative as a whole is not affected. In the treatment of the two figures who act as observers of the story in the two great philosophical poems, the element of comedy affects the structure of the whole work. Without Pandarus and Theseus, handled as Chaucer handles them, the stories in which they play a part would have totally different implications – as, indeed, we can actually see if we look at the sources, in which these characters are not treated as Chaucer treats them.

In Pandarus's case, comedy arises mainly from the fact that he represents a different view of the world to that of the other characters. In a sense he is in closer touch with actuality – he can recognize a farm cart when he sees one, unlike Troilus – and, as we have seen, he helps to link the intensity and self-centredness of the love story to a wider, more diffuse context. But there is also comedy in the fact that, however accurate his vision is where facts are concerned, he is all at sea when values are involved. Troilus's assessment of the nature of his loss, and of his own tragedy, is more truthful than Pandarus's.

There is no indication that Theseus's view of the world is a false or mistaken one. On the contrary, the whole structure of the poem depends on its acceptance as true. The denouement, in fact, can only work when we realize that the divergent views on the nature and function of love of the two lovers and of Theseus have at last converged in an understanding of the function of married love as a unifying and ordering force. Like Pandarus, however, Theseus is a link with a wider, less obsessive world, and the humour arises from the discrepancy between the lovers' view of life and life as we see it in this wider world, not from their clash with Theseus. In both poems, it is obvious, the inclusion of a character which in some sense belongs to comedy results in the enlargement of the scope of the whole work and, in these two great philosophical poems, in a widening and deepening of our comprehension of the themes.

So far, humour plays a strictly subordinate part in Chaucer's work – neither Theseus nor Pandarus are wholly comic characters, and the poems to which they belong never fail to keep in strict perspective our perception of a kind of comic disproportion which is, perhaps, inherent in reality itself, but which never for a moment invalidates or hinders our sympathy with the seriousness of the central situation. In many of the *Canterbury Tales*, comedy is more complete, and we have numerous characters presented in a wholly comic spirit in tales which have no overt serious aspect.

In developing the characters in tales of this kind, or in the frame, Chaucer uses methods of which there is no sign in the earlier works – and for which there was no need. Comedy is always particular – it exploits the way in which the individual case fails to fit the norm, the discrepancies between reality and a particular, partial view of the facts. Tragedy takes a wider sweep, and its characters do not need the kind of minute particularization required by comedy. In the Prologue to the *Canterbury Tales*, for example, Chaucer presents the characters through a cumulative list of details, in which every item helps to mark this particular figure off from any other. He avoids, however, the catalogue-type of visual description and mingles details of appearance, dress, etc. with those of occupations and habits, of past history and present employment. The section on the Squire provides a good example of this method at its most straightforward. He is not, it is true, an altogether comic figure, but there is an element of comedy in his behaviour as a lover and in his youth, which gives a certain extravagance to his occupations and dress not found, for example, in the more sober portrait of the Knight:

> With hym ther was his sone, a yong SQUIER,
> A lovyere and a lusty bacheler,
> With lokkes crulle as they were leyd in presse.
> Of twenty yeer of age he was, I gesse.
> Of his stature he was of evene lengthe,
> And wonderly delyvere, and of greet strengthe.
> And he hadde been somtyme in chyvachie
> In Flaundres, in Artoys, and Pycardie,
> And born hym weel, as of so lytel space,
> In hope to stonden in his lady grace.
> Embrouded was he, as it were a meede
> Al ful of fresshe floures, whyte and reede.
> Syngynge he was, or floytynge, al the day;
> He was as fressh as is the month of May.
> Short was his gowne, with sleves longe and wyde.
> Wel koude he sitte on hors and faire ryde. . . .
>
> (I, 79–94)

The narrative method here, with its apparent lack of organization, its rapid transitions from a detail noticed in the figure before the eye to a bit of information about its history, helps to ensure that we react as to an individual seen at a specific moment of time. What Chaucer, in fact, does is to present himself, as narrator, as reporting to us on what he sees before him. He gives us a detail as it happens to catch his eye, coming back, after each digression into the history or habits of the figure, to its actual appearance at the moment of speaking. Thus, after a reference to the Squire's habitual singing or fluting, Chaucer returns to the actual figure on horseback as it rides at that moment in the pilgrimage.

With all the emphasis on individualization and particularization, we must not lose sight of the fact that, for Chaucer, the figures of the Prologue, as of many of the comic tales, also represent clearly recognizable types, with vices or virtues which are commonly attributed to persons of their order.[3] In some cases, however, this conformity to type only results in a sharper focus on the individual. The joke against lovers is, after all, that 'thise loveris al' indulge in the same antics, however different their characters may be. In the Prioress's case, conformity to the convention which equips wealthy and fashionable ladies with little dogs is, given her ecclesiastical rather than worldly status, a decidedly individualizing trait.

Simple as the description of the Squire seems, it depends for its effect almost entirely on our acceptance of the observer – in this case of the narrator who presents him to us. The observer, indeed, often used in much more complicated ways, is an essential part of the machinery of Chaucerian comedy. He is, however, an unobtrusive figure, only emerging into the foreground with a comment on rare occasions. These calculated emergences, in fact, as well as his equally calculated withdrawals, convey a great part of the comedy of the *Canterbury Tales*. His elusiveness and the method by which straight description, without the slightest indication of evaluation, is tellingly interspersed with a rare, unemphatic comment or a half concealed allusion compel us to join him and to become observers ourselves. This is characteristic of Chaucer's approach to his subject-matter in comedy. If we identify ourselves with anyone, it is with the half-glimpsed narrator. We are carefully kept at a distance from the characters: our sympathy may be from time to time engaged, but never as a participant in the action and seldom even as a partisan. It is, indeed, rather that, as Raleigh said of the best of Boccaccio's stories,[4] we react to something 'so entirely like life that the strongest of the emotions awakened in the reader is not sympathy or antipathy, not moral approval or moral indignation, but a more primitive passion than these – the passion of curiosity'.

These results are largely achieved by the exploitation of variations in style similar to those we have already seen in the earlier works and, above all, in the *House of Fame*. For comedy Chaucer uses as the basic medium the simple style, with mainly coordinate or paratactic sentence structure. This style is typical of earlier narrative poetry in English, although it is also, of course, found in French. There is no doubt that, to build up the narrator's attitude to and evaluation of his story, the more complex periodic sentence is needed; it is through the connectives – a reluctant 'although', a 'nevertheless' or an apologetic 'but yet' – that a complex attitude is most easily conveyed, and the subordination of one part of a lengthy sentence to another generally coincides with the writer's estimate of its value to the whole. In the descriptions in the Prologue, Chaucer uses simple, paratactic structure so as to allow detail to pile on detail without the slightest overt indication of their relation to each other or their relative value – we are left to supply our own assessment, guided by the narrator's hidden skill in timing and placing:

> He was nat pale as a forpyned goost.
> A fat swan loved he best of any roost.
> His palfrey was as broun as is a berye.
>
> (205–7)

Here the effect depends on the ironical reversal of positive and negative: he was *not* pale, as a monk properly devoted to asceticism should be; he *did* enjoy fat swans and good horses. The unemphatic line opening 'He was nat' is, as it were, counterbalanced and contradicted by the emphatic position before the line pause, of 'loved he'.

> His typet was ay farsed ful of knyves
> And pynnes, for to yeven faire wyves.
> And certeinly he hadde a murye note:
> Wel koude he synge and pleyen on a rote;
> Of yeddynges he baar outrely the pris.
> His nekke whit was as the flour-de-lys;
> Therto he strong was as a champioun.
>
> (233–9)

The emphatic placing of the apparently conventional epithet 'faire' in the second line, where it carries the penultimate stress, causes it to linger in our minds and so to reinforce the sensuous and virile description of the last two: such a man would certainly be likely to pick out the prettiest women as the recipients of his gifts.

> Wel koude he stelen corn and tollen thries;
> And yet he hadde a thombe of gold, pardee.
> A whit cote and a blew hood wered he.
> A baggepipe wel koude he blowe and sowne,
> And therwithal he broghte us out of towne.
>
> (562–6)

Here the effect depends upon the ambiguity of the opening 'wel'. The first impression is of a line of good humoured praise for a good point in the character, but the smoothly running first half 'wel koude he . . .' is set against the heavily regular stress of the last 'stelen corn and tellen thries'. The narrator's amiable praise turns out to be directed at skill in thievery, unambiguously described. The apparently apologetic 'and yet' with the reinforcing affirmation tagged on like an innocent afterthought at the end of the line, develops the irony further. The proverb 'an honest miller has a golden thumb' is not altogether appropriate to this one. He is, the narrator indulgently adds, after all as honest as such men usually are, and we are left to decide for ourselves whether the golden thumb benefits its owner or his customers. The apparently inconsequent piling up of the details of dress and equipment in the last three lines helps to build up the portrait, developed in the passage as a whole, of a colourful, vulgar figure. The bagpipes, of course, were not a refined instrument.

The longer, consecutive or periodic sentences, which do indicate a definite attitude to the matter in hand, stand out sharply in contrast. The passage in which the good priest is compared to the 'shiten shepherde' provides a good example:[5]

> This noble ensample to his sheep he yaf,
> That first he wroghte, and afterward he taughte.
> Out of the gospel he tho wordes caughte,
> And this figure he added eek therto,
> That, if gold ruste, what shal iren do?
> For if a preest be foul, on whom we truste,
> No wonder is a lewed man to ruste;
> And shame it is, if a prest take keep,
> A shiten shepherde and a clene sheep.
>
> (496–504)

Or again, in one of the rare passages in which the narrator actually joins in the conversation, he commends the logic with which the monk argues against confinement to the cloister in a paragraph of complex structure:

> And I seyde his opinion was good.
> What sholde he studie and make hymselven wood,

Upon a book in cloystre alwey to poure,
Or swynken with his handes and laboure,
As Austyn bit? How shal the world be served?
Lat Austyn have his swynk to hym reserved!
(183–8)

And he continues with a telling 'therefore':

Therfore he was a prikasour aright;

and justly indulges 'al his lust', sparing no expense in his pursuit
of the chase (177–92).

The technique of bare statement is not, of course, restricted to
the Prologue. It is often used in the comic tales themselves. For
example:

A theef he was for sothe, of corn and mele,
And that a sly, and usaunt for to stele.
His name was hoote deynous Symkyn.
A wyf he hadde, ycomen of noble kyn;
The person of the toun hir fader was.
(*CT* I, 3939–43)

Or:

This carpenter out of his slomber sterte,
And herde oon crien 'water' as he were wood,
And thoughte, 'Allas, now comth Nowelis flood!'
He sit hym up withouten wordes mo,
And with his ax he smoot the corde atwo,
And doun gooth al. . . .
(*CT* I, 3816–21)

Here the syntax produces the effect of speed in the narrative and
also, with its plain enumeration of detail after detail without
comment on the narrator's part, helps to build up the outrageous
climax. The same effect is produced by the relentless accumulation
of detail in the *Reeve's Tale*. Narrator and audience alike are helpless
before the ineluctable logic of events:

> This John stirte up as faste as ever he myghte,
> And graspeth by the walles to and fro,
> To fynde a staf; and she stirte up also,
> And knew the estres bet than dide this John,
> And by the wal a staf she foond anon,
> And saugh a litel shymeryng of a light,
> For at an hole in shoon the moone bright;
> And by that light she saugh hem bothe two,
> But sikerly she nyste who was who,
> But as she saugh a whit thyng in hir ye.
> And whan she gan this white thyng espye,
> She wende the clerk hadde wered a volupeer,
> And with the staf she drow ay neer and neer,
> And wende han hit this Aleyn at the fulle,
> And smoot the millere on the pyled skulle,
> That doun he gooth, and cride, 'Harrow! I dye.'
>
> (*CT* I, 4292–307)

Such gross overworking of the conjunction 'and' with the minimum
of explanatory 'buts' and 'fors' would be easy to parallel from many
English narrative poems before Chaucer. But we should find no
parallel to its deliberate exploitation for a comic effect which depends
on the cumulative weight of the sentence structure.

This strict selectiveness in the style works together with another
kind of selectiveness which is characteristic of the *fabliau*. This is the
narrative selectiveness, which pares down all accompanying or
background detail to the bare minimum which is actually needed for
the exposition of the plot. There is no exuberance in the description
of the settings; any detail that is mentioned is mentioned in explanation of the action, as Muscatine has pointed out.[6] The passage just
quoted from the *Reeve's Tale* provides an excellent example of the
technique. As in the passage in the *Troilus* in which Pandarus
introduces Troilus into Criseyde's bedroom, each detail helps us
to understand and visualize the exact progression of events, and
nothing is mentioned which is outside this immediate purpose.
Everything is given the most precise definition. The inadequate
light is 'a litel shymeryng'. This is because although the moon, its
source, is bright, it comes 'at an hole'. It is 'that light' by which
the Miller's wife sees 'a whit thyng in hir ye'. This 'white thyng'
looks to her like a 'volupeer' worn by one of the clerks. With care

and accuracy 'the staf she drow ay neer and neer', with the result that she, of course, succeeds in placing her blow on the white thing, now only too clearly identified as the miller's 'pyled skulle'.

Passages showing a similar method could be quoted from most of the *fabliau* tales, and it is this new precision of style, with its exact selection of relevant detail and its accurate timing and placing which is the great innovation of Chaucer's comic art. The more obviously literary earlier works allowed a good deal of slacker writing – passages which, if not padding, are at least leisurely and make their mark through cumulative effect rather than imme- diate impact. The success of the *fabliau* style and its novelty in English were fully appreciated by Chaucer's immediate successors.[7]

The technique of the comic tales assumes, but never openly states, a standard and a norm which is shared by narrator and audience, and it is in this implicit comparison of the characters and their behaviour with something accepted as normal and desirable that the comedy largely consists. In these tales, this is where the clash of interests and standards comes, not, as in the *Knight's Tale* or the *Troilus*, in the conflicting views of reality held by different characters within the story. In the comic tales, all the characters accept the foibles on which the plot depends in the same way. Their reactions may differ – husbands of erring wives do not view their error in the same light as their lovers do – but they all inhabit the same world, a world in which fraud and cuckoldry are accepted as the norm, and the only valid motto for those possessed of money or wives is *sauve qui peut*. The reader stands with the narrator on the edge of this narrow comic vista and, it is flatteringly assumed, is capable of appreciating other views of reality and of setting the limited comic norm over against one of more universal validity. He is capable, too, of appreciating what is not necessarily apparent to the characters within the tale: the justice and satisfactory fittingness of the denouements. In a work like the *Troilus*, on the other hand, comedy consists in an internal clash of viewpoints which is inherent in the story itself, and the conclusion involves a resolution, not the restoration of a sense of order and decorum temporarily in abeyance.

To press the exclusion of the audience from the tales too far, however, would be to oversimplify. Chaucer's art as a story-teller ensures its involvement as far as continued and vivid interest is concerned, and we cannot say that our sympathies are never engaged. How far and at what point interest passes into sympathy is a delicate matter – the boundary probably comes at a slightly different point for every reader. There is always a moment at which sheer delighted appreciation of the perfection and completeness of the character and situation which develops before our eyes passes into something indistinguishable from sympathy, even though it does not necessarily carry with it acquiescence in the standards of conduct involved. This is, perhaps, most obviously true in the case of that most complex and complete of Chaucer's comic creations, the Wife of Bath. A simpler case is that of Alisoun in the *Miller's Tale*. Taken at its face value, there is certainly nothing sympathetic about her conduct towards either of her lovers. She yields easily to one and helps play a somewhat brutal joke on the other. Moreover, her story consists in nothing but the immediate satisfaction of impulse; it has no reverberations beyond the moment. In Chaucer's hands, however, this is more than enough. Alisoun, like so many of Chaucer's comic characters, absorbs us through the sharpness of the definition; she is herself to a superlative degree:

> There nys no man so wys that koude thenche
> So gay a popelote or swich a wenche.
>
> (*CT* I, 3253–4)

Judging from May's indignant, and unjustified, cry that she is 'a gentil womman and no wenche', this places Alisoun with exactitude.[8] Chaucer develops her portrait through comparisons with birds and young animals:

> But of hir song, it was a loude and yerne
> As any swalwe sittynge on a berne.
> Therto she koude skippe and make game,
> As any kyde or calf folwynge his dame.
> Hir mouth was sweete as bragot or the meeth,
> Or hoord of apples leyd in hey or heeth.
> Wynsynge she was, as is a joly colt,
> Long as a mast, and upright as a bolt.
>
> (*CT* I, 3257–64)

The birds and young animals share the same characteristic of total absorption in their own vigorous and, from the human point of view, quite incalculable life and happiness. Alisoun, by the comparison, is thus invested with a kind of liveliness and also a kind of innocence, which is certainly not centred in the specifically human virtues. This is not quite to say that she is what we should call amoral. It is rather that her conduct is made fully explicable, and in this sense fully 'right', in natural rather than moral terms. Nicholas's wooing of her takes full account of this. He shows his 'subtlety' as a clerk by paying lip-service to a more sophisticated form of love-making (although his words echo popular vernacular lyric rather than the tremulously respectful pleas of a lover like Troilus):[9]

> And seyde, 'Ywis, but if ich have my wille,
> For deerne love of thee, lemman, I spille'
> (3277–8)

and:

> 'Lemman, love me al atones,
> Or I wol dyen, also God me save!'
> (3280–1)

But his actions are even less sophisticated:

> And prively he caughte hire by the queynte . . .
> (3276)

> And thakked hire aboute the lendes weel . . .
> (3304)

Alisoun takes no more notice of his words than the swallow would have done, but reacts predictably to his actions:

> And she sproong, as a colt dooth in the trave,
> And with hir heed she wryed faste awey,
> And seyde, 'I wol nat kisse thee, by my fey!
> Why, lat be,' quod she, 'lat be, Nicholas,
> Or I wol crie "out, harrow" and "allas"!'
> (3282–6)

This is, of course, only the prelude to her practical and unemotional consent to

been at his comandement,
Whan that she may hir leyser wel espie.
(3292–3)

In the end, when she makes her final contribution –

'Tehee!' quod she, and clapte the wyndow to –
(3740)

the intensity of our pleasure in her is in proportion to the unflawed perfection with which she acts out the nature Chaucer has given her. We can say with the narrator:

This passeth forth; what wol ye bet than weel?
(3370)

In the *Reeve's Tale* the characters are probably even less sympathetic, in any normal sense of the word, than those of the *Miller's Tale*, and the elaborate manœuvres of the communal bedroom scene would be almost too shallow if they were not for a moment brought to life by the reactions of Malkin. She is a plain girl, left unmarried by the haggling methods of her family in the conduct of marriage negotiations (she is twenty; the Wife of Bath, like the young bride of the *Clerk's Tale*, started her married career at twelve; May was eighteen when she married January). Whatever her parents suffer, she, at least, enjoys her night with the clerk and parts with him on the best of terms:[10]

'Fare weel, Malyne, sweete wight!
The day is come, I may no lenger byde;
But everemo, wher so I go or ryde,
I is thyn awen clerk, swa have I seel!'
'Now, deere lemman,' quod she, 'go, far weel!'
(*CT* I, 4236–40)

And she also, of course, contributes the necessary turn to the plot by gratefully telling him of the whereabouts of the stolen cake.

Even the *Summoner's Tale*, which illustrates his own vice of *ira*,[11] gives us a figure, in the maddening friar, which is made enjoyable and so far, in a sense, sympathetic by the very perfection and completeness of its self-consistency. Every tone of his voice seems to reflect his nature, and his unconscious self-betrayal in a gesture like the putting aside of the cat, which, in the nature of things, would have been occupying the most comfortable place on the bench, completes the picture:[12]

> '*Deus hic!*' quod he, 'O Thomas, freend, good day!'
> Seyde this frere, curteisly and softe.
> 'Thomas,' quod he, 'God yelde yow! ful ofte
> Have I upon this bench faren ful weel;
> Heere have I eten many a myrie meel.'
> And fro the bench he droof awey the cat,
> And leyde adoun his potente and his hat,
> And eek his scrippe, and sette him softe adoun.
>
> > (*CT* III, 1770–7)

The conclusion of this tale is interesting, because in it Chaucer shows us the reaction of an audience placed within the story to the plot enacted in it – and by so doing, suggests, I think, the way in which he intends his own audience to react. Thomas has set the outrageous and insoluble problem of the division of the fart and with it provoked a burst of anger in which the friar appears 'as dooth a wood leoun' (2152). We are then shown the reactions of the 'lord of that village', to whom the story is told. First the lady reacts with fascinated astonishment:

> 'Ey, Goddes mooder,' quod she, 'Blisful mayde!
> Is ther oght elles? telle me feithfully.'
>
> > (2202–3)

Then the lord's even greater astonishment is described:

> The lord sat stille as he were in a traunce
> And in his herte he rolled up and doun,
> 'How hadde this cherl ymaginacioun
> To shewe swich a probleme to the frere?
> Nevere erst er now herde I of swich mateere,
> I trowe the devel putte it in his mynde.
> In ars-metrike shal ther no man fynde,
> Biforn this day, of swich a question.'
>
> > (2216–23)

The tale, in fact, makes its point on both the internal and the external audiences by the sheer perfection in virtuosity of each of its participants. The begging friar is a prince among his kind. The churl calls forth exclamations of maddened and delighted astonishment at his brilliant improvisation, and the squire, of course, further astonishes and delights the audience by providing a solution even more outrageous than the original insult.

The reactions of an internal audience are important in other tales. In the *Merchant's Tale*, for example, the denouement is played out before the audience of fairy gods as well as the suddenly sighted January. In the *Shipman's Tale* of the young monk who cheats his friend out of his wife and his money, the internal audience is also put to subtle use. It helps to build up and to make at once credible and tolerable this rather dubious ecclesiastic, in that no opportunity is lost of describing his popularity and the effects of his charm on those he meets with. This results in a comic clash of values between what we actually see him doing, and know him to be, and the kind of man the characters in the story think he is.[13]

The *fabliau*, as we have said, depends on an in-built, if rough, sense of justice. The denouement, in which the characters who act with vice or folly are fittingly punished – or, in the case of most of the erring wives, escape punishment by a stroke of superlative wit which brings retribution on their husbands' heads instead – depends on a standard of what is at least socially acceptable being shared by narrator and audience. Thus, in the *Reeve's Tale*, the elaborate build-up concerning the false social aspirations of the miller's family, even more than his actual dishonesty, makes the ending not only poetic, but desired justice; while the pretensions of Absolon and the folly of the carpenter make their somewhat violent punishment at least tolerable. To go beyond this, however, and to apply a sensitive or puritanical scale of moral values to the tales would be as far beside the mark as to dispute the question of *meum* and *tuum* with the swallows Alisoun resembles.

It is, however, another question altogether, as to whether we can regard the tales, within the whole complex of the pilgrimage, as reflecting, or helping to reflect, a view of the world which belongs neither to the individual character who is presented as narrator nor to the individual tale, but to Chaucer himself, whose perceptions are, obviously, a good deal more comprehensive as well as a good deal more sensitive than those of his Miller or Reeve. Here, it seems to me that to press the issue too hard is to destroy the effect of the tales. In the last resort it means turning them into allegory of a curiously ill-managed and unsatisfactory kind.[14] Nevertheless, in trying to define the special nature of Chaucerian comedy, we cannot ignore the fact that in all his purely comic writing he has chosen to set the piece within a framework. He has left us no isolated or entirely self-contained comic poem. This, in fact, seems to bring us very near the heart of Chaucerian comedy. It is not only that, as we have seen, we are imperceptibly lead to play the part of external audience to, rather than participator in, the individual tales: through the organization of the tales within the framework of the *Canterbury Tales* as a whole, we get the effect of comic worlds within worlds, of layers of different perceptiveness, arising from the fact that the tales exist in and for themselves but at the same time reflect, in varying degrees, the minds and limitations (in themselves part of the stuff of comedy) of the tellers. These, in their turn are reflected – together with their tales – in the mirror of the larger audience of the pilgrims, while we, as final audience, through all the devices of Chaucerian description and presentation, are inevitably drawn into the position of the final mirror of all.

More than this, the comic tales are an inextricable part of a series which includes the serious and 'noble' tales. They are only more closely linked to the special characteristics of their tellers because comedy, as we have seen, gains from particularization, while tragedy does not. It is for this reason, I think, rather than because of greater maturity in his art or any change in purpose in the *Canterbury Tales*, that Chaucer exploits the individual characteristics and foibles of the pilgrims more fully in the comic tales than elsewhere.[15] Here the character of Harry Bailey, the Host, is important. His reactions to the tales and tellers emphasizes their precise position within the whole. He has an unfailing appreciation of order and degree. His submission to the authority of the Knight is unquestioning, and he shows more delicacy in his approach to the Prioress than some of her modern critics. He has, also, an unfailing flair for the order of disrespect. His reaction to the Pardoner is crucial, and he strikes exactly the right note for the sub-comedy of the pilgrim Chaucer. He has an equally unfailing zest in his praise and dispraise of the entertainment provided, and the very naïvety of his reactions – always to the content in the most superficial sense, never to the art of the tales – enhances the comedy, in the case of the humorous tales, by helping to pin-point the special comic involvement of the teller through his pet vice or cherished misfortune;[16] and also gives a wider perspective to some of the serious ones. His extravagant reaction to the pathos of the *Physician's Tale*:

> Oure Hooste gan to swere as he were wood;
> 'Harrow!' quod he, 'by nayles and by blood!'
> (*CT* VI, 287–8)

should at least give us to think before we dismiss it as a rather colour-less and characterless example of Chaucer's art. It would seem that here, as, perhaps, in the *Clerk's Tale*, Chaucer is relying on a sensi-bility which we do not altogether share with his age.[17] There is no more reason to reject the validity of the Host's reaction here than there is to reject his appreciation of the Knight. Nevertheless, the form it takes is vulgar and exaggerated, and there is no doubt that his impassioned championship of Virginia does bring her pathetic fate within the confines of the comic world. I do not think that, through this somewhat subtle manœuvre, Chaucer invalidates the pathos of the tale or calls its internal values in serious question. He merely once more demonstrates – and this is the essence of comedy – that there is more than one way of looking at a thing and, through the very fervour of the simple Host's undiscriminating agreement, suggests the possibility of a different reaction.

The Host is not, however, the only means of achieving this interweaving of the comic and serious in the *Canterbury Tales*. Nor is he the only literary critic. Just as he puts a stop to the in-tolerable din of Chaucer's own drasty rhyming, so the Knight, like Theseus in a similarly unbearable situation, calls 'Ho' and puts a stop to the Monk's depressing flood of tragedies. The effect, like that of the Host's overexuberant appreciation of the *Physician's Tale*, is again to bring the tales into juxtaposition with another viewpoint. The Knight, too, has to act as mediator between the Pardoner and the Host and is thus involved, as is the Parson, in a clash with some of the characters of comedy.[18] The Clerk, in spite of the serious nature of his tale, ends with a humorous reference to the Wife of Bath; and we are made vividly aware of the 'gentles' as part of the audience of the more outrageous tales when they all protest in chorus against the kind of tale they fear the Pardoner is about to tell, or share in the laughter produced by the Miller's 'nyce cas'. In the same way, after the *Prioress's Tale*, which is perfectly serious and perfectly seriously received:

> Whan seyd was al this miracle, every man
> As sobre was that wonder was to se
>
> (*CT* VII, 691–2)

the silence is broken by the Host's return to a jesting mood.

The choice of tale for teller is at times used as another means of producing this kind of juxtaposition and interpenetration of the comic and the serious. The Man of Law, the Physician and the Franklin are all presented as having their share of folly, if not vice; that is, they are typical figures of comedy. Yet they tell fundamentally serious tales. The *Franklin's Tale* is perhaps not entirely serious: there is incipient comedy in the exuberance with which it treats the important virtue it exemplifies. Dorigen and her husband are extravagantly honourable: Dorigen could not normally be considered bound by a promise whose fulfilment would involve her in the sin of adultery. Nevertheless, it is a gracious story, graciously told, and I think that to see it as a parody of courtliness is to underrate it grossly. In the *Man of Law's Tale*, Chaucer may occasionally smile at the conflicts with which saintliness at large in the world is inevitably faced – whether in bed or in those situations, so common to heroines of this kind, in which would-be ravishers are repelled with uncompromising violence.[19] Chaucer, indeed, treats with unqualified approval the god-sent 'vigour' of Constance, when she pushes the 'renegat' overboard to his death. The only hint of any other point of view lies in the elaboration of the rhetoric with which he praises it; and I think that this is here to be taken at its face-value.[20]

In the case of the Wife of Bath, Chaucer seems first to have planned to give her a tale (which we know as the Shipman's) typical of the kind of marital strategy sketched out by La Vieille in the *Roman de la Rose*. There is no doubt that it was a good second thought by which he gave her a story which has an element of romance as well as *fabliau* and which, while it certainly develops the view of woman as dominating over man by her wit (which the Wife shares with La Vieille), also has room for serious themes like that of patient poverty and true gentility.[21] This helps to fill out the impression we have of her through her Prologue – an impression which is immeasurably more complex than that of Jean de Meun's Vieille.

Another method of linking the comic to the serious is by the juxtaposition of the tales themselves, irrespective of the tellers. In the absence of Chaucer's final order, it is not easy to say how much use he intended to make of this method. In the groups which we can accept with most probability, we have some extreme contrasts like that between the *Shipman's* and the *Prioress's Tales*. This transition is made without emphasis by the Host:

> 'But now passe over, and lat us seke aboute,
> Who shal now telle first of al this route
> Another tale.'
>
> (*CT* VII, 442–4)

In this, as in other cases, Chaucer seems quite content to allow free play to the principle of variety and contrast, which his choice of the frame mechanism ensures. There is, however, one case in which he himself seems to direct us to read the two contrasting tales together. This is the case of the *Knight's* and the *Miller's Tales*, which are elaborately linked. The Host calls on the Monk as a proper person to provide something to 'quite with' the *Knight's Tale* but is interrupted by the drunken Miller who, echoing the praise of the Knight's 'noble storie' offers a 'noble tale' of his own 'With which I wol now quite the Knyghtes tale' (*CT* I, 3127). Since the meaning of 'quite' here is obviously 'be a return or equivalent for, to balance' (*OED* II, 11, c.), the Miller is offering his story as in some way directly comparable to the Knight's. It is obvious, as we read, that the equivalence is indeed fully worked out in the tale, as most commentators have pointed out.[22] We have the pair of lovers – perhaps with the significant reversal that, while it is the man of action who fails to win the lady in the *Knight's Tale*, in the *Miller's Tale* Nicholas, who is as 'sodeyn' as Diomede, is more successful than the gentler parish clerk Absolon. We also have the lady who, unlike Emely, is perfectly ready to cope with a love affair; and the astrological pretensions of Nicholas, which provide an important part of the plot machinery, replace the epic machinery of the planet-gods in the *Knight's Tale*. There is even the significant verbal echo of the line 'Allone, withouten any compaignye' (*CT* I, 3204) which, in the *Knight's Tale*, is movingly used of Arcite's death, but in the *Miller's Tale* is used to indicate a gap in Nicholas's life shortly to be filled by Alisoun.

Some critics have gone so far as to see in all this a straightforward parody of the *Knight's Tale*. This, I think, is to impoverish our understanding of both tales. It is, surely, rather that, having whole-heartedly, and certainly without the slightest poetic reservation, given us a poem which embodies everything that is most noble and most profound in the poetry of his day in the *Knight's Tale* – but always, we must remember, with that leavening of the heroic tone which Theseus continually introduces – Chaucer now chooses to show us how a superficially similar arrangement can be handled to totally different effect, as well as how a totally different perception of life can have its own validity. He has already indicated as much in his treatment of the different types of birds and their contrasting viewpoints in the *Parlement of Foules*. It is now as if he actually showed us the love story of the noble birds re-enacted by a troop of ducks. There is no doubt that we emerge from the experience of plunging out of the *Knight's Tale* into the *Miller's Tale* with our understanding of the themes of both much enriched, but the enrich-ment comes from the perception of difference as well as from a pleasant apprehension of sameness under differing disguises. We do not really think that the nobility of Palemoun and Arcite is debased by the comparison, though we may feel that their undoubted moments of folly are pointed up. But our chief gain, I think, is insight into the way in which Nature crams the world full of differing creatures, whose difference tends to find its most common ground at the point where Nature and Venus join hands to work out their plan for even further increase, until

> erthe, and eyr, and tre, and every lake
> So ful was that unethe was there space
> For me to stonde, so ful was al the place.
> (*Parlement*, 313–15)

It is, of course, true that human beings, even more than the birds, tend to abuse Nature's laws and that not all their manœuvres help to fulfil her plan. Nevertheless, even these deviations can be seen as an expression of her infinite variety. If there is any moral in the juxtaposition of the *Knight's* and the *Miller's Tales*, it seems to me to lie more in this direction than in that of a heavy-handed comment on the noble, but not always strictly practical, flights of heroical love. The latter, we must also remember, do yet culminate in a marriage in strict accordance with Nature's mandates, while, ironically, the uncomplicated lovers of the *Miller's Tale* never get beyond an adulterous union which is, from Nature's point of view, disruptive and useless.

So far, in considering Chaucerian comedy, we have seen characterization handled in various ways and on various levels, but always subordinated to plot. In three cases Chaucer does something different and shifts the emphasis from the telling of the tale to the presentation of the character. In each case this results in a new synthesis of prologue, or links, and tale. These three cases are those of the Pardoner, the Wife of Bath and the Mal Marié, January, in the *Merchant's Tale*, which has its own internal prologue. Each of these is differently developed, but they have this in common: they are all derived from stock figures of earlier satirical or comic genres. The Wife of Bath, as, again, has often been pointed out, follows closely in the steps of La Vieille, in the *Roman de la Rose*, who is herself a stock figure of anti-feminist writing.[23] January has affinities with *fabliau*, but he is also closely modelled on another figure of the anti-feminist tradition, Jean de Meun's Le Jaloux.[24] The Pardoner stands alone, in that his development as a character is not connected with any wider thematic development. The figures of the Wife of Bath and of January are so inextricably involved in the marriage theme that their discussion in full must be held over to chapter 4.

The Pardoner, as has often been pointed out, has clear affinities with the kind of self-revealing and self-describing vice figures common in allegorical writing.[25] In particular, Chaucer has borrowed much from the confessions of Faux Semblant in the *Roman de la Rose*.[26] Characters of this kind are often made into ecclesiastical hangers-on. Langland, for example, gives his Fals and Favel, figures belonging to the same tradition, an ecclesiastical-legal retinue.[27]

In the nature of things, figures of this kind are neither sensitively nor naturalistically treated in the kinds of writing to which, traditionally, they belong. The allegorical vice figure, indeed, needs no sympathy. It is a self-contained, self-conditioned entity, operating according to the laws of its nature with perfect self-satisfaction.[28] Any mitigating circumstances or softening traits would merely destroy the allegorical meaning. Falsehood can be conquered or replaced by Truth, but it cannot become less false and still remain a convincing part of the allegory. The convention by which such figures describe their own characteristics is firmly entrenched as a normal part of the machinery of allegorical satire. Such confessions do not need either motivation or excuse. They are merely a part of the exposition. Thus Langland, for example, may give some air of probability to his self-characterizing vices by using the general framework of the confessional; but he has no hesitation in departing from this frame whenever it suits him – giving, for example, actions as well as words to Glutton, or allowing the confessions to become cheerful descriptions of activities quite satisfactory to the confessing figures, as in the case of Avarice, who evades all Conscience's efforts to bring him to a state of contrition. There is little or no satire involved in the presentation of figures of this kind, and comedy only arises through their grotesqueness and through their obvious deviation from what is normally acceptable.

Anyone who reads through fragment C of the Chaucerian translation of the *Roman de la Rose*,[29] which contains most of the confession of Faux Semblant, will see that, although there is an obvious relationship between this hypocrite who prefers ecclesiastical disguise, and whose only devotion is to money, and the Pardoner who interprets the dictum 'Radix malorum est cupiditas' in an original way, to imply that vice exists only to be exploited for his own profit, there are also important differences. In the *Roman*, the figure of Faux Semblant is manipulated so as to serve two main purposes. There is a pleasing irony in the fact that the love story, on whose thread Jean de Meun keeps a firm hold in spite of all his digressions, is advanced by the strangling of Slander by Hypocrisy and False (i.e., pretended) Abstinence. The God of Love, like Venus in the *Parlement of Foules*, employs some dubious servants – in this case, one whose character is so sinister that, Jean seems to imply, his acceptance by Love amounts to an act of self-destruction, as the following exchange shows:

> 'Wolt thou wel holden my forwardis?'
> 'Ye, sir, from hennes forwardis;
> Hadde never youre fadir heere-biforn
> Servaunt so trewe, sith he was born.'
> 'That is ayenes all nature.'
> 'Sir, putte you in that aventure.
> For though ye borowes take of me,
> The sikerer shal ye never be

> For ostages, ne sikirnesse,
> Or chartres, for to bere witnesse.
> I take youresilf to recorde heere,
> That men ne may in no manere
> Teren the wolf out of his hide,
> Til he be flayn, bak and side,
> Though men hym bete and al defile.
> What! wene ye that I nil begile
> For I am clothed mekely?
> Ther-undir is all my trechery;
> Myn herte chaungith never the mo
> For noon abit in which I go.'
>
> (C, 7301–20)

This speech gives us a very exact definition of the allegorical vice figure. Such a figure is, obviously, an important part of Jean de Meun's satirical technique. Faux Semblant exists not merely to advance the story by his actions and reactions, but to help lay out a body of material which, branching out from the problems of the particular kind of love involved in the story of L'Amant and the Rose, includes the topical question of new and dangerous beliefs and movements among the co-called Béguins and Joachimite Friars,[30] as well as much general criticism of hypocrisy, with special, though not exclusive, reference to the clergy.

Chaucer has little to do with either purpose. The *Pardoner's Prologue* and *Tale* have nothing to do with love, and the topic of popular religious movements is not one that touches him. Langland is still concerned over the debate about religious poverty, but for Chaucer the tag phrase 'patient poverty' means something different.[31] He is not interested, either, in Jean de Meun's manning of the university barricades.[32] What does interest him is the figure itself, and the way in which it enthusiastically exposes its own nature so as to both shock and titillate the audience. The reaction of Love and his barons to Faux Semblant's revelations is reasonably polite:

> The god lough at the wondir tho,
> And every wight gan laugh also,
> And seide, 'Lo, heere a man aright
> For to be trusty to every wight!'
>
> (C, 7293–6)

They show, however, something of the same mixture of outrage
and amusement with which the Host and the Knight, between them,
finally silence the Pardoner, in the course of which the Host at
least is far from polite:

> 'Now,' quod oure Hoost, 'I wol no lenger pleye
> With thee, ne with noon oother angry man.'
> But right anon the worthy Knyght bigan,
> Whan that he saugh that al the peple lough,
> 'Namoore of this, for it is right ynough!
> Sire Pardoner, be glad and myrie of cheere;
> And ye, sire Hoost, that been to me so deere,
> I prey yow that ye kisse the Pardoner.
> And Pardoner, I prey thee, drawe thee neer,
> And, as we diden, lat us laughe and pleye.'
> Anon they kiste, and ryden forth hir weye.
>
> (CT VI, 958–68)

The difference is that, where the reactions of Love and his barons
underlines the idea which the allegory expresses – that is, of the
inevitable relation of evil things to love of this kind – the Host
and Knight react in an individual way to a particular situation
which has arisen through the behaviour of another individual.
In fact, much as he owes to a method developed for allegorical
exposition, Chaucer's approach is fundamentally a naturalistic
one. How far he has succeeded in reconciling these two opposing
techniques in the Pardoner's case, has always been a matter for debate
among critics.

Faux Semblant and the Pardoner have in common an enthusiasm
in self-exposure which, as we have said, is an accepted convention
in the case of the vice figure and which passes smoothly enough
for motivation in the case of the more realistically conceived
character. Faux Semblant, commanded by Love to describe his way
of life, says:

> 'I shal don youre comaundement,
> For therto have I gret talent.'
>
> (C, 6133–4)

The Pardoner's enthusiasm is more subtly indicated, but we are left in no doubt that he shares the pleasure he confidently expects his audience to feel, as he describes how:

> 'Myne handes and my tonge goon so yerne
> That it is joye to se my bisyness, . . .'
>
> (*CT* VI, 398–9)

and he asserts that no reasonable man could fail to be pleased with his performance:

> 'By God, I hope I shal yow telle a thyng
> That shal by reson been at youre likyng.'
>
> (457–8)

There is a difference, however, between the Pardoner's claim to success and popularity and Faux Semblant's pleasure in fulfilling his allegorical destiny. The fact that both figures are, according to the kind to which they belong, treated with subtlety, only points up the difference. Faux Semblant is not mechanically handled. He is shown approaching Love with fear and shame-facedness:

> 'But Fals-Semblant dar not, for drede
> Of you, sir, medle hym of this dede,
> For he seith that ye ben his foo;
> He not if ye wole worche hym woo.'
>
> (C, 6049–52)

It is only when he is sure of a place at Love's court, as 'kyng of harlotes', that he is able to give expression to his true nature. This is convincing both in terms of the personification, which is given added liveliness by its doubts and hesitations, and of the allegorical argument. In allegorical terms, it is only when it has been established that the dubious practices to be described are an essential part of the kind of love story on which L'Amant is embarked, that they can fall into place within the structure of the exposition. Love's doubtful behaviour then runs parallel to, and in some sort reflects, the behaviour of the world at large, and the satire widens out to include issues which have little to do with love. In the case of the religious deviants, however, there is, no doubt, a particularly savage irony in the fact that the most common accusations against them were of sexual licence of a kind which throws a lurid light on the apparently gentle love story of the *Roman*. Much of the savage mood of Chaucer's *Merchant's Tale* is to be found in the *Roman*, not only in the more obviously satirical digressions, but also as an ineradicable element in the main plot – the story of Love pursued in defiance of Reason and in doubtful accord with Nature.[33]

But naturalism is not the method by which this very complex ordering of the material can be achieved, and Faux Semblant, for all his liveliness, remains a purely allegorical figure. At times he seems to split up, and we hear of a whole troop of deceivers, referred to as 'we', who carry out activities obviously too extensive for a single one – for example:

> 'Another custome use we:
> Of hem that wole ayens us be,
> We hate hem deedly everichon,
> And we wole werrey hem, as oon.'
>
> (C, 6923–6)

He shifts his dress, occupation, and even sex:

> 'For Protheus, that cowde hym chaunge
> In every shap, homly and straunge,
> Cowde nevere sich gile ne tresoun
> As I; for I com never in toun
> There as I myghte knowen be,
> Though men me bothe myght here and see.
> Full wel I can my clothis chaunge,
> Take oon, and make another straunge.
> Now am I knyght, now chasteleyn,
> Now prelat and now chapeleyn. . . .
> Somtyme a wommans cloth take I;
> Now am I a mayde, now lady.'
>
> (C, 6319–46)

The description of his dwelling is significant. It is a purely allegorical palace, not meant to be visualized in the ordinary way, but not without iconographical significance:

'My paleis and myn hous make I
There men may renne ynne openly,
And sey that I the world forsake,
But al amydde I bilde and make
My hous, and swimme and pley therynne,
Bet than a fish doth with his fynne.'

(C, 7003–8)

We are inevitably reminded of the common depiction of Luxuria swimming in the sea.[34]

The end of the passage brings us back, in a particularly skilful way, to the bones of the allegory. We are always aware that we are not watching an autonomous character in a story, but are learning, through the brilliant series of images, something about love. The more 'digressive' parts of Faux Semblant's confession shows us that Love is only part of a tangled web of human behaviour, operating through every aspect of life. The conclusion then returns to love in the narrower sense of L'Amant's pursuit of the Rose and shows it voluntarily, if blindly, involving itself with a dangerously destructive force. Or, to put it another way, 'the blinde lust', although it is potentially allied to Nature and can have its creative aspects, is all too likely to prove a destructive power. After all the ironies and ambiguities, Jean de Meun's conclusion leaves no room for doubt:

And Love answerde, 'I truste thee
Withoute borowe, for I wole noon.'
And Fals-Semblant, the theef, anoon,
Ryght in that ilke same place,
That hadde of tresoun al his face
Ryght blak withynne and whit withoute,
Thankyng hym, gan on his knees loute.

(C, 7328–34)

It is obvious that Chaucer approaches the figure of the Pardoner in a totally different way, although he uses many of the same devices to lay out his self-revelation. The initial reluctance of Faux Semblant, which serves as a warning of what is to come, is transferred to the more respectable part of the Pardoner's audience. He himself shows no reluctance to come forward. The gentils express it for him:

> But right anon thise gentils gonne to crye,
> 'Nay, lat hym telle us of no ribaudye!
> Telle us som moral thyng, that we may leere
> Som wit, and thanne wol we gladly heere.'
>
> (*CT* VI, 323–6)

This is a deliberate reminder of the figure presented to us in the General Prologue, certainly one of the most disreputable among the pilgrims and, moreover, set apart from them by his physical characteristics:

> A voys he hadde as smal as hath a goot.
> No berd hadde he, ne nevere sholde have;
> As smothe it was as it were late shave.
> I trowe he were a geldyng or a mare.
>
> (*CT* I, 688–91)

Chaucer does not re-emphasize this disability in any way which might be unacceptable to the gentle part of the audience until the end of the Pardoner's self-exposure, when he returns to it in no uncertain terms by pitting the Pardoner against Harry Bailey, the Host. The Host, as we have seen, acts, in many ways, as the norm for his section of the community, just as the Knight does for his and the Parson for the third, clerical, estate, Harry Bailey, the plain man, has his disadvantages as well as his advantages and can certainly not be taken as expressing standards which are Chaucer's own. As a literary critic, as we have seen, he knows what he likes and has a flair for the inept comment. His reaction to his fellow men is also a simple one, in so far as it is not restrained by the politeness due to the orders definitely above him. Confronted by a male, his mind runs on masculinity of an obvious kind. His remarks on the appearance of the Monk (and perhaps of the Nun's Priest)[35] are to the point:

> 'Thou woldest han been a tredefowel aright.
> Haddestow as greet a leeve, as thou hast myght,
> To parfourne al thy lust in engendrure,
> Thou haddest bigeten many a creature.
> Allas, why werestow so wyd a cope?'
>
> (*CT* VII, 1945–9)

He would certainly have approved of L'Amant's attitude to Nature's endowments in the *Roman*. The Pardoner, unfortunately, is not in a position to share L'Amant's enthusiasm, and the Host harps mercilessly on this theme in his angry rejection of the Pardoner's invitation to be the first to kiss his relics. The whole ending, by which the Pardoner's discourse merges into the link by being interrupted, rather than concluded, by the heated comments of the Host[36] and the hasty peacemaking of the Knight, is brilliantly contrived to expose the Pardoner, not as he sees himself – he has already done this – but as he really is. It leaves him as a personality which, for all his dubious friendship with the Summoner, cannot win popularity from the Harry Baileys of his world (the world of the gentles is, of course, utterly closed to him). Chaucer builds up this section on the basis of the Pardoner's attempt to conquer this difficult part of his audience through a personal attack on the Host, aimed either at his subjugation or at the turning of the rest decisively against him by making him a laughing stock:

> 'Looke which a seuretee is it to yow alle
> That I am in youre felaweshipe yfalle,
> That may assoille yow, bothe moore and lasse,
> Whan that the soule shal fro the body passe.
> I rede that oure Hoost heere shal bigynne,
> For he is moost envoluped in synne.
> Com forth, sire Hoost, and offre first anon,
> And thou shalt kisse the relikes everychon,
> Ye, for a grote! Unbokele anon thy purs.'
>
> (*CT* VI, 937–45)

Then comes the Host's ruthless and accurate counterattack, followed by the almost disproportionate intensity of the Pardoner's reaction, after the supreme self-confidence of his confessions:

> This Pardoner answerde nat a word;
> So wrooth he was, no word ne wolde he seye.
>
> (956–7)

This sudden reversal of his euphoric mood brings home to us the reality of his problem of gaining appreciation and recognition. Finally, the Host's contemptuous dismissal:

'I wol no lenger pleye
With thee, ne with noon oother angry man.'

(958-9)

confirms the total failure of his attempt. Far from winning over his audience to laugh with him, they are now united against him: 'al the peple lough'. The Knight's intervention to resolve a situation which has become a serious threat to the good order of the pilgrimage further emphasizes the explosive quality of this strange eruption of feeling. The whole episode clearly points up the difference between the Pardoner and Faux Semblant. Faux Semblant is only describing the nature of those things which he symbolizes. His confessions cannot arouse personal feeling. An occasional expression of outraged amusement from his audience is the most that can be allowed; and this is only a device to break up his speeches and enliven the discourse by giving it the semblance of dialogue. In the case of the Pardoner, we are shown, by the final clash with the Host, the fundamental cleavage between his view of the world and that of his audience, as well as a subtle distinction between his view of his own evil-doing – frank as it is – and that of an unsympathetic on-looker.

To overemphasize the Pardoner's lack of normal masculinity and its social consequences would be misleading. We must not introduce twentieth-century perceptiveness or twentieth-century tolerance into a comic situation which, in the main, depends on the assumption of medieval ideas about the *eunuchus ex nativitate*.[37] We cannot, however, ignore Chaucer's own deliberate confrontation of the two characters whom he has caused to stand for an almost aggressively normal masculinity and its equally obvious lack. To see the whole nature and problem of the Pardoner, and his special needs and reactions, as the carefully worked out result of his deviation from the physical norm would be to saddle Chaucer with preoccupations which he almost certainly does not have. Besides the *eunuchus ex nativitate*, he shows us a go-getter, a successful huckster, a man dominated by a vanity which makes it impossible for him to believe that others do not, at bottom, share his view of life. All these characteristics help to provide a naturalistic motivation for the extravagance of his frankness about himself. This kind of motivation is, of course, never needed for the confessions of personifications like Faux Semblant, but the way in which the character of the Pardoner is worked up suggests that Chaucer was well aware that, in borrowing the self-revelatory device proper to the allegorical vice for a figure conceived in naturalistic terms, much care was needed in providing a measure of probability for the confession. Like the corresponding vice figure, the Pardoner is aware of the virtue which, as it were, stands opposite to him; but, unlike the vice figure, he sees this as a part of the justification of his own cleverness. His acknowledgement of the falseness of his own pardons, and his brazen admission of his understanding of where truth really lies, comes as the crowning stroke to the whole confidence trick:

> 'I yow assoille, by myn heigh power,
> Yow that wol offre, as clene and eek as cleer
> As ye were born. – And lo, sires, thus I preche.
> And Jhesu Crist, that is oure soules leche,
> So graunte yow his pardoun to receyve,
> For that is best; I wol yow nat deceyve.'
>
> (913–18)

This is, too, the justification of the violence of the Host's reaction. Like Faux Semblant, the Pardoner has no redeeming features – unless, seeing him as a figure of comedy rather than of satire, we take into account his supremacy in life and vigour. But, while the fact that Love, the personification, admits Faux Semblant to his retinue, in spite of the knowledge that he is 'Right blak withinne and whit withoute', gives us information about love as an idea, the fact that the pilgrims do not accept the Pardoner on such easy terms, and do not share his view either of himself or of the world, gives us information about him, and them, as individuals. That they see in him cause for laughter, extends his impotence from the physical to the moral sphere – a sphere in which Faux Semblant is, of course, effective.

Faux Semblant shares with the Pardoner knowledge of the good whose rejection is a condition of his own existence. It is an essential part of the method of the satire that he should refer to the 'cursedness' and 'orribilite' of the Joachimite work which the good clerks of Paris expose, even while he still refers to it as 'our book', and remarks sadly:

> 'But hadde that ilke book endured,
> Of better estat I were ensured.'
>
> (C, 7209–10)

In the same way he speaks frankly about the good Christian's opposition to him and to his works:

> 'But he in Cristis wrath hym ledith,
> That more than Crist my britheren dredith.
> He nys no full good champioun,
> That dredith such simulacioun,
> Nor that for peyne wole refusen
> Us to correcte and accusen
> He wole not entremete by right,
> Ne have God in his eye-sight,
> And therfore God shal hym punyshe.'
>
> (C, 7225-33)

This kind of double vision is a fundamental part of Jean de Meun's satiric method and is, indeed, common to most vice figures. They tend to inhabit a world in which they automatically call into being their opposites and exist as the half of a kind of double image. Thus, most self-exposés contain warnings against the vice involved and reminders of the fate which will result from indulgence in it.[38] For medieval allegorical satirists, in fact, the idea that evil is the absence of good is ever present. To present vice without showing that it is only the attendant shadow of the corresponding virtue is unacceptable. In the Pardoner's case, however, the success of his trickery depends on his own appreciation of the reality for which he offers a shoddy substitute. If pardon for sin were not a reality for which mankind craved, it would not be possible for him to batten on their need. The result is something much more shocking than is the portrait of a Faux Semblant which teaches intellectual understanding of truth by the method of opposites.

Much of our understanding of the Pardoner and of his situation comes from his contacts with his fellow pilgrims at the beginning and end of his 'sermon'. But, by a skilful stroke, Chaucer extends the revelation through the discourse. All that the Pardoner says, in the introductory section on swearing and gluttony, and in the tale of the search for death (one of the most effectively constructed in the whole series), adds up to 'an honest thyng'. It is thus not only that the Pardoner condemns himself through his direct version of the way in which, like the wicked who ask Fame to grant that they be known as wicked, he would like to be regarded. He also, inexorably and

226

at length, gives full expression to values which are the reverse of those he himself holds and which, if he were an allegorical vice personification, would belong to his better half. The whole complex – prologue, introduction, tale and end-link – is designed as a whole, rounded and complete, and Chaucer achieves this result by taking over and adapting in an extremely subtle way the methods of allegorical satire. The result, although the tendency is certainly towards a naturalistic conception of character, is still, perhaps, not wholly naturalistic. Chaucer has not quite bridged the gap between the kind of presentation in which the confession can be accepted as a necessary and inevitable part of the exposition and that in which it needs a motivation in keeping with the laws of probability. In his treatment of the other two figures which are derived from the stock types of allegorical satire – the Wife of Bath and January – he is able to solve the problem more completely, largely because the figures can take their *raison d'être* from their close involvement with the marriage theme. This gives them both a convincing environment and good reason for all they say and do.[39]

Chaucerian comedy has, typically, little in common with romantic comedy, if we can take the latter as characteristically involving the audience sympathetically with the characters and action. His method is, rather, to present us with typical individuals – that is, with figures which are not so particularized as to stand quite apart from the class or sub-section of society to which they belong, but which are also far from standing only for a type or class – who, through folly, eccentricity, out-and-out vice or even (in the Pardoner's case) physical abnormality, are at odds with an accepted and socially desirable norm. These he develops by all possible methods: detailed description; self-revelation within and without the tales; reaction to and from other individuals. At the same time he establishes the norm partly through characters who are not foolish, wicked or in any other way obviously abnormal (we have noticed that he gives us, significantly, one for each order of society – the Knight and Parson, who may be taken as providing absolute standards; and the Host, who has the cruder and more limited, but still sound, approach of his part of the social order) – and partly by oblique reference or even significant absence of reference, which helps to establish the importance of the observer, in whose function the reader is made to share and whose view of the world is always a wider one than that of the comic characters.

227

We cannot, I think, say of the spirit of Chaucerian comedy that it is especially kindly. This is hardly the epithet for the rough justice of broken arms and heads or 'scalding in the tout'. The illusion of a wide tolerance, too, surely arises mainly from the obliqueness of the narrator's comments and in part from a connoisseur's delight in the surpassing excellence of the specimens under the microscope. Chaucer's praise of the steed of brass in the *Squire's Tale*, that it 'was so horsly', could, *mutatis mutandis*, be applied to most of the pilgrims. There are, it is true, the moments of understanding of the most unpromising characters – Malkin's pleasure in her clerk; the Wife of Bath's momentary loss of confidence when she remembers her age; the appreciation of May's predicament in bed with January – but, by and large, Chaucer treats his characters with an open-eyed consistency in which justice is the ruling principle. In the case of the Pardoner, his eyes are perhaps even too widely open for modern taste. Yet Chaucer's comedy, with all this, is never inhuman; there is never any suggestion of a mere mechanical casting up of accounts in which everyone gets their true deserts. Probably the best summing up on the characters of his comic world is that of a poet writing near his own time:[40]

> It seemith vnto mannys heerynge
> Not only the word but verely the thing.

7

The *Canterbury Tales*:
major themes

To show in detail how all the recurring themes, major and minor, are worked out in the *Canterbury Tales* would require a line-by-line reading and cross-referencing; and, in the process, there would be some danger that the integrity and effectiveness of the tales themselves would be lost sight of. This, after all, is the great achievement of the *Canterbury Tales*: that while it is true, as T. W. Craik puts it, 'that the story itself, *as* story, has a personality of its own',[1] yet it is still essential, if we are to appreciate the full force and the many dimensions of Chaucerian poetry, to read the series as a whole. There is danger if we are too forcible in disengaging ideas and themes from their context within a tale; but, on the other hand, the tales lose in depth of meaning if we fail to realize that they are often involved in a thematic development which extends beyond their individual context.

The method here will, therefore, be to take only a few major themes – those of Fortune and free will; of marriage in relation to Nature, and to order and disorder; of the nobleness of man[1a] – and to try to show their place both in the achievement of the individual tales in which they are important and in the development of the series as a whole. All these themes have already been discussed in relation to poems outside the Canterbury group and, within it, to the *Knight's Tale*. They form a closely related nexus, or, rather, they are part of a philosophically consistent way of looking at the world. There is, first, the fundamental theme of order *versus* disorder, which we have already seen as the leading one of the *Knight's Tale*. Order partakes of the nature of the One, perfect, stable, eternal, and is therefore directly ruled over by God. Disorder, on the other hand, partakes of the nature of multiplicity, instability and impermanence – all characteristics of the created world below the moon, which becomes more and more imperfect the further it is removed from the One from which it takes its being. The world below the moon is subject to Fortune and, in close association with Fortune, to the planets. These have power delegated to them from the One, as does Nature. Nature symbolizes the divine purpose of achieving a modicum of order out of the disorder of the world, so far removed from the perfection from which it originally sprang. But it is the very perfection of the originating One which ensures the infinite variety of Nature. Nature, therefore, while she works for order, also works with Venus, natural sexual passion, to bring about the continued propagation of the whole gamut of creatures. In the case of mankind, however, Venus all too often goes astray, divorces herself from Nature and nullifies her plan by making passion barren. Man, in fact, occupies a key position in the world of change. On the one hand, he can spoil the order which the divine plan is always working to introduce into its multiplicity. On the other, because, unlike any other creature, he is made in the image of the One, he has a potential for order far beyond any other of Nature's charges. If man is considered from the point of view of this key position in the natural world, marriage becomes the point at which he is able to exert the greatest force in either direction – for order or disorder. This is because it is through marriage that mankind achieves its fullest expression and perfection in the natural order – as Langland puts it, mankind is incomplete unless it develops into a trinity of man–wife–child.[2] Through the negation of marriage – the refusal to allow this trinity to come into being – mankind can bring about the maximum disruption in the natural order. It must, of course, be emphasized (although Langland goes pretty far in his parallelism of the human and divine trinities) that this is not the only possible way of looking at man. Yet to see man as the turning point in the natural order, by means of his direct link with the originating One, bypassing, as it were, all the descending hierarchies and so becoming the means of a fulfilment in perfection otherwise denied to Nature, is certainly to give him no insignificant position in the universe.

As far as individuals are concerned, this means that, for good, the emphasis is on the 'noble' man or woman, created in God's image and behaving 'gentilly'. In the case of women, the ideal is the good wife, 'womanly' and not 'mannish wood', who acts as an influence for order both in her husband's affairs and in the affairs of nations. On the opposite side, motivated not by love but by 'the blinde lust', we have mankind in pursuit of all the deadly sins, but especially of the violation of marriage either through direct adultery or through the barren and fleeting love outside marriage which brings with it strife and jealousy, sickness of mind and body, and every sort of disorder. This is the picture we are shown, above all, in the *Knight's Tale* and which underlies the *Canterbury Tales* as a whole.

In the *Knight's Tale* the major themes are formally presented, through the deliberate patterning of the story and through passages which are explicitly philosophical. This method of presentation is balanced by the equally formal methods, in another mode, of the *Parson's Tale*. But in between, the method is often quite different, and it is here, in tales like the Miller's and the Reeve's, the Pardoner's and the Nun's Priest's, that, if we try to see the total meaning of the *Canterbury Tales* as equally present in every part, we shall seriously distort the nature of Chaucer's art. In fact, instead of giving us the comparatively systematic exposition of ideas and themes of, for example, Langland or Jean de Meun, Chaucer places us within a world where such ideas are ruling principles, whose presence or absence is an important factor in the lives of the people who inhabit it. Unlike the allegorists, Chaucer handles his themes naturalistically, as Shakespeare was to do in drama and Henry James in the novel. Langland utilizes the basically non-naturalistic convention of allegory, which always follows a logic of its own and which can, at any given moment, cut straight across the logic of naturalism. In this sense allegory is always analytic rather than descriptive: that is, the whole selection and ordering of the material is conditioned by the structure of the ideas to be expressed, and it is no concern of the poet if clarity of exposition is obtained at the expense of natural probability. There is, thus, no reason within allegory why a character called *Activa Vita* should not be presented with a concomitant which, to begin with, seems meant to be visualized – a dirty cloak – but which turns out to be a purely explanatory device for introducing a structurally essential résumé of the material of an earlier part of the poem. Chaucer, as we have seen, deliberately rejects this method in the case of Nature in the *Parlement*, when he refuses to describe just such a garment as *Activa Vita* was wearing and places its ornaments, as living creatures in a real woodland, at their lady's feet.³ Any exercise of critical ingenuity designed to get the goose, cuckoo and duck back on the fabric is inevitably perverse; and, in the same way, the characters of the churls' tales cannot, by more than the most distant implication, be pinned down within the strict schema of either the *Knight's* or the *Parson's Tales*.

It is important to emphasize the difference between the two methods. If we regard Chaucer as hiding under the variety of his tales the expository, schematic method, we shall find that we are introducing clearcut dividing lines where he has placed none. We shall, in fact, begin to regard all the characters who are not wholly good as wholly bad – with the result that the spirit of comedy will be lost. In fact, Chaucer presents us with a much more complex world, in which important contributions to the themes of *gentilesse* and patience – essential parts of true nobility – are made by the far from ideal Wife of Bath and in which the Pardoner, a character on whose behalf very little can be said, reaffirms the theme of the stable Lord of unstable Fortune and indicates the boundary between permanence and impermanence in no uncertain terms. We are never presented with anything approaching a *psychomachia* in the *Canterbury Tales* – or, indeed, anywhere in Chaucer's poetry. Far from externalizing the inevitable conflicts in the human soul, Chaucer does more to internalize them than any medieval writer before him and has, as a result, an approach to characterization which is both complex and essentially naturalistic. We need only compare the characters of an old-fashioned religious romance, the *Man of Law's Tale*, where the types do to some extent stand out clearcut, like vices and virtues in conflict, with even those of the *Clerk's Tale*, where the treatment is still not entirely naturalistic, to see clearly the direction in which Chaucer is moving. If we go on from there to his presentation of the Wife of Bath or of the Pardoner, we can form some estimate of the distance he actually travelled.

It is not only in his approach to characterization that Chaucer favours complexity. His view of the natural world, as I have tried to show in the case of the *Knight's Tale*, is not that it is simply divided between order and disorder. Nature, ruler of the creatures which inhabit the delusive world of change, is God's vicaire and works to bring about His plan of ordered change. Venus can work with her, as well as against her. Fortune, even though men abuse her, is also part of the divine plan and acknowledges God as her lord. Even the apparent conflict between submission to Fortune and the exertion of human free will is not a true confrontation. It consists rather in putting Fortune in the right place in the scheme of things than in setting her aside.[4] Most of the characters of the *Canterbury Tales* abuse their freedom of will and willingly bind themselves to Fortune's wheel, just as most of the plaintiffs in the *House of Fame* willingly submit to Fame's rather similar vagaries. But there are a number who do not, and who show us the reverse side of the picture.

Fortune and free will

The most clearcut discussion of the problem of Fortune and free will is provided by the *Man of Law's Tale*. The *Knight's Tale* had stated the problem and had examined it and provided a solution in philosophical terms. The *Man of Law's Tale* uses the hagiographic romance to present the explicitly Christian solution. This operates in two ways. In the first place, although Constance is shown as being peculiarly the victim of Fortune and of adverse planetary influences, she is also shown as exercising an unswerving freedom of will towards Christian virtue. Secondly, in support of Constance's will to virtue, we are shown direct divine intervention in the world, running, apparently, counter to the machinations of Fortune. As these two things – the heroic sovereignty of the human will and the possibility of direct divine intervention in the world – were precisely what the saint's legend was developed to demonstrate, Chaucer's choice of a story of this kind is particularly apt.[5] Nevertheless, I think that the importance of the tale to him, as far as its inclusion in the Canterbury series is concerned, was as a further comment on the theme of Fortune and free will; it is not developed as a religious poem in its own right. Here again, the hybrid form – this is not a saint's legend pure and simple, but a saintly romance (an equally well established, but different, genre)[6] – lends itself well to Chaucer's purpose. The tale of Constance, moreover, is particularly well adapted to this purpose. Her very name reminds us of the most essential Christian virtue with which Fortune must be opposed, and her sea voyages (although Chaucer does not stress the point) cannot fail to suggest one of the most usual figures for the Christian life on earth.

From the beginning of the tale, the astrological indications, which are bad, are carefully set against prayers for God's intervention. The fate of the pagan Sowdan is treated summarily. In his case the decree of the heavens cannot be circumvented:

> Paraventure in thilke large book
> Which that men clepe the hevene ywriten was
> With sterres, whan that he his birthe took,
> That he for love sholde han his deeth, allas!
> For in the sterres, clerer than is glas,
> Is writen, God woot! whoso koude it rede,
> The deeth of every man, withouten drede
>
> (*CT* II, 190–6)

Apart from the adverse state of the stars at his nativity, the moment chosen for the marriage is a bad one:

> O firste moevyng! crueel firmament,
> With thy diurnal sweigh that crowdest ay
> And hurlest al from est til occident
> That naturelly wolde holde another way,
> Thy crowdyng set the hevene in swich array
> At the bigynnyng of this fiers viage,
> That crueel Mars hath slayn this mariage.
>
> Infortunat ascendent tortuous,
> Of which the lord is helplees falle, allas,
> Out of his angle into the derkeste hous!
> O Mars, o atazir, as in this cas!
> O fieble moone, unhappy been thy paas!
> Thou knyttest thee ther thou art nat receyved;
> Ther thou were weel, fro thennes artow weyved.
>
> (295–308)

To set against this dark picture[7] we have first the narrator's appeal:

> Now, faire Custance, almyghty God thee gyde!
> (245)

then the prayers of the people for a marriage which is planned 'in encrees of Cristes lawe deere' (237):

> And notified is thurghout the toun
> That every wight with greet devocioun
> Sholde preyen Crist that he this mariage
> Receyve in gree, and spede this viage;
>
> (256–9)

and, lastly, Constance's own prayer:

> 'But Crist, that starf for our redempcioun
> So yeve me grace his heestes to fulfille,
> I, wrecche womman, no fors though I spille!'
>
> (283–5)

All this helps to build up two ideas: that God might yet intervene to nullify the portents of the stars, as far as Constance is concerned; and, secondly, that the stars, in any case, rule over a world whose values are not necessarily those of the Christian. Constance is prepared to accept the evil fate the stars indicate, but suggests that Christ may yet bring good out of it.

It is not only the stars which are in opposition to Constance. She is also assailed, like the Stoic good man, by the inevitable alternations of Fortune. The marriage feast ends in the slaughter of the Sowdan and all the Christians except Constance:

> O sodeyn wo, that evere art successour
> To worldly blisse, spreynd with bitternesse!
> The ende of the joye of oure worldly labour!
> We occupieth the fyn of oure gladnesse.
> Herke this conseil for thy sikernesse:
> Upon thy glade day have in thy mynde
> The unwar wo or harm that comth bihynde.
>
> (421–7)

The same pattern manifests itself at the end of Constance's story:

> This kyng Alla, whan he his tyme say,
> With his Custance, his hooly wif so sweete,
> To Engelond been they come the righte way,
> Wher as they lyve in joye and in quiete.
> But litel while it lasteth, I yow heete,
> Joye of this world, for tyme wol nat abyde;
> Fro day to nyght it changeth as the tyde.

235

Who lyved euere in swich delit o day
That hym ne moeved outher conscience,
Or ire, or talent, or som kynnes affray,
Envye, or pride, or passion, or offence?
I ne seye but for this ende this sentence,
That litel while in joye or in plesance,
Lasteth the blisse of Alla with Custance.

(1128–41)

In neither passage, it is true, is Fortune actually mentioned. That it is meant is shown, I think, partly by the familiar Boethian pattern of alternations, partly by the phrase 'Lord of Fortune' used, at line 448, of Christ.[8] In lines 1128–41 Chaucer joins the Stoic idea of enslavement by the passions to the idea (also Stoic) of involvement in the inevitable chances and changes of the world. The best result of such involvement is only 'joye of this world' which, throughout the tale, by implication or direct statement, is carefully contrasted with 'the joye that lasteth everemo' (1076). He uses much the same phrase for the couple's time of bliss – 'in joye and in quiete' – as he does for that of Troilus and Criseyde which also proved brief and deceptive.[9] Indulgence of the passions, of course, lays a man peculiarly open to the adverse influences of the stars as well as to the blows of Fortune. Thus, at the beginning, Chaucer is careful to state that the Sowdan actually encounters the fate written for him in the stars because he succumbs to his passion for Constance:

al his lust and al his bisy cure
Was for to love hire while his lyf may dure.

(188–9)

'Lust' can mean 'pleasure' without any pejorative overtones; but with the intensifying 'al' and with the sense Chaucer elsewhere gives to 'business', of an entangling preoccupation with worldly affairs,[10] it seems likely that this is the 'blinde lust' which, in a cruder form, in the case of the wicked Steward, also terminates in death. The good king Alla, on the other hand, disclaims any 'lust' which is not in accord with Christ's pleasure:

'Welcome the sonde of Crist for everemoore
To me that am now lerned in his loore!
Lord, welcome be thy lust and thy plesaunce;
My lust I putte al in thyn ordinaunce.'

(760–3)

236

Here 'lust' includes Alla's love (a natural and virtuous one) of his wife and child; and, while the Sowdan was in the expectation of the joyful fulfilment of his 'lust', Alla speaks at a moment of great sorrow:

> Wo was this kyng whan he this lettre had sayn, –
>
> (757)

The incident in the plot which brings about this situation is not in itself very convincing. Chaucer takes no special trouble to give an air of probability to the unlikely news of the monstrous nature of the child born to Constance. He is not, indeed, concerned in this tale with realistic plot construction, but he *is* concerned with the exposition of certain themes and ideas, and for this purpose the old folk-tale motifs are well adapted. The tale is a suitable vehicle to show the good Christian undeservedly opposed to those alterna-tions of joy and sorrow which are characteristic of the movement of Fortune. These alternations pose the same problem which troubled the lovers, and especially Arcite, in the *Knight's Tale*. In the *Man of Law's Tale* the same question is asked by the messenger, but in a tone of not irreverent wonder, rather than with the passionate sense of injustice of Palamoun:[11]

> 'O myghty God, if that it be thy wille,
> Sith thou art rightful juge, how may it be
> That thou wolt suffren innocentz to spille,
> And wikked folk regne in prosperitee?'
>
> (813–16)

Constance meets this problem with unquestioning steadfastness:

> But nathalees she taketh in good entente
> The wyl of Crist, and knelynge on the stronde,
> She seyde, 'Lord, ay welcome be thy sonde!'
>
> (824–6)

The end of the poem, especially, is built round the idea of the inevitable alternations of joy and woe which make up earthly experience, contrasted with the permanent joy of heaven. Sorrow and joy are formally juxtaposed in the matching pair of stanzas which describe the recognition scene; and, again, the exposition of the theme becomes more important than probability. There is nothing in the situation which really justifies such lengthy lamentations, but there is good thematic reason for an excursus on woe to balance one on joy:

> Long was the sobbyng and the bitter peyne,
> Er that hir woful hertes myghte cesse;
> Greet was the pitee for to heere hem pleyne,
> Thurgh whiche pleintes gan hir wo encresse.
> I pray yow alle my labour to relesse;
> I may nat telle hir wo until to-morwe,
> I am so wery for to speke of sorwe.

> But finally, whan that the sothe is wist
> That Alla giltelees was of hir wo,
> I trowe an hundred tymes been they kist,
> And swich a blisse is ther bitwixt hem two
> That, save the joye that lasteth everemo,
> Ther is noon lyk that any creature
> Hath seyn or shal, whil that the world may dure.
>
> (1065-78)

This joy culminates in the couple's happy life together, 'wheras they live in joye and in quiete'; but the warning contained in the proviso 'save the joye that lasteth everemo' proves necessary. This, for Alla and Constance, is not the everlasting joy any more than it was for Troilus and Criseyde. It is the joy which belongs to the world, and, like the world, it does not 'dure'. It is, in fact, brought to an end by the death of Alla. Constance suffers this vicissitude as she does all others:

> Wepynge for tendrenesse in herte blithe,
> She heryeth God an hundred thousand sithe.
>
> (1154-5)

The narrator gives a final emphasis to the theme in the prayer with which such romances customarily end:

> Now Jhesu Crist, that of his myght may sende
> Joye after wo, governe us in his grace,
> And kepe us alle that been in this place!
>
> (1160-2)

Here the joy that Christ sends after sorrow is, no doubt, the everlasting joy of heaven; but the prayer is also an assertion of a faith, like that which Constance shows, in God as the origin of all the events, woeful or joyful, which can befall us. In fact, the substitution of Christ for Fortune, as the source of alternating joy and sorrow in the world, is complete.

This is a process which begins much earlier in the poem and which is, indeed, its main contribution to the development of the theme of Fortune and free will. After the *exclamatio* 'O sodeyn wo, that evere art successour / To worldly blisse . . .' (421 ff.), Chaucer gives us a brief description of the calamity which ends with the placing of Constance 'in a ship al steerelees'. The narrator then intervenes with a plea for her safety:

> O my Custance, ful of benignytee,
> O Emperoures yonge doghter deere,
> He that is lord of Fortune be thy steere!
> (446–8)

This is immediately followed by Constance's own prayer to the Cross, not for safety but

> 'Me fro the feend and fro his clawes kepe,
> The day that I shal drenchen in the depe.'
> (454–5)

Constance sails on the sea 'yeres and dayes', and the narrator again pauses to comment, and to answer any possible objections:

> Men myghten asken why she was nat slayn
> Eek at the feeste? who myghte hir body save?
> (470–1)

The answer concerns, first, the general purpose of miracles:

> God liste to shewe his wonderful myracle
> In hire, for we sholde seen his myghty werkis;
> (477–8)

and, secondly, affirms the goodness of God's providence, that is, answers in advance the question of why he suffers harm to come to innocents:

> Crist, which that is to every harm triacle,
> By certeine meenes ofte, as knowen clerkis,
> Dooth thyng for certein ende that ful derk is
> To mannes wit, that for oure ignorance
> Ne konne noght knowe his prudent purveiance.
>
> (479–83)

The examples of divine intervention are all well-known instances of God's direct action to alter the natural order of things, taken from the Old Testament. They are: the preservation of Daniel in the lion's den, Jonah and the whale, and the Israelite's crossing of the Red Sea. Then, in answer to the question 'Where myghte this womman mete and drynke have?' (498), the examples of the feeding of 'the Egipcien Marie in the cave' and of the feeding of the five thousand with the loaves and fishes are given. The point, in fact, is made at length, and with emphasis, that God alters the natural order of things in Constance's case, as he had done in other cases recorded in the Bible and in the Lives of the Saints. Since the natural order includes the manifestations of Fortune, which belongs, because of its changeable nature, to the world below the moon, it is obvious that 'he that is lord of Fortune' may also alter the fate which is prepared for Constance by the alternations of Fortune's wheel or by the stars. This, indeed, God does by preserving her miraculously from what appears to be a certain death by drowning; but Constance's true victory over Fortune and the stars is to come through the freedom of her will. The pattern of woe after joy, therefore, continues to work itself out in her life to the end. Her freedom consists not in God's removal of her troubles, but in her persistence in carrying out the injunction Chaucer gives us in *Truth*:

> Know thy contree, look up, thank God of al.

To preserve the heroine to the end, it is true, 'open myracle' is more than once needed, as each temporary period of ease is predictably followed by a new woe; but this does not alter her essential function, which is to stand as a type and example of the constant Christian assailed by Fortune. After she is falsely accused before Alla and her terror is described:

> Have ye nat seyn somtyme a pale face,
> Among a prees, of hym that hath be lad
> Toward his deeth, wher as hym gat no grace?
>
> (645–7)

Chaucer pauses to address 'queenes, lyvynge in prosperitee' and to contrast her fate with theirs. It would be familiar and normal to follow the opening lines of this stanza with a reference to the inevitable reversal in the lot of the queens – such prosperity, according to the way of the world, must be followed by its reverse. Instead, Chaucer makes Constance herself stand for the expected reversal of fortune and thus emphasizes her function in the poem:[12]

> O queenes, lyvynge in prosperitee,
> Duchesses, and ye ladyes everichone,
> Haveth som routhe on hire adversitee!
> An Emperoures doghter stant allone;
> She hath no wight to whom to make hire mone.
> O blood roial, that stondest in this drede,
> Fer been thy freendes at thy grete nede!
>
> (652–8)

This, like many other stanzas containing what is technically an *exclamatio*, or *invocatio*, is not really a sign of Chaucer's addiction to formal rhetoric in this poem, but rather of the way in which he chooses to step aside from his narrative and to emphasize its thematic material. We may feel that he shows greater art in poems in which the plot and the thematic development are more intimately related; but in the special case of the hagiographical narrative, this intimate relation is very difficult to achieve. The hagiographical plot is apt to be inherently improbable and to lack the specifically human values which make a more naturalistic treatment rewarding. It is essential that each stage of the action is placed not within the ordinary scheme of cause and effect which conditions ordinary human life, but within the particular manifestation of a divine purpose which the story is intended to describe. Chaucer shows a clear grasp of both the potentialities and the limitations of the saint's legend, both here and in the *Second Nun's Tale*; and, to judge from the *Retractions*, where he mentions with pride 'bookes of legendes of seyntes', he considered this an important part of his work. We can only judge his achievement in it with due consideration to the nature of the kind he is attempting, although in the case of the *Man of Law's Tale*, we can also admire the success with which he has used the genre to further the development of the theme of Fortune and free will and to provide the Christian answer to the problem as a complement to the philosophical solution of the *Knight's Tale*.

The heroine of the *Clerk's Tale*, like the heroine of the *Man of Law's Tale*, could stand as a type of the good Christian who resists the assaults of Fortune – this time by patience, the Christian virtue closely related to constancy.[13] A recent analysis of the tale by Barbara Bartholomew (*Fortuna and Natura: A Reading of Three Chaucer Narratives*) shows how far Chaucer has gone in relating the alternations of her affairs to the idea of chance and Fortune. The husband who, in her case, acts as the immediate cause of her misfortunes, is linked to Fortune from the moment when he is first introduced:

> A markys whilom lord was of that lond,
> As were his worthy eldres hym bifore;
> And obeisant, ay redy to his hond,
> Were alle his liges, bothe lasse and moore,
> Thus in delit he lyveth and hath doon yoore,
> Biloved and drad, thurgh favour of Fortune,
> Bothe of his lordes and of his commune.
>
> (64–70)

He is represented not only as 'the child of Good Fortune', but also as having the kind of impulsive nature which, as it causes him to indulge his passions freely, would place him peculiarly at Fortune's mercy. He thinks of marriage without any care for the future: 'on his lust present was al his thoght' (79). When he begins to try Griselda, the wish to do so is an overmastering, emotional one not a reasoned purpose:

> This markys in his herte longeth so
> To tempte his wyf, hir sadnesse for to knowe,
> That he ne myghte out of his herte throwe
> This merveillous desir his wyf t'assaye.
>
> (451–4)

Just so is Troilus unable to put his desire for Criseyde out of his mind or to see where it is leading him. In the event, because Griselda remains immovable and never for a moment abnegates her function as a true wife, Walter suffers no ill effects from his self-indulgence and, finally overcome, accepts marriage in its true function as a perfecting and unifying force. Marriage in the *Clerk's Tale*, in fact, has the same high significance which it had in the *Knight's Tale*. The closing stanzas emphasize this with a triple repetition:

242

> Ful many a yeer in heigh prosperitee
> Lyven thise two in *concord and in reste*,
> And richely his doghter maryed he
> Unto a lord, oon of the worthieste
> Of al Ytaille; and thanne in *pees and reste*
> His wyves fader in his court he kepeth,
> Til that the soule out of his body crepeth.
>
> His sone succedeth in his heritage
> In *reste and pees*, after his fader day,
> And fortunat was eek in mariage . . .
>
> (1128–37)

The reconciliation of Walter and Griselda in a perfect marriage brings a similar reconciliation to the other characters, and the peace and unity which is produced extends even to a later generation. To lead up to this satisfactory conclusion is certainly one of the main purposes of the tale – and if it were the only purpose, we should be in no difficulty over it. The Clerk's final comment, however, suggests another, additional purpose:

> This storie is seyd, nat for that wyves sholde
> Folwen Grisilde as in humylitee,
> For it were inportable, though they wolde,
> But for that every wight, in his degree,
> Sholde be constant in adversitee
> As was Grisilde; therfore Petrak writeth
> This storie, which with heigh stile he enditeth.
>
> (1142–8)

This suggests that we are to take the sufferings and triumph of Griselda as in some sense an allegory of the ways of God with the soul – and this too, would enable us to take a straightforward view of the story. Chaucer, however, hastens to disabuse us of this idea, in any simple sense:

> For, sith *a womman* was so pacient
> *Unto a mortal man*, wel moore us oghte
> Receyven al in gree that God us sent.
>
> (1149–51)

We are not, in fact, to think of Walter as anything but a mortal man or of Griselda as anything but a real wife. Indeed, after the careful build-up of Walter as the man of impulse – Will opposed to Griselda's Wit, or Sensuality to her Reason – we could hardly with propriety see him as standing for divine providence itself, although he is certainly its unconscious instrument.

The narrator is not the only one to reprove Walter for his conduct. Griselda herself shows a perfectly clearsighted appreciation of it; and, at the one point in the story where the utterance of a rebuke is possible without detriment to her wifely obedience, she does not hesitate:

> 'O thyng biseke I yow, and warne also,
> That ye ne prikke with no tormentynge
> This tendre mayden, as ye han doon mo:
> For she is fostred in hire norissynge
> Moore tendrely, and, to my supposynge,
> She koude nat adversitee endure
> As koude a povre fostred creature.'
>
> (1037–43)

This is the only point at which Griselda clearly tells Walter that his conduct is open to criticism. There is, however, one other point in the story which shows her as a living, reacting recipient of his torments, not merely as suffering them in passive endurance. This passage is important in establishing that Griselda, like Constance, opposes a free will to the onslaughts of Fortune. This is the moment when Walter dismisses her from his house, and she contrasts her own faithfulness:

> 'God shilde swich a lordes wyf to take
> Another man to housbonde or to make!'
>
> (839–40)

with his changeableness:

> 'But sooth is seyd – algate I fynde it trewe,
> For in effect it preeved is on me –
> Love is noght oold as whan that it is newe.'
>
> (855–7)

At this moment in the story, and at this moment only, Griselda is allowed an outburst of feeling which makes both touching and credible her final plea to Walter, as much for his sake as hers, when he attempts to send her naked away:

> 'O goode God! how gentil and how kynde
> Ye semed by youre speche and youre visage
> The day that maked was oure mariage! . . .
> Ye koude nat doon so dishonest a thyng,
> That thilke wombe in which youre children leye
> Sholde biforn the peple, in my walkyng,
> Be seyn al bare.'
>
> (852–79)

Yet it is in this very passage, in which both Walter and Griselda appear as most human, that there are the strongest overtones of something more than particular and individual humanity. Griselda's expression of her faithfulness, for one thing, is cast in the form of a resolution to live well in the life of widowhood just as she had done in that of virginity and marriage:

> 'Ther I was fostred of a child ful smal,
> Til I be deed, my lyf ther wol I lede,
> A wydwe clene in body, herte, and al.
> For sith I yaf to yow my maydenhede,
> And am youre trewe wyf. . . .'
>
> (834–8)

This reference to the three states of human life, in all of which Griselda lives in perfection, places her as an ideal type of humanity rather than as Walter's individual wife.[14] Again, in:

> 'Naked out of my fadres hous', quod she,
> 'I cam, and naked moot I turne agayn',
>
> (871–2)

the reminiscence of the burial service suggests that her plight is generalized into that of all mankind. Even more significant is the line:

'Lat me nat lyk a worm go by the weye'
(880)

which is hardly, as Robinson suggests, 'a stock comparison',[15] but a reference to Psalm 21:7: 'But I am a worm and no man; the reproach of men and the outcast of the people.' Since this verse was commonly applied to Christ,[16] the reference makes of Griselda's departure a *via dolorosa* in imitation of Christ. The suggestion that she lives out her life as an *imitatio Christi* is supported by other Biblical echoes. Her humble upbringing is described in terms which recall the Nativity:

But hye God somtyme senden kan
His grace into a litel oxes stalle
(206–7)

and:

And she set doun hir water pot anon,
Biside the thressh-fold, in an oxes stalle.
(290–1)

We might even see a similarity to the Blessed Virgin's reception of the Annunciation in Luke 1:38 – 'And Mary said: Behold the handmaid of the Lord; be it done to me according to thy word' – and Griselda's reply to Walter:

She seyde, 'Lord, undigne and unworthy
Am I to thilke honour that ye me beede,
But as ye wole youreself, right so wol I.'
(359–61)

Her silence and submission in her time of trial certainly recall that of Christ, and the comparison to the lamb points up the similarity:[17]

And as a lamb she sitteth meke and stille,
And leet this crueel sergeant doon his wille.
(538–9)

The cumulative effect of this treatment is to give to the figure of Griselda a depth of significance with which – and this is the crux of the matter – her wilful husband seems to have little to do. The poem fails – if it does fail – because the two main characters seem to operate on different planes of meaning. It is not, we feel, really quite fair to expose Walter to a quintessence of virtue more appropriate to the problems which humanity encounters in the religious life than to marriage. Griselda tames her husband, but an 'arche-wyve', 'strong as is a greet camaille', would have done it quicker and, perhaps, in a way more satisfactory to our sense of justice. So much, indeed, Chaucer seems to hint in his somewhat frivolous envoy. The story, in fact, suffers in part from an excess of meaning, in part from the very urbanity which makes it impossible for Chaucer to come down emphatically on one side or the other, and which ensures his success in so many other works. The themes of Fortune and free will, of marriage as a force for order and unity, of the soul in its *imitatio Christi* and also as the bride of a divinely incalculable bridegroom,[18] and of a conflict of Wit and Will – in which the normal order is amusingly inverted and Will, usually 'te fulitohe wif',[19] becomes the husband – are altogether too much for both the old folk-tale and the Chaucerian method of dealing unemphatically and sophisticatedly with the world of ideas. In his religious poetry, and even in the Man of Law's religious romance, Chaucer shows no such sophistication, but gives us a simple, single-hearted approach. In contrast, in its mingling of apparently secular elements with religious significances, the *Clerk's Tale* is like one of the religious artifacts of the fourteenth to fifteenth centuries which, increasingly, include the secular in their design – the richly bordered pages of missals, for example, which seem to aim as much at entertainment as piety, or the reliquaries in which the setting has little to do with the object of devotion.[20] Such works represent an aspect of late medieval sensibility with which it is, perhaps, difficult for us to come to terms. The secular and religious content seem to pull in different directions; and in a poem, which necessarily lacks the unifying factor of visible form and design, the difficulty is even greater than in a work of visual art. We must, however, accept it as a historical fact that works of this kind were popular and, presumably, capable of making an effective statement in the late fourteenth and early fifteenth centuries.

The characterization, too, which is partly in keeping with the older method, by which a character only exists in accordance with the requirements of a particular scene, or a given moment in the narrative, and is not required to show a consistency which extends through the story as a whole, involves a conflict with the newer, more naturalistic type which Chaucer usually prefers. Walter, like Emely, is called on by the narrative to stand at one moment in opposition to marriage through his apparent lack of love for his wife, and his separation of first mother and child and then even of the partners to the union, and at the next to take his place within a perfect married state – 'in concorde and in reste' – and unless he does so without reservation the story will not work. Yet in between he is consistently represented as a dominating, wilful character. In the same way, Griselda's lapses into naturalism tend to give the lie to behaviour which seems, in other places, to show her to us as a figure of symbolical depth and resonance. This poem, I believe, is Chaucer's one attempt to exploit that density of Christian significance and reference which is utilized with such virtuosity by Langland and by the *Pearl*-Poet. Although, in the process, he undoubtedly adds much to the development of his major themes in the *Canterbury Tales*, the method does not seem to have suited him. It needs a firmer choice between naturalism and the special formalism of allegory and its related kinds, and it needs, too, a stronger didacticism than Chaucer's urbanity ever makes possible to him.

The theme of Fortune is inevitably linked to that of free will, as far as Chaucer is concerned. This arises both from the Stoic conception of the inner self-sufficiency which stands unharmed in the face of all that Fortune can do, and from the Boethian conception of the freeing of the will as consisting in the clearing away of the clouds and mists of ignorance. For Boethius, and for Chaucer after him, a free choice is, inevitably, a choice of the good.[21] This means that it is not a theme which can play much part in the comic tales, where the wills of the characters are hardly free in this sense; they are certainly subject to the reversals of Fortune, but they contribute to their fate by their bad choices. The Miller gets his skull cracked, Absolon is scalded in the tout, old John the carpenter breaks his arm, and the begging Friar is humiliated through the ineluctable logic of events which they themselves help to set in motion, through their own folly or vice. In this sense we can say that even the lowest of the churls inhabit the same world as that in which their betters debate with high seriousness about Providence, destiny and free will; but unless we share some of their unawareness of such debates, we shall, as I have suggested, miss most of the comedy. An appreciation of the fundamental rightness of the rough justice of the tales and its ultimate compatibility with the world of the *Knight's Tale* is a part of our appreciation of Chaucerian comedy. But more than this has not been built into the tales, and any further reflections are ours, not Chaucer's.

Nevertheless, there are points at which the theme of Fortune and free will is allowed to penetrate the world of comedy. The *Monk's Tale* consists simply of a series of *exempla* of reversals of Fortune from good to bad, in illustration of the maxim:

> For certein, whan that Fortune list to flee,
> Ther may no man the cours of hire with-holde.
> Lat no man truste on blynd prosperitee,
> Be war by thise ensamples trewe and olde.
>
> (*CT* VII, 1995–8)

This is material which Chaucer uses perfectly seriously elsewhere – and, indeed, there is no reason to suppose that the *Monk's Tale* is not serious, as far as it goes. There is, however, an unusual flatness, a complacent, pounding beat in the verse which matches the flat superficiality of the conclusion. Certainly, the Monk does not go on to suggest any solution to the problem of Fortune's ravages, and the Knight is quick to point out the one-sidedness of his handling of the subject:

> 'Hoo!' quod the Knyght, 'good sire, namoore of this!
> That ye han seyd is right ynough, ywis. . . .
> I seye for me, it is a greet disese,
> Whereas men han been in greet welthe and ese,
> To heeren of hire sodeyn fal, allas!
> And the contrarie is joye and greet solas,
> As whan a man hath been in povre estaat,
> And clymbeth up and wexeth fortunat,
> And there abideth in prosperitee.
> Swich thyng is gladsom, as it thynketh me.'
>
> (*CT* VII, 2767–78)

This is the same criticism of incompleteness, delivered in much the same tone of voice, as that of the Eagle, when he points out that Chaucer the poet has so far had nothing to say about 'Loves folk yf they be glade'. The Host, in full agreement with the Knight, then gives his plain man's opinion. He has not understood a word, but he knows what he likes:

> 'Ye,' quod oure Hooste, 'by seint Poules belle!
> Ye seye right sooth; this Monk he clappeth lowde.
> He spak how Fortune covered with a clowde
> I noot nevere what; and als of a tragedie
> Right now ye herde, and, pardee no remedie
> It is for to biwaille ne compleyne
> That that is doon, and als it is a peyne,
> As ye han seyd, to heere of hevynesse.'
>
> (2780–7)

The *Nun's Priest's Tale* is closely linked to these reactions to the Monk's anecdotes of ill fortune, since it is to the Nun's Priest that the Host turns 'with rude speche and boold' to provide the desired contrast. It is not therefore surprising that the themes of Fortune and free will are woven into the burlesque tale of the cock and the fox, along with other solemnities.

From the beginning the actual farm-yard, described in plain terms, is set against the sophisticated accomplishments of its inhabitants:

> A yeerd she hadde, enclosed al aboute
> With stikkes, and a drye dych withoute,
> In which she hadde a cok, hight Chauntecleer.
> In al the land, of crowyng nas his peer.
> His voys was murier than the murie orgon
> On messe-dayes that in the chirche gon.
>
> (*CT* VII, 2847–52)

As the words lengthen and become more learned, so the cock's capabilities become more impressive:

> Wel sikerer was his crowyng in his logge
> Than is a clokke or an abbey orlogge.

> By nature he knew ech ascencioun
> Of the equynoxial in thilke toun;
> For whan degrees fiftene weren ascended,
> Thanne crew he, that it myghte nat been amended.
>
> (2855–8)

His wife, Dame Pertelote, shows an equally profound knowledge, this time of medicine, nicely adjusted to the hen-run:

> 'Now sire,' quod she, 'whan we flee fro the bemes,
> For Goddes love, as taak som laxatyf.
> Up peril of my soule and of my lyf,
> I conseille yow the beste, I wol nat lye,
> That bothe of colere and of malencolye
> Ye purge yow; and for ye shal nat tarie,
> Though in this toun is noon apothecarie,
> I shal myself to herbes techen yow
> That shul been for youre hele and for youre prow;
> And in oure yeerd tho herbes shal I fynde
> The whiche han of hire propretee by kynde
> To purge yow bynethe and eek above.'
>
> (2942–53)

Both are learned in the matter of dreams, which, Chauntecleer explains, may be prophetic and relate to the alternations of Fortune:

> '. . . dremes been significaciouns
> As wel of joye as of tribulaciouns
> That folk enduren in this lif present,'
>
> (2979–81)

He gives examples of dreams which warn a man of

> '. . . his aventure or his fortune,
> That us governeth alle as in commune; . . .'
>
> (2999—3000)

or of the disaster that comes about

> 'Noot I nat why, ne what *myschaunce* it eyled.'
>
> (3100)

His conclusion is 'That I shal han of this avisioun / Adversitee,' (3152–3), and he proceeds immediately to demonstrate that he is in full possession of the joy that comes before such inevitable woe:

> 'For whan I feele a-nyght your softe syde,
> Al be it that I may nat on yow ryde,
> For that oure perche is maad so narwe, allas!
> I am so ful of joye and of solas,
> That I diffye bothe sweven and dreem.'
> And with that word he fley doun from the beem,
> For it was day, and eke his hennes alle,
> And with a chuk he gan hem for to calle,
> For he hadde founde a corn, lay in the yerd.
> Real he was, he was namoore aferd.
>
> (3167–76)

Chauntecleer is at the top of Fortune's wheel, both as king of his farm-yard – 'as a prince is in his halle' – and as successful lover:

> He fethered Pertelote twenty tyme,
> And trad hir eke as ofte, er it was pryme.
>
> (3177–8)

His fall is inevitable:

> For evere the latter ende of joye is wo.
> God woot that worldly joye is soone ago,
>
> (3205–6)

and the sad contrast provokes a long passage of learned lamentation from the Nun's Priest, in the course of which he insinuates part of the answer to the problem which had been lacking in the *Monk's Tale*. This consists, of course, in the discussion of necessity and free will – as to which the Nun's Priest refuses to adjudicate since 'My tale is of a cok, as ye may heere':

> O Chauntecleer, acursed be that morwe
> That thou into that yerd flaugh from the bemes!
> Thou were ful wel ywarned by thy dremes
> That thilke day was perilous to thee;
> But what that God forwoot moot nedes bee,

> After the opinioun of certein clerkis,
> Witnesse on hym that any parfit clerk is,
> That in scole is greet altercacioun
> In this mateere, and greet disputisoun,
> And hath been of an hundred thousand men.
> But I ne kan nat bulte it to the bren
> As kan the hooly doctour Augustyn,
> Or Boece, or the Bisshop Bradwardyn,
> Wheither that Goddes worthy forwityng
> Streyneth me nedely for to doon a thyng, –
> 'Nedely' clepe I symple necessitee;
> Or elles, if free choys be graunted me
> To do that same thyng, or do it noght,
> Though God forwoot it er that it was wroght;
> Or if his wityng streyneth never a deel
> But by necessitee condicioneel.
> I wol nat han to do of swich mateere;
> My tale is of a cok, as ye may heere.
>
> (3230–52)

The passage is a nice instance of the manner in which Chaucer suggests ideas clearly known to him, and, it is assumed, to his reader, through the modest confusion of a less percipient character. In the same way, though to sadder effect, Troilus gives a confused and partial rendering of the argument.

When Chauntecleer has finally encountered the inevitable reversal of Fortune, Chaucer breaks into a further lengthy passage of mock-heroic ejaculation, whose opening lines, the appeal to destiny and to Venus, make it perfectly clear on which side he stands in the argument of destiny and free will. Why, he asks, did Chauntecleer and Pertelote not use their freedom of choice to better effect and so avoid the unavoidable:

> O destinee, that mayst nat been eschewed!
> Allas, that Chauntecleer fleigh fro the bemes!
> Allas, his wyf ne roghte nat of dremes!
>
> (3338–40)

Moreover, it happened on a Friday, the day dedicated to Venus:

253

> O Venus, that art goddesse of plesaunce,
> Syn that thy servant was this Chauntecleer,
> And in thy servyce dide al his poweer,
> Moore for delit than world to multiplye,
> Why woldestow suffre hym on thy day to dye?
>
> (3342-6)

Chauntecleer, it would seem, has been indulging his passions in a manner contrary to Nature's purpose – the Venus invoked is the fallen one. He has thus placed himself peculiarly at the mercy of Fortune – and, as the *moralitas* points out, has got exactly what he asked for:

> Lo, swich it is for to be recchelees,
> And necligent, and truste on flaterye.
>
> (3436-7)

Unlike the ostensible attitude of the rhetorically magnificent passages of lamentation over the cock's fate, the *moralitas* comes down bluntly on the side of personal responsibility. Fortunately for Chauntecleer, however, the fox is equally 'recchelees', and the story, as required by the host, ends happily – a double joy, not, as in Troilus's case, a double sorrow. The fox in his turn experiences a reversal of Fortune:

> Lo, how Fortune turneth sodeynly
> The hope and pryde eek of hir enemy!
>
> (3403-4)

The whole story thus depends on the theme of Fortune, which had been dealt with by the Monk without the complementary one of free will and is now restored to its proper proportions. But there is much more to the tale than this. The very fact of the humorous, mock-heroic treatment adds a new dimension to the whole discussion of Fortune. It is salutary to watch the silly cock, with ideas above his station, tripping up through precisely the same kind of obtuseness and self-deception as the characters of the serious, philosophic poems. 'My tale is of a cok, as ye may heer', and the Nun's Priest does not force us to translate the behaviour of the birds into human terms, any more than Chaucer himself enforces the comparison between

Chauntecleer's sensuous delight in Pertelote, 'whan I feele a-nyght your softe syde', with that of Troilus in Criseyde, when 'Hire sydes longe, flesshly, smothe, and white / He gan to stroke'. This is not parody nor the debasement of a noble passage, but a reminder that Nature deals with all her creatures in ways which are basically the same. Chaucer's strength is that he never shows an inclination to deny dissimilitude through the assertion of similarity. His mood is as far as possible from Lear's in his sickness of mind, or even from the more light-heartedly sardonic insinuations of the Middle English Lyric:[22]

> Wormes woweþ vnder cloude;
> Wymmen waxeþ wounder proude.

Chaucerian comedy does not thrive through the debasing of the subtle and the beautiful. It has a place for the cock, whose sensuous satisfaction is somewhat diminished by the exigencies of the perch, and also for the man, who has other problems. If it compares, it is to differentiate as much as to draw together.

Another element in the tale arises through the Monk's attitude to Fortune. He had failed to distinguish between cases of bad luck and cases of bad judgement in his opening examples – the fall of the angels, for which he apologizes himself, and the fall of Adam, which were due to the abuse of free will.[23] The fall of Adam is also a type of the failure of marriage and the disruption in the order of things which it causes, since the marriage of Adam and Eve in Paradise, in which they are joined by God himself, is the type of all good marriages. Within the limitations of the humorous, mock-heroic tale, the Nun's Priest picks up the idea of the failure of Adam and Eve to use their free will rightly and also glances at the rôle of Eve as the wife who did her husband no good. Appropriately to the new setting, the story is stood on its head – it is poor Pertelote's housewifely medical advice and sound common sense which has to bear the blame for Chauntecleer's downfall.

As the catastrophe draws near, the first, oblique, comparison of Chauntecleer's state to that of Adam is made:

> Whan that the month in which the world bigan,
> That highte March, whan God first maked man,
> Was compleet, and passed were also,
> Syn March bigan, thritty dayes and two,

> Bifel that Chauntecleer in al his pryde,
> His sevene wyves walkynge by his syde,
> Caste up his eyen to the brighte sonne. . . .
>
> (3187–93)

Chauntecleer inhabits the yard which is his paradisial garden in a state of pride and outdoes Adam in the ownership of seven wives, all, alas, utilized 'Moore for delit than world to multiplye!' His experience is, however, so much like Adam's that even one of the seven is enough for his undoing:

> Wommennes conseils been ful ofte colde;
> Wommannes conseil broghte us first to wo,
> And made Adam fro Paradys to go,
> Ther as he was ful myrie and wel at ese.
>
> (3256–9)

Adam's happiness in paradise is made to sound very like Chauntecleer's – 'I am so ful of joye and of solas'. Just as Adam came to grief by paying attention to his wife's bad advice, so the foolish cock falls into the fox's jaws through attending not so much to his wife's common sense, as to her charms – 'Ye been so scarlet reed aboute youre yen' – which lull him into false security. The comedy of folly and conceit, solemnly examined in terms of destiny and free will, is enhanced by the oblique comparison with the Fall. But comedy is eliminated if we press the comparison too hard. The splendid bathos of the final human intervention in the story after the high flight, in which the woeful hens are compared to Priam's mourning wives and to Nero's senators when Rome was burned, would hardly make its point if the tale were to be taken as a moral allegory:[24]

> Ran Colle oure dogge, and Talbot and Gerland,
> And Malkyn, with a dystaf in hir hand;
> Ran cow and calf, and eek the verray hogges,
> So fered for the berkyng of the dogges
> And shoutyng of the men and wommen eeke,
> They ronne so hem thoughte hir herte breeke.
> They yolleden as feendes doon in helle;
> The dokes cryden as men wolde hem quelle;
> The gees for feere flowen over the trees;
> Out of the hyve cam the swarm of bees . . . .

Of bras they broghten bemes, and of box,
Of horn, of boon, in whiche they blewe and powped,
And therwithal they skriked and they howped.
It seemed as that hevene sholde falle.

(3383–401)

With this final crescendo of noise and confusion, Chaucer makes an abrupt transition back to the quiet, even tone of the fable narrative and the deluded world of the animals:

Now, goode men, I prey yow herkneth alle:
Lo, how Fortune turneth sodeynly
The hope and pryde eek of hir enemy!

(3402–4)

and so on to the final trickery which saves the cock.

The juxtaposition of the human and animal world is an essential part of the comic method in this tale. Chauntecleer, his seven wives and his kingdom of the farm-yard do not form an autonomous world, as is sometimes the case in fable. They are the possessions of a good widow, quite seriously and fully described in the opening as living the life of patient poverty in widowhood – the kind of life Griselda proposed going back to after her rejection by her husband:

This wydwe, of which I telle yow my tale
Syn thilke day that she was last a wyf,
In pacience ladde a ful symple lyf.

(2824–6)

Her life is described in the manner of the General Prologue:

No deyntee morsel passed thurgh hir throte;
Hir diete was accordant to hir cote.
Repleccioun ne made hire nevere sik;
Attempree diete was al hir phisik,
And exercise and hertes suffisaunce.

(2835–9)

It is out of this good widow's spare and sober way of life that all the exuberance and all the delusions of the world of Chauntecleer and Pertelote grow, until at last the human world erupts into the animal one, in an energetic and breathless attempt to rescue a valuable piece of property. This treatment of the human and the animal on two different levels, each blissfully unaware of the other's mode of experiencing life and each pursuing its ends with equal vigour and determination, is responsible for much of the comic effect of the tale.

Marriage

The *Knight's Tale*, as we have seen, depends for its denouement on a philosophical conception of marriage, both as a symbol of perfection and completeness and as an actual means of producing creative order in the natural world. The *Man of Law's Tale* and the *Clerk's Tale* develop the idea of marriage on a similarly philosophical basis. In the *Man of Law's Tale* philosophy is given a specifically Christian orientation, and marriage, like everything else below the moon, is seen primarily as part of the pattern of change which characterizes the world and contrasts with heaven. This viewpoint is not denied in the *Knight's Tale*. It is rather that the end of this tale shows us the pattern which marriage imposes on events, as it were, for a moment outside time, with the emphasis on achievement rather than on the continuity of the process. In the *Man of Law's Tale* all the emphasis is on temporal process, since life is always seen from the explicitly Christian viewpoint, *sub specie aeternitatis*. Constance achieves happiness through marriage and respite from change, but, since her eyes are fixed on the eternal stability, this moment of rest in the cyclic alternations of the world is not abstracted. It remains a part of the never-ending pattern of change, and her happiness in marriage, like everything else in nature, is brought to an end by death.

Although Constance's marriages thus certainly tend towards the achievement of some degree of stabilization in her own life and in the proper conduct of political affairs,[25] the achievement of stability within the temporal process is not the main theme. In the *Clerk's Tale*, on the other hand, as in the Knight's the degree to which marriage can bring about stability in the life of the individual and the state is one of the main interests.[26] Chaucer does not explicitly look beyond this within the framework of the tale, although other values are suggested by the Clerk's epilogue and are implicit in the way in which the figure of Griselda is treated.

These three tales – the Knight's, the Man of Law's and the Clerk's – all give us more or less abstract treatments of marriage as an archetype of order and stability in the natural world. The *Nun's Priest's Tale* provides a comic reversal of the picture in which the married life of the cock and his hens contributes to his downfall and leads to disorder instead of order. But this is by no means Chaucer's only interest in the theme of marriage. The ideal pattern, seen as a part of the mechanics and, indeed, of the very stuff of which the natural world is made, is important to him. But he shows, in numerous tales, that he also appreciates that the pattern is worked out as much through the interaction of human personalities as in the marriage of numbers which subdues the war of opposites and holds together the fabric of matter. This more personal aspect of marriage is important in all the tales of the so-called marriage group.[27] This consists of the *Wife of Bath's Prologue* and *Tale*; the *Clerk's Tale* and *Envoy*, with its references to the Wife of Bath and all her sect; the *Merchant's Tale*, which is linked to the Envoy to the *Clerk's Tale*; and the *Franklin's Tale*, included because of its subject-matter, although it is planned to stand after the *Squire's Tale*. Marriage is discussed, in all these tales, in terms of the dominance of one partner over another. This approach, apart from its sound basis in experience, would be natural to Chaucer from both his theological and secular reading. On the one hand, there is the ideal Christian marriage, as St Augustine, for example, described it and as Chaucer's Parson was to do after him.[28] This is based on mutual love and equal companionship, although the husband has a certain dominance, arising from a natural difference between the sexes, in that he must lead and protect the wife. On the other hand, there was the fashionable idea of sophisticated love-making, consisting in abject service of the lady while she is still to be won. This is described in many French and Italian sources. It was apt to involve a view of marriage not nearly so enlightened as the patristic one, either excluding it, on the assumption that it implied a masculine dominance incompatible with love, or abruptly reversing the rôles of the sexes so that the woman's brief period of importance ends with the lover's achievement of his purely sensual aim. This is the viewpoint, implied by Pandarus's bewilderment at Troilus's tragic refusal to 'unlove' Criseyde once he has had his will, when we are shown the artificiality of that faithfulness which it is the courtly lover's part to swear and to which Pandarus himself pays lip-service. Chaucer, indeed, had a *locus classicus* for the exposure of the shallowness of the sophisticated idea of love in the *Roman*, in a passage in which L'Ami pauses in his account of the trials of the jealous husband to set out the basic problem of the marriage relationship in terms which Chaucer clearly echoes in the *Franklin's Tale*:

> E se fait seigneur de sa fame,
> Qui ne redeit pas estre dame,
> Mais sa pareille e sa compaigne,
> Si con la lei les acompaigne,
> E il redeit ses compainz estre,
> Senz sei faire seigneur ne maistre. . . .
> Ja de sa fame n'iert amez
> Qui sires veaut estre clamez;
> Car il couvient amour mourir
> Quant amant veulent seignourir.
> Amour ne peut durer ne vivre
> S'el n'est en cueur franc e delivre.
>   Pour ce reveit l'en ensement
> De touz ceus qui prumierement
> Par amour amer s'entreseulent,
> Quant puis espouser s'entreveulent,
> Enviz peut entr'aus avenir
> Que ja s'i puisse amours tenir,
> Car cil, quant par amour amait,
> Sergent a cele clamait
> Qui sa maistresse soulait estre,
> Or se claime seigneur e maistre
> Seur li, que sa dame ot clamee
> Quant ele iert par amour amee.

(9425–54)

(And he sets himself up as lord over his wife, she who ought to be, not lady over him, but his equal and companion – this is the relationship in which they are joined together by law. And, in his turn, he ought to be her companion, not her lord and master. . . . The man who wants to be called master will never be loved by his wife; love dies when the lover wants to rule as lord. Love can only live and last in hearts which are generous and free. Therefore it happens to all those who begin as lovers that, when they embark on marriage, love is at an end. For the man who, while he was her lover, swore to be the servant of his lady, whom he desired to have as his mistress, now claims to be lord and master over one whom he called lady when he was her lover).

The point, of course, is not the praise of love outside marriage, but the need for a true relationship within it.[29]

In the tales of the marriage group, Chaucer deals systematically with the problem of the relationship of the partners to marriage. In the *Wife of Bath's Prologue* and *Tale*, he examines the woman's attempt to be the dominant partner. In the *Clerk's Tale* and the *Merchant's Tale*, the man dominates. All these attempts to establish an imbalance either end in disaster or need to be corrected. The *Franklin's Tale* describes a marriage in which the partners 'walk together and observe where they are walking'. The three most generalized and philosophical considerations of the marriage theme – the *Knight's*, *Clerk's* and *Man of Law's Tales* – have little to do with any courtly or sophisticated ideas concerning love.[30] Neither has the *Wife of Bath's Prologue*; but her tale has courtly leanings. And, in their different ways, both the *Franklin's* and the *Merchant's Tales* use ideas of this kind as a point of reference.

The *Franklin's Tale*, whenever it was actually written, is the conclusion to any 'marriage debate' which Chaucer may have planned for the *Canterbury Tales*, but it will be best to consider it first, since it gives us the norm – the marriage in which a proper balance between the partners has been achieved and which is therefore established on a sound basis. It also gives us a more detailed view of the somewhat rarefied unions of the more philosophical poems, set out in more naturalistic and more light-hearted terms.

Chaucer is at some pains, as he describes the culmination of Arveragus's courtship of Dorigen, to answer Jean de Meun's criticisms and to reconcile the courtly conception of a long and arduous pursuit in which the woman, through her power of refusal, is the dominating figure, while the man suffers every degree of frustration, with that of a continued relationship after the lady has succumbed within the partnership of marriage. Arveragus is a lover after the usual pattern:

> In Armorik, that called is Britayne,
> Ther was a knyght that loved and dide his payne
> To serve a lady in his beste wise;
> And many a labour, many a greet emprise
> He for this lady wroghte, er she were wonne.
> For she was oon the faireste under sonne,
> And eek therto comen of so heigh kynrede
> That wel unnethes dorste this knyght, for drede,
> Telle hire his wo, his peyne, and his distresse.
>
> (*CT* V, 729–37)

The conclusion is not an illicit love, but marriage, and the keyword 'lady' is replaced by 'lord', 'lordshipe':

> . . . she fil of his accord
> To take hym for hir housbonde and hir lord,
> Of swich lordshipe as men han over hir wyves.
>
> (741–3)

But, having established the themes of service and lordship, Chaucer's conclusion is not the same as that of L'Ami in the *Roman*. Marriage does not mean the end of love, because each partner offers submission to the other, and the resulting balance is described in Chaucer's favourite formula for the achievement of stability, temporary or permanent, in love: 'Thus been they bothe in quiete and in reste' (760):

> Of his free wyl he swoor hire as a knyght
> That nevere in al his lyf he, day ne nyght,
> Ne sholde upon hym take no maistrie
> Agayn hir wyl, ne kithe hire jalousie,
> But hire obeye, and folwe hir wyl in al,
> As any lovere to his lady shal,
> Save that the name of soveraynetee,
> That wolde he have for shame of his degree.
> She thanked hym, and with ful greet humblesse,
> She seyde, 'Sire, sith of youre gentillesse

Ye profre me to have so large a reyne,
Ne wolde nevere God bitwixe us tweyne,
As in my gilt, were outher werre or stryf.
Sire, I wol be youre humble trewe wyf;
Have heer my trouthe, til that myn herte brest.'
Thus been they bothe in quiete and in reste.

(745–60)

The narrator now adds a long passage of comment, in which the problem is further analysed, not within the sophisticated limitations proper to the love vision, but in terms of the actual difficulties likely to be encountered in the establishment of a permanent relationship between two people. The discussion starts from a conventional tag:[31]

Love wol nat been constreyned by maistrye.
Whan maistrie comth, the God of Love anon
Beteth his wynges, and farewel, he is gon!

(764–6)

But the tag is invoked not in support of love outside marriage, but of friendship:

For o thyng, sires, saufly dar I seye,
That freendes everych oother moot obeye,
If they wol longe holden compaignye.

(761–3)

In equating the lasting love and companionship of marriage with *amicitia* rather than *amor*, Chaucer is in agreement with Reason in the *Roman* when she distinguishes between the transitory, contradictory love which is contrary to Nature and the love which is not subject to Fortune.[32] In Andreas Capellanus's *Art of Love*, the lady in one of the dialogues takes up the same position when she shrewdly defines *amor*: 'Love seems to be nothing but a great desire to enjoy carnal pleasure with someone'.[33] This, of course, as the dialogue goes on to say, can be as much a sin within marriage as outside it.[34] Chaucer, therefore, has nothing to say concerning *amor* in his discussion of the relationship of Arveragus and Dorigen. It is not rejected; but, in the limited sense in which the term is used

of sophisticated lovers, it is only one element in that permanency
of relationship which is established through *amicitia*. The Franklin
places the difficulty of establishing such a relationship firmly in the
day to day annoyances and inconveniences of life, and the solution
in mutual trust and forbearance:

> Looke who that is moost pacient in love,
> He is at his avantage al above.
> Pacience is an heigh vertu, certeyn,
> For it venquysseth, as thise clerkes seyn,
> Thynges that rigour sholde nevere atteyne.
> For every word men may nat chide or pleyne.
> Lerneth to suffre, or elles, so moot I goon,
> Ye shul it lerne, wher so ye wole or noon;
> For in this world, certein, ther no wight is
> That he ne dooth or seith somtyme amys.
> Ire, siknesse, or constellacioun,
> Wyn, wo or chaungynge of complexioun
> Causeth ful ofte to doon amys or speken.
> On every wrong a man may nat be wreken.
> After the tyme moste be temperaunce
> To every wight that kan on governaunce.
> And therfore hath this wise, worthy knyght,
> To lyve in ese, suffraunce hire bihight,
> And she to hym ful wisly gan to swere
> That nevere sholde ther be defaute in here.
>
> (771–90)

The Wife of Bath's contention 'Wommen, of kynde, desiren
libertee' (768) is given a new meaning by this definition of a life
of freedom; and, moreover, it is completed so as to become an
observation about humanity in general: 'And so doon men, if I
sooth seyen shal' (770). The conclusion makes formal, rhetorical
play with the key terms, 'service' and 'lordship', of L'Ami's speech
in the *Roman* and brings them into accord with each other and with
'the law of love':[35]

> Heere may men seen an humble, wys accord;
> Thus hath she take hir servant and hir lord, –
> Servant in love, and lord in mariage.
> Thanne was he bothe in lordshipe and servage.

> Servage? nay, but in lordshipe above,
> Sith he hath bothe his lady and his love;
> His lady, certes, and his wyf also,
> The which the lawe of love acordeth to.
>
> (791–8)

The point of the story, as it develops after this preamble, is that this ideal marriage is nevertheless challenged in a way which affects its very basis. Dorigen engages her honour by her foolish promise. If she keeps it, she will have to deal her husband, and her marriage, the worst possible blow through her – albeit enforced – adultery. If she does not keep it, her very identity and value as a separate person will be injured, since 'Trouthe is the hyeste thyng that man may kepe' (1479). In this predicament, Arveragus is steadfast in keeping the vows he made to his wife on their marriage. He approaches the problem as it affects her as an individual, not as a wife whose identity is not separate from his own or who is thought of as his possession. This is the generosity in which his 'gentilesse' consists, and it is so remarkable that it triggers off all the subsequent acts of *gentilesse* which ensure the happy ending.

Arveragus is motivated solely by his love for Dorigen, but this love is the lasting *amicitia* which Reason urges on L'Amant in the *Roman*, not the momentary *amor* which is restricted to 'carnal pleasure':

> This housbonde, with glad chiere, in freendly wyse
> Answerde and seyde as I shal yow devyse:
> 'Is ther oght elles, Dorigen, but this?'
> 'Nay, nay,' quod she, 'God helpe me so as wys!
> This is to muche, and it were Goddes wille.'
>   'Ye, wyf,' quod he, 'lat slepen that is stille.
> It may be wel, paraventure, yet to day.
> Ye shul youre trouthe holden, by my fay!
> For God so wisly have mercy upon me,
> I hadde wel levere ystiked for to be
> For verray love which that I to yow have,
> But if ye sholde youre trouthe kepe and save.
> Trouthe is the hyeste thyng that man may kepe' –
> But with that word he brast anon to wepe
>
> (1467–80)

This gives us, in naturalistic terms, a realization of Jean de Meun's humane conception of the lasting love in which reason has a share, which results in a marriage of true companionship. I do not think that we can doubt that in developing such ideas Chaucer is perfectly serious, or that we can detect either irony or sentimentality in his approach to the main theme of the tale. The story itself is certainly fantastical, and Dorigen is made to play out a comedy of errors, but it is a comedy which involves the characters in serious issues. Dorigen's troubles arise from her efforts to improve the reasonableness of God's world. This seems to her to be, in the matter of the Breton rocks, very imperfect:

> 'Eterne God, that thurgh thy purveiaunce
> Ledest the world by certein governaunce,
> In ydel, as men seyn, ye no thyng make.
> But, Lord, thise grisly feendly rokkes blake,
> That semen rather a foul confusion
> Of werk than any fair creacion
> Of swich a parfit wys God and a stable,
> Why han ye wroght this werk unresonable? . . .
>
> (865–72)

Her speech contains the same doubts and arguments which are put forward, with varying degrees of defiance, by many of Chaucer's characters – with the difference that here every cadence and turn of phrase develops the comedy by echoing the speaking voice. The only true solution, of course, is the exercise of free will in the face of Fortune, to whose realm such accidents as the rocks may cause obviously belong, and a patient endurance of what is sent by God's 'purveiaunce' – the solution, in fact, put into practice by Constance. Dorigen's obsession with the rocks and her lack of patience (ironically, the very virtue which ensures the success of her marriage) lead to her rash promise which, in turn, induces the subtle Breton clerk to put in motion the machinery of 'magyk natureel' in order to achieve her desire. This interference with the natural order of things – unlike the 'open myrakle' of Constance's story – is, Chaucer is careful to point out, only illusion:

> But thurgh his magik, for a wyke or tweye,
> It semed that alle the rokkes were aweye.
>
> (1295–6)

Dorigen herself analyses her plight with accuracy. She has been trapped and subjected to the influence of Fortune by her wish to eliminate Fortune's power in the case of the rocks:

> 'Allas,' quod she, 'on thee, Fortune, I pleyne,
> That unwar wrapped hast me in thy cheyne,
> Fro which t'escape woot I no socour,
> Save oonly deeth or elles dishonour.'
>
> (1355–8)

The elaboration of the magical marvels by which her immediate dilemma has been brought about adds to the irony of the situation. Chaucer is careful to point out that such practices are 'supersticious cursednesse' (1272) and only what 'hethen folk useden in thilke dayes' (1293). Nevertheless, they help to create a serious moral dilemma which challenges the whole basis, sound as it is, of the marriage. Appropriately, the trap is sprung, and Fortune defeated, by the very qualities of generosity and forbearance on which the marriage is built. It is in ironies of this gentle kind that the comedy of the tale depends, not on the view of marriage, of *amor* and *amicitia*, which it sets forth.

The *Clerk's Tale*, among other things, displays a marriage, in contrast to that of Arveragus and Dorigen, in which the dominance is all on the husband's side and in which the husband shows so little respect for his wife's separate identity as to call forth a final rebuke even from her patience. The Wife of Bath, on the other hand, develops the theme of feminine dominance. She describes her ideal husband bluntly:

> An housbonde I wol have, I wol nat lette,
> Which shal be bothe my dettour and my thral,
> And have his tribulacion withal
> Upon his flessh, whil that I am his wyf.
> I have the power durynge al my lyf
> Upon his propre body, and noght he.
> Right thus the Apostel tolde it unto me;
> And bad oure housbondes for to love us weel.
> Al this sentence me liketh every deel.
>
> (*CT* III, 154–62)

The Wife of Bath has nothing to say concerning *amicitia*, but she develops the idea of *amor* as 'a great desire to enjoy carnal pleasure with someone', within the frame of marriage, in a way which is frequently outrageous and always extremely funny.

The first three of her five husbands fall short of her ideal, although, in compensation, they endow her richly with this world's goods. Dame Alisoun is not, like Jean de Meun's Vieille, reduced to poverty and disgrace through her dealings with the male sex, but remains in the end a prosperous widow. The fourth husband was more suited to her tastes:

> My fourthe housbonde was a revelour;
> This is to seyn, he hadde a paramour;
> And I was yong, and full of ragerye,
> Stibourn and strong, and joly as a pye!
>
> (453–6)

But the fifth, although he gave her more trouble than all the rest, was her real love:

> Now of my fifthe housbonde wol I telle,
> God lete his soule nevere come in helle!
> And yet was he to me the mooste shrewe;
> That feele I on my ribbes al by rewe,
> And evere shal unto myn endyng day.
> But in oure bed he was so fressh and gay,
> And therwithal so wel koude he me glose,
> Whan that he wolde han my *bele chose*,
> That thogh he hadde me bete on every bon,
> He koude wynne agayn my love anon.
> I trowe I loved hym best, for that he
> Was of his love daungerous to me.
>
> (503–14)

For La Vieille, indulgence in love, rather than self-interest, proved disastrous;[36] but Alisoun does not come too badly out of her troubles with her fifth husband. He is a clerk, and his attacks on her, when they are not physical, are made through a book – 'He cleped it Valerie and Theofraste' (674) – not through disreputable conduct. In the end, the couple fight it out fairly, and Alisoun wins the victory.

After dealing her a blow which knocks her senseless, her husband is alarmed:

> And neer he cam, and kneled faire adoun,
> And seyde, 'Deere suster Alisoun,
> As help me God! I shal thee nevere smyte
> That I have doon, it is thyself to wyte,
> Foryeve it me, and that I thee biseke!'
> And yet eftsoones I hitte hym on the cheke,
> And seyde, 'Theef, thus muchel am I wreke;
> Now wol I dye, I may no lenger speke.'
> But atte laste, with muchel care and wo,
> We fille acorded by us selven two.
> He yaf me al the bridel in myn hond,
> To han the governance of hous and lond,
> And of his tonge, and of his hond also. . . .
> After that day we hadden never debaat.
> God helpe me so, I was to hym as kynde
> As any wyf from Denmark unto Ynde,
> And also trewe, and so was he to me.
>
> (803–25)

Dame Alisoun thus achieves stability and peace in marriage through a truth which is rather different from that exemplified in the marriage of Arveragus and Dorigen, but which, nevertheless, has a certain validity in terms of her own vigorous nature. In her honest satisfaction with the degree of good she has been able to achieve, there is comedy which contrasts sharply with the satire of Jean de Meun's presentation of La Vieille. The difference between the two figures, and the two methods, can be clearly seen if we compare the original lines with Chaucer's version. In the *Roman*, La Vieille attempts to cheer herself by her memories:

> Par Deu! si me plaist il encores
> Quant je m'i sui bien pourpensee;
> Mout me delite en ma pensee
> Et me resbaudissent li membre
> Quant de mon bon tens me remembre
> E de la joliete vie
> Don me cueurs a si grant envie;

> Tout me rejovenist le cors
> Quant j'i pens e quant jou recors;
> Touz les bien dou monde me fait
> Quant me souvient de tout le fait,
> Qu'au meins ai je ma joie eüe
> Combien qu'il m'aeint deceüe.
> Jenne dame n'est pas oiseuse
> Quant el meine vie joieuse,
> Meïsmement cele qui pense
> D'aquerre a faire sa despense.
>
> (12932–48)

Apart from the cynicism of the last two lines, these words of the 'fausse vieille e serve' (12988) are to be read within the context of her numerous and bitter lamentations for what she has irretrievably lost.[37] Chaucer renders the passage thus, omitting lines 12945–8 entirely:

> But, Lord Crist! whan that it remembreth me
> Upon my yowthe, and on my jolitee,
> It tikleth me aboute myn herte roote,
> Unto this day it dooth myn herte boote
> That I have had my world as in my tyme.
> But age, allas! that al wole envenyme,
> Hath me biraft my beautee and my pith.
> Lat go, farewel! the devel go therwith!
> The flour is goon, ther is namoore to telle;
> The bren, as I best kan, now moste I selle;
> But yet to be right myrie wol I fonde.
>
> (469–79)

Dame Alisoun's momentary recognition of the power of age to poison a life such as hers is at once checked by the resilience and vital enthusiasm which has by no means left her. She is still 'stibourn and strong', and she deals with her own doubts with the same good-humoured determination which she brings to the quarrelsome interruptions to her tale – 'Al redy, sire,' quod she, 'right as yow lest' (854) – and even to her own deficiencies in the art of sustained discourse:

'But now, sire, lat me se, what shal I seyn?
A ha! by God, I have my tale ageyn.'

(585–6)

She does not solve her problems, great or small, through any depth of character or by any virtue, but by her sheer inability to loose her hold on life as she understands it.

Her tale gives a slightly romanticized version of the theme of her prologue. The heroine undergoes a transformation from age to perfect youth and beauty – thus solving the only problem which causes Alisoun any real disquiet. The hero escapes punishment for rape – a crime which, if it does not satisfy the requirements of either a romantic hero or a virtuous husband, at least shows vigour in the direction most favoured by Alisoun – by agreeing to marry the hideous old woman who supplies him with the answer to the riddle on which his life depends. In his despair he gives his wife that total sovereignty which Alisoun finally achieved in her fifth marriage:

This knyght avyseth hym and sore siketh,
But atte laste he seyde in this manere;
'My lady and my love, and wyf so deere,
I put me in youre wise governance;
Cheseth youreself which may be moost plesance
And moost honour to yow and me also.
I do no fors the wheither of the two;
For as yow liketh, it suffiseth me.'

(1228–35)

There is irony in the use of such terms by a husband whose feelings are thus described:

Greet was the wo the knyght hadde in his thoght,
Whan he was with his wyf abedde ybroght;
He walweth and he turneth to and fro.

(1083–5)

And there is added irony in the teller of the tale's easy assumption that such lip-service to courtesy – with a dash of magic to make everything comfortable – will ensure a perfect marriage. This is described in a phrase which echoes the conclusion of the *Knight's Tale*:

And thus they lyve unto hir lyves ende
In parfit joye –

but, incorrigibly, the Wife of Bath adds her definition of such joy, which is very unlike Theseus's:

. . . and Jhesu Crist us sende
Housbondes meeke, yonge, and fressh abedde,
And grace t'overbyde hem that we wedde.
(1257–60)

The fairy-tale couple have no life outside the marriage bed, and the teller of the story does not envisage any. Whether or not we are willing to go quite so far as Huppé, in his conclusion – '*Prologue* and *Tale* are a single, dramatic entity in which Chaucer searches with humour and with sympathy the mind of a worldly woman whose vivacity and laughter hide the soul of a lost and wandering pilgrim' – his final words cannot be bettered: 'It is a profound study of the highest comic seriousness.'[38]

As was the case with the Pardoner, the shift from satire to comedy is achieved in part, at any rate, through the change from the method of allegory to that of naturalism. The Wife of Bath is even more closely modelled on La Vieille than the Pardoner on Faux Semblant, but she is given a much clearer definition as a 'real' character through her function of furthering the development of the marriage theme. We have seen how the very wide field of reference of Faux Semblant, the shape-shifter, makes real individualization impossible, and how, although the field is greatly reduced, even the Pardoner does not achieve completely convincing individuality. In the case of the Wife of Bath, the wide field of the satire against women, and against sensuality in general, is narrowed to the problems and pre-occupations of her own particular marriages. Since there are five of them – 'withouten other compaignie in youthe' – the range is still wide, but the focus on her single figure is constant. La Vieille is, like Faux Semblant, involved in an improbable variety of affairs; she is at one moment bitterly vengeful, at another, triumphant in her 'joliete'. She is now in the gutter, betrayed by the male sex in general and her last husband in particular, now the trusted and prosperous guardian of Bel Aceuil. In all these metamorphoses she unswervingly serves the purposes of the allegory and allows the poet to develop the satire on a much wider front than would be possible with a character conceived in more consistently naturalistic terms.

Jean de Meun's method is comparatively straightforward. La Vieille is bluntly offered us as a detestable character – 'fausse' and 'serve'. We have fair warning that her doctrines are not likely to be true, and the satire, for the most part, consists in her description of her own practices, which are, clearly, bad ones. In spite of her dependence on Nature in her defence of promiscuity:

> 'Mais prenez bien garde a Nature
> Car, pour plus clerement voeir
> Come ele a merveilleus poeir,
> Mainz essemples vous en puis metre,'
>
> (13936–9)

('But pay due attention to Nature, for so that you may see more clearly how great her power is, I can give you innumerable examples,')

she is at odds with the son of Venus and does not, in fact, recommend love in any but the most limited sense:

> 'Qui veaut qu'amanz ait le cueur large,
> E qu'en un seul leu le deit metre:
> C'est faus textes, c'est fausse letre.
> Ci ment Amours li fiz Venus,
> De ce ne le deit creire nus.
> Qui l'en creit chier le comparra,
> Si come en la fin i parra.'
>
> (13030–6)

('If anyone teaches that a lover should have a generous heart and ought to bestow it in one place only, it is a false text and a a false doctrine. Love, the son of Venus, lies in this and ought not to be believed. If anyone does believe him, he will pay dearly for it, as I shall make plain.')

Worse than this, in at least two passages Jean de Meun allows something of the joy of love to come through La Vieille's discourse, but uses it only to give a sharper edge to the satire by the immediacy of her cynical disavowal. This is the case in the passage in which she recalls the pleasures of her youth, which Chaucer uses touchingly, but which is negated in the *Roman* by the conclusion 'a young girl can't be accused of idleness while she leads a life of joy – and especially if she keeps her eye on the profits'. Elsewhere (*Roman*, 14293–304), La Vieille gives a description of the mutual bliss of lovers which would not be entirely inappropriate to the consummation scene of the *Troilus*. But here, too, the *volte face* is immediate: 'and if the woman doesn't feel like this, she'd better take care to pretend she does!' We are reminded that love is not La Vieille's real subject – the more sharply for our brief reorientation towards a world in which other values prevail.

La Vieille's purpose is to achieve vengeance on the male sex, for the troubles it has brought upon her, by teaching Bel Aceuil how to avoid a similar fate by concentrating on rich men and a sound investment policy:

> Car aquerre, s'il n'i a garde,
> Ne vaut pas un grain de moustarde.
>
> (14455–6)

(Having without holding is not worth much.)

This device allows the satire to be as inclusive as its author cares to make it – any trick that the woman can play is relevant. The Wife of Bath, on the other hand, is shown grappling with life as she finds it, from her first marriage at the age of twelve to the moment in which she rides on the pilgrimage. Whereas La Vieille is made to present each point against women simply as a part of her own activity and experience, whose values the reader must reverse, the Wife of Bath argues out the case, with the same combative zest with which she tames her husbands. Her repeated 'thou seyst . . . seydest', 'thou liknest' (256 ff.), indeed, make the argument a part of the taming process, since they form the framework of the type of speech she was accustomed to address to her husbands. She may reciprocate a blow on the ear, but she is not motivated by any general desire for vengeance, and rides her waves as they reach her. Her love of her fifth husband is not seen as a disastrous backsliding, but as a fulfilment of her general hopefulness towards matrimony – in which she nevertheless shows no surprise when the rough comes with the smooth. There is, indeed, no room in her mind for *arrières pensées*. The singleness of vision which shows her nothing but the immense desirability of Jankin's handsome legs as she follows her fourth husband's bier, rules her life and even gives her a kind of innocence – or at least shows her in that analogous state of genuine inability to appreciate even the existence of any other point of view – and also a degree of positive achievement. She lives out her life wholeheartedly according to her lights. That they are not everyone's lights is obvious – her own career is sufficiently checkered to show them as somewhat unreliable. Comedy lies in her own almost complete self-satisfaction – and the very thin crack which Chaucer allows us to glimpse in this satisfaction only enhances the comedy. That her values are not accepted by all her audience is shown by the Clerk's reaction and by the amused comment of the Friar. The remarks of the Pardoner and Summoner show no comprehension of the issues involved and merely offer a clamorous insistence on their own experience of the world, in its way as limited as hers.[39] Her tale, like that of the Pardoner, has built into it an implicit criticism of her point of view, through its references to true 'gentilesse' and patience and to the truth on which marriage ought to be founded. Ironically, however, none of these virtues are required. In the make-believe world of the tale, the happy ending is achieved without them. Chaucer, characteristically, guides his reader's reactions through the total context, but not by any straightforward directives of the kind which Jean de Meun employs when he openly tells us that characters are good or bad. Neither, in the comic world to which the Wife of Bath belongs, do we necessarily make our decisions in the clearcut terms which satire demands.

The interest of the three most complex figures of the *Canterbury Tales* – the Pardoner, the Wife of Bath and January (to whom we must now turn) – as far as technique is concerned, is not only that, in their creation and presentation, Chaucer shows a unique interest in naturalism. He uses naturalism elsewhere within the series, as well as outside it – notably in the *Troilus*. Nor is it the case, as we have seen in connection with the Pardoner, that his methods with these three are, on analysis, exclusively naturalistic. It is rather that in their case he explores and exploits more fully than had ever been done before all the opportunities for the development of character afforded by the device of the series of tales within a frame. No other way of laying out a work could give the poet quite the same oppor-

tunities for self-revelation, oblique or direct, on the part of the characters or could place them in quite the same complexity of relationships
with other figures. Chaucer is able to have the best of two worlds.
He can, if he chooses, exploit the isolated tale – amuse his audience
by a 'nice cas', a dilemma which is particular and has little reference
beyond itself – or he can, as is the case with the marriage theme,
gain something of the width of generality which belongs to allegorical
satire – but gain it without the sacrifice of personality which is
necessary for the proper development of this genre. Jean de Meun's
Jaloux is dissolved, as far as individuality is concerned, in a flood
of generalizations about jealousy. January is defined and delimited
with the accuracy and particularly of all the figures of the *Canterbury
Tales*, although, as he wrestles with his own special problems,
he casts a flood of light on the general topic of good and bad
marriages.

The *Clerk's Tale* and the *Wife of Bath's Tale* form a pair, in that
they show marriages in which the domination is, respectively, on
the male and on the female sides. The *Merchant's Tale* also shows us
an attempt at male dominance, but it is really the converse of the
true marriage of the *Franklin's Tale*. Its marriage is everything
which Chaucer and Jean de Meun tell us that marriage should not
be. In it, the wife is a chattel, bought by the marriage settlements.
The husband is exacting and jealous. No confidence exists between
the two. The husband's only thought is to use his wife for his own
enjoyment, the wife's is to escape in any way she can. This is the
kind of situation which Jean de Meun develops through the speeches
of Le Jaloux; but, once again, Chaucer treats the same subject in
a way which is both more particular and less extreme. Jean de
Meun sets out to give an exhaustive study of the effect of jealousy
on marriage and examines every possible permutation of events to
which it can give rise. Le Jaloux and his wife are every jealous
husband and abused wife. January and May are a particular
couple, although their predicament is described in such a way as
to give it reference beyond their individual case. They contribute
to the marriage discussion, but, as in the case of the Wife of Bath,
their contribution cannot be entirely disengaged from Chaucer's
handling of them as naturalistically conceived characters.

As far as marriage is concerned, January demonstrates what
happens when the husband approaches it for the sake of selfish
lechery and of nothing else. His sole aim in marrying is to legitimize

pleasures to which he has long been habituated, and which age affects only in so far as some fear for the ultimate destination of his soul is now forcing itself on his consciousness. This complexity of motivation is, in itself, enough to mark him off from the allegorical or type figure which is, necessarily, dominated by a driving force as single as it is strong, since in such figures we see the quintessence of what they stand for. January is not a quintessential figure. He is an ingenious old man who plans to have his cake and eat it:

> Whilom ther was dwellynge in Lumbardye
> A worthy knyght, that born was in Pavye,
> In which he lyved in greet prosperitee;
> And sixty year a wyflees man was hee,
> And folwed ay his bodily delyt
> On wommen, ther as was his appetyt,
> As doon thise fooles that been seculeer.
> And whan that he was passed sixty yeer,
> Were it for hoolynesse or for dotage,
> I kan nat seye, but swich a greet corage
> Hadde this knyght to been a wedded man
> That day and nyght he dooth al that he kan
> T'espien where he myghte wedded be . . .
> (*CT* IV, 1245–57)

The long series of speeches in which the theme is developed serves as a kind of internal prologue to the *Tale*. Like the Wife of Bath, January uses material which in fact proves the opposite of what he wants to prove, since, like her, his aim is to show that marriage legitimizes lust. Even the logicians of Andreas Capellanus's dialogues know better than this.

January is the traditional figure of the *Senex Amans* only in so far as age makes him repulsive. His boast:

> For, God be thanked! I dar make avaunt,
> I feel my lymes stark and suffisaunt
> To do al that a man bilongeth to,
> (1457–9)

is so far justified that he does get May with child – and so gives her an excuse for an urgent longing for small green pears, to his

ultimate undoing. Chaucer dwells on the lechery of January in
line after relentless line descriptive of his enjoyment of May, writing
with a savagery and remorselessness of unpleasant detail which is
unparalleled elsewhere in his work. The ultimate triumph of sensuality for two well-matched lovers in the *Troilus* is firmly, but delicately, drawn. There is no delicacy and no restraint in the *Merchant's
Tale*, where sexuality is deliberately used as the chief weapon of the
satire against both marriage partners, in a comedy of a kind which
we do not encounter anywhere else in Chaucer's work. It is a double
comedy: both the main characters are equally self-deluded in their
attempts to delude each other – in contrast to the *Roman*, where Le
Jaloux's wife is merely the victim (not an altogether unresisting one)
of his persecution. May marries for money, as Chaucer shows by his
emphasis on the marriage settlements and the luxury of the feast:

> I trowe it were to longe yow to tarie,
> If I yow tolde of every scrit and bond
> By which that she was feffed in his lond.
> > (1696–8)

She shows no dissatisfaction with her bargain. She is described at
the feast as:

> Mayus, that sit with so benyngne a chiere,
> Hire to beholde it semed fayerye,
> > (1742–3)

and her acquiescence to all January's demands continues to the
end. Chaucer questions her thoughts, but not her words or actions,
when he describes her in bed with January:

> He was al coltissh, ful of ragerye,
> And ful of jargon as a flekked pye.
> The slakke skyn aboute his nekke shaketh,
> Whil that he sang, so chaunteth he and craketh.
> But God woot what that May thoughte in hir herte,
> Whan she hym saugh up sittynge in his sherte,
> In his nyght-cappe, and with his nekke lene.
> > (1847–53)

In a similar situation, the knight of the *Wife of Bath's Tale* expresses his feelings freely. There is no 'rape of May', but rather a willing prostitution, in which the silence with which she receives all January's advances acts like a savage parody of Griselda's silence in the face of her husband's persecution.

January thus has no reason to complain, as has Le Jaloux, that his wife does everything she can to hinder his enjoyment.[40] In fact, Chaucer borrows a detail from Le Jaloux's speech and turns it to an opposite effect. Le Jaloux complains at length of his wife's extravagance. The splendour of her clothes, he says, is nothing but useless ostentation:

> Que me fait ele de profit?
> Combien qu'ele aus autres profit,
> A mei ne fait ele fors nuire;
> Car, quant me vueil a vous deduire,
> Je la treuve si encombreuse,
> Si grevaine e si enuieuse
> Que je n'en puis a chief venir.

(What good is it to me? However much you may please other people, it's nothing but a nuisance to me. For, when I want some pleasure from you, I find them so much in the way, such an encumbrance and such an inconvenience, that I never manage to get anywhere.)

(8851–7)

This play on the various meanings of 'profit' is witty. Chaucer, however, does not borrow the passage for the purpose of wit. January indulges his lust at all times of the day or night and

> Anon he preyde hire strepen hire al naked;
> He wolde of hire, he seyde, han som plesaunce,
> And seyde hir clothes dide hym encombraunce.
> And she obeyeth, be hire lief or looth.

(1958–61)

There is no wit here; but the casually demanding, near querulous note which Chaucer contrives to put into January's reported speech is one of the most telling strokes in the attack on him.

May is bought, and gives value for the money – a fact which

mitigates the sympathy aroused by the reference to her inevitable thoughts. Sympathy is further dispelled by the fact that she is soon shown to be as lustful as January. Her courtship by Damyen is as swift and easily successful as that of Alisoun by Nicholas – but it lacks the freshness and the charm. May is, she insists, 'a gentil womman and no wenche' (2202), and Chaucer accordingly deals with her rapid surrender with all the trappings proper to the sophisticated ploys of *fin' amour* – the joke, of course, is not at the expense of *gentilesse* in love, but at May's assumption of it. Damyen languishes in bed like Troilus and achieves May's acceptance of a letter; but the ready wit by which she immediately understands Damyen, and finds at once the privacy to read his letter and a good way of disposing of the evidence, has little to do with Criseyde:

> She feyned hire as that she moste gon
> Ther as ye woot that every wight moot neede;
> And whan she of this bille hath taken heede,
> She rente it al to cloutes atte laste,
> And in the pryvee softely it caste.
>
> (1950–4)

In pursuance of the joke, Chaucer sets her careless speech of acceptance:

> 'Certeyn', thoghte she, 'whom that this thyng displese,
> I rekke noght, for heere I hym assure
> To love hym best of any creature,
> Though he namoore hadde than his sherte'
>
> (1982–5)

between two passages in the grand style on destiny and chance, and on the pity that belongs to *gentilesse*, both topics which he uses with serious force in the philosophical love poems. The line, indeed, in which he sums up May's soliloquy – 'Lo pitee renneth soone in gentil herte' (1986) is a key one, which he uses in all sincerity of his noble heroines, and which he here turns against May with terrible effect.[41]

Chaucer uses, too, another theme which is familiar from his more philosophical treatments of love. January, he laments, suffers a reversal, common to mankind, from the joy in which he is living with a wife, as we know, already determined to betray him:

> And in this wyse, many a murye day,
> Lyved this Januarie and fresshe May.
> But worldly joye may nat alwey dure
> To Januarie, ne to no creature.
>
> (2053–6)

January becomes blind, and for a time the state of May and Damyen is worse than before, since he adds jealousy to his other advantages as a husband. Our sympathy even veers a little towards May. 'This noble Januarie free' – Chaucer gives him a formula implying the highest virtue, to correspond to May's gentle pity[42] – becomes so exacting in his jealousy

> That neither in halle, n'yn noon oother hous,
> Ne in noon oother place, neverthemo,
> He nolde suffre hire for to ryde or go,
> But if that he had hond on hire alway;
> For which ful ofte wepeth fresshe May,
> That loveth Damyan so benyngely. . . .
>
> (2088–93)

Chaucer, however, is quick to unsettle any feelings of this kind by beginning to build up a little sympathy for January. After the outrageous speech in which he addresses May in a paraphrase of the Song of Songs – 'swich olde lewed wordes', as they indeed become in his mouth – Chaucer makes him express a love for his wife which we may, if we choose, take as having a meaning that is a little deeper than his prevailing characteristic of lust:

> 'Now wyf,' quod he, 'heere nys but thou and I,
> That art the creature that I best love.
> For by that Lord that sit in hevene above,
> Levere ich hadde to dyen on a knyf,
> Than thee offende, trewe deere wyf!
> For Goddes sake, thenk how I thee chees,
> Noght for no coveitise, doutelees,
> But oonly for the love I had to thee.
> And though that I be oold, and may nat see,

Beth to me trewe, and I wol telle yow why.
Thre thynges, certes, shal ye wynne therby:
First, love of Crist, and to youreself honour,
And al myn heritage, toun and tour;
I yeve it yow, maketh chartres as yow leste;
This shal be doon to-morwe, er sonne reste. . . .'

(2160–74)

The ambiguities and ironies are nicely balanced. True, January
did not marry for 'coveitise'; but May did, as we know. Equally
true, he was dominated in his choice by 'love'; but a love which, as
we have had ample opportunity to judge, was lust pure and simple.
It may be that he now values 'truth' in a wife, but hardly with any
real understanding of a concept which is, of course, a central one to
Chaucer's view of marriage. He is, in fact, addressing a wife who,
far from being true, has already betrayed him in intention and is
about to do so in fact, and the only persuasion he can offer with any
hope that it will prove effective is to buy her once again — to
add new 'chartres' to the deeds of the marriage settlement. The fact
that both he and May discuss the matter with perfunctory reference
to Christian virtue enhances the irony. January promises her 'love
of Crist', before he hurries on to detail the endowment he proposes
to make, and May remarks, with some indignation:

'I have', quod she, 'a soule for to kepe
As wel as ye.'

(2188–9)

The whole tale develops an ironical interchange of the idea of
gentilesse and its reverse as applied to May. The narrator comments
admiringly on her 'gentil' pitifulness. She makes her claim to be a
'gentil womman and no wenche'. January hopes to buy truth from
her – 'the hyeste thyng that man may kepe', in Arveragus's words –
and, finally, the whole elaborate irony is brought to a point in
January's outraged bewilderment when his wife is revealed to him
as she really is:

'Out! help! allas! harrow!' he gan to crye.
'O stronge lady stoore, what dostow?'

(2366–7)

He roars out a confusion of epithets, appropriate and the reverse, among which, by a cunning positioning in the line, the one word, 'lady', which May claimed for herself, and to which she now has no claim whatsoever, bears witness to a lingering obstinacy in self-deception which paves the way for January's final, total subjugation by his ingenious wife. If we need a further comment on May, we can find it in the *Manciple's Tale*, where the teller, commenting on women who 'werke . . . amys', remarks:

> . . . the gentile, in estaat above,
> She shal be cleped his lady, as in love;
> And for that oother is a povre womman,
> She shal be cleped his wenche, or his lemman.
> (*CT* IX, 217–20)

The conclusion of the Manciple, who apologizes for himself as 'a boystous man', is unkindly appropriate to May:

> And, God it woot, myn owene deere brother,
> Men leyn that oon as lowe as lith that oother.
> (*CT* IX, 221–2)

It is the continual interplay in delusion between the two main characters – to which only a line-for-line analysis could do full justice – each equally duped and duping, in which the savage comedy of the *Merchant's Tale* consists. It is in this interplay, too, that we can see the fundamental difference between Chaucer's and Jean de Meun's approach to the subject of the *Mal Marié*. January is a comic figure because he is placed in the common human predicament of longing for something only dimly understood. In satisfying an apparently clear and limited desire, he finds himself with other desires still unsatisfied. He has some distant inkling of the worth of a true wife and of the true joys of marriage, but without any real understanding of what is involved and without the slightest idea of how to get them. These complexities are necessarily absent from Le Jaloux, who serves the satire as the quintessence of jealousy and unreasonableness in marriage and has no shades or half-tones about him. Both poets develop the theme with consummate skill, but they develop it differently.

Notes

1 The urbane manner

1 See Robinson, ed., *Works of Chaucer*, p. 523. It is, however, possible that the poem was written earlier and provided with a new envoy for this occasion.

2 *Ibid.*, p. 523.

3 *Ibid.*, pp. 422–3. The couplet is in both versions of the Prologue. Unfortunately the dating and order of composition of the two are still uncertain. The first version could have been written as early as 1385, the second, generally assumed to be the revised one, in which the couplet still stands, and is therefore presumably still topical, as late as 1395. See *ibid.*, pp. 839–40, for a summary of the discussion with full references, and R. D. French, *A Chaucer Handbook* (New York, 1947; 2nd ed.,) pp. 126 ff.

4 Agreement on the occasion and date of this poem is general, that is, that it commemorates the death of Blanche, Duchess of Lancaster, in September 1369 and was written very soon after this event. For a dissenting voice (although the date need not necessarily be affected), see Bernard F. Huppé and D. W. Robertson Jr, *Fruyt and Chaf: Studies in Chaucer's Allegories* (Princeton, 1963), pp. 32 ff. The Prologue to the *Legend of Good Women* is, in fact, a fourth love vision, but here the form is only used as a device to introduce the unrelated matter of the tale-collection.

5 The miniature in MS 61, Corpus Christi College, Cambridge (see cover), may even represent his usual method of publication although it is, obviously, an idealized scene. On the relationship of Chaucer to his audience see further J. Lawlor, *Chaucer* (London, 1968).

6 See Clemen, *Chaucer's Early Poetry*, p. 23; Muscatine, *French Tradition, passim*. It must be remembered, however, that interest in French poetry does not exclude the possibility of knowledge and enjoyment of earlier works in English.

7 It has often been claimed that the *Pearl*-Poet had first-hand knowledge of Dante. See P. M. Kean, *The Pearl: An Interpretation* (London, 1967), pp. 120 ff. He is, however, the only contemporary of Chaucer for whom such a claim could be made.

284

8 W. W. Skeat, ed., *The Lay of Havelok the Dane*, revised by K. Sisam (Oxford, 1915), l. 195. This may, of course, mean no more than 'discuss marriage'; but, in the context, it seems to me to have a more precise sense. It is a sign of maturity in a twelve-year-old princess that she 'couþe of curtesye / Don, and speken of luue-drurye'. Though her marriage is certainly contemplated (196–203), this couplet seems to refer to fashionable adult behaviour in general.

9 We cannot, of course, prove that these serious poems were, in fact, intended for the same audience as the love poems, but it is significant that they show exactly the same interest in experimentation with verse forms. It is also true that Chaucer generally mingles moral and philosophical themes with that of love. This is not only the case in his most complex works – the *Parlement of Foules*, the *Troilus* and the *Knight's Tale* – but also of simpler ones like the *Complaint of Mars* and the *Book of the Duchess*.

10 Deschamps' short moral poems tend to use the same abrupt, familiar openings addressing the reader as do Chaucer's, and usually continue in the same half argumentative, half exhortatory style. His metrical virtuosity is not so great as the English poet's, but the same basic way of writing is used by both. See the 'Balades de Moralitez', *Œuvres Complètes d'Eustache Deschamps*, I and II, SATF (Paris, 1880).

11 This is not, of course, to say that either Deschamps or Chaucer would not have regarded Seneca as a Christian author. It is, of course, possible that either, or both, used a *florilegium* rather than a comprehensive volume of Seneca's works.

12 Cf., e.g., Balade cxci, 12–14; Balade clxxxvii, 19–20. The only specifically Christian note introduced by Chaucer is in *Truth*, 18–19, on the pilgrimage of life and the duty of thanking God for all – and this is distinctly less specific than most of Deschamps' references.

13 See Robinson, notes to lines 7, 11, 17.

14 See p. 31.

15 See, e.g., R. M. Gummere, ed., *Seneca ad Lucilium: Epistulae Morales* (Cambridge, Mass. 1961, Loeb edition), xxiv, 4; xxviii, 8; lxx, 9; lxxi, 17; xcviii, 12.

16 *Ibid.*, vii, 1. All quotations are from the text and translation of the three-volume Loeb edition.

17 See Robinson, note to *Truth*, 2.

18 For this idea cf., e.g., Epistles vii, xiv, xix, xxvii, all on the same theme of worldly business and the need to avoid it.

19 It is also possible that it has an allegorical meaning of a topical kind and refers to current events and personalities (see Robinson, notes, for references). J. D. North, 'Kalenderes Enlumyned ben They: Some Astronomical Themes in Chaucer', *RES*, N.S. XX (1969), pp. 137 ff., considers that the poem reflects the state of the heavens in 1385–1386.

20 Elias Ashmole, *Theatrum Chemicum Britannicum* (London, 1652; reprinted New York, 1967), pp. 415 ff.

21 Muscatine, *French Tradition*, p. 107. For a full discussion of the *Book of*

the Duchess, see Clemen, *Chaucer's Early Poetry*, pp. 23 ff. and the references there given.

22 Most successfully, no doubt, by the Scottish Chaucerians; but cf., e.g., a passage like lines 372 ff. of the *Flower and the Leaf*, in which the company that has been drenched by the storm is rescued by the good offices of their rivals, or the dialogue of the *Assembly of Ladies*, to which the poem owes most of its charm.

23 See Martin M. Crow and Clair C. Olson, eds, *Chaucer Life-Records* (Oxford, 1966), pp. 13 ff.

24 On the themes of the *House of Fame*, see pp. 55 ff.

25 For accounts of the French love vision literature in relation to Chaucer see Clemen, *Chaucer's Early Poetry*, chs 1, 2 and 3, Muscatine, *French Tradition*, ch. 4. Robinson, notes, contains reasonably complete references to the individual poems Chaucer is likely to have known and used.

26 E. Hoepffner, ed., *Œuvres de Guillaume de Machaut* SATF (Paris, 1908), I, pp. 57 ff.

27 *Book of the Duchess*, l. 531. Both phrases can be translated 'acting, speaking proudly', but the alternative senses of 'over-elaborate' for 'quaint' and 'brusque' or 'rude' for 'tough' seem to fit the context better. Both are well evidenced.

28 *Œuvres de Machaut*, I, pp. 11 ff.

29 M. A. Scheler, ed., *Œuvres de Froissart* (Brussels, 1870), I, 1 ff.

30 The same stylistic device is used by Froissart when, in lines 1–12 of the *Paradys d'Amour*, the rhyme-scheme involves the repetition of parts of the verb 'veiller'. The effect is thus the opposite of Chaucer's, with the emphasis on wakefulness. Lines 13 ff. of the *Paradys* do contain numerous repetitions of parts of the verb 'dormir', but this material is not used by Chaucer until he reaches line 240 of his own poem.

31 Deities or allegorical personages, especially female ones, are often somewhat arbitrary in their commands – but it seems to me that, just as Fame, in the *House of Fame*, is exceptionally free in her language, so here the colloquialism goes further than it could do in the more consistent language of Chaucer's French prototypes. Compare, for example, a similar command in the *Jugement dou Roy de Navarre*, where the general level of style is lower than in some French love visions:

> Lors un escuier appealla
> Et li dist: 'Vois tu celui la
> Qui bel se deduit et deporte?
> Va a lui, et si me raporte
> Qui il est, et revien en l'eure,
> Sans la faire point de demeure.'
> (559–64)

32 It is used in the *Troilus* by Pandarus, for example:

His nece awook, and axed, 'Who goth there?'
'My dere nece,' quod he 'it am I.'

(III, 751–2)

In the *Legend of Good Women* the context is one of even more formal politeness:

This god of Love on me hys eyen caste,
And seyde, 'Who kneleth there?' and I answerde
Unto his askynge, whan that I it herde,
And seyde, 'Sir, it am I,' and com him ner,
And salwed him.

(F, Prologue, 311–15)

33 Although I would agree with Huppé and Robertson that 'the hart is symbolically complex' (*Fruyt and Chaf*, p. 54, n. 26), I can see no sign of the 'allegorization of God as the Hunter-King hunting after the human soul' (*ibid.*, p. 49).

34 On the relationship of the Dreamer and the Man in Black, see Clemen, *Chaucer's Early Poetry*, pp. 42 ff. and the references there given, especially in n. 1, p. 43.

35 For Chaucer the heart is the location of the rational soul. In his description of Arcite's death (*Knight's Tale*, *CT* I, 2797 ff.), first the 'vital strength' is lost, to the accompaniment of coldness; then, when death affects the heart, in which the intellect dwells, the process is complete and his spirit leaves his body. The 'vital strength' seems equivalent to the 'spirits' here – the means by which body and soul are normally held together. Their failure produces at first paralysis and unconsciousness, and then, if it is continued, death. For a good short account of the spirits in this sense, see C. S. Lewis, *The Discarded Image* (Cambridge, 1964), pp. 166 ff. On Arcite's death, with particular reference to the heart as the seat of the rational soul, see W. C. Curry, *Chaucer and the Medieval Sciences* (London, 1960; 2nd ed., pp. 299 ff.) and J. A. W. Bennett, *Chaucer: The Knight's Tale* (London, 1954, pp. 141–4). It is clear that the state of the Man in Black is a potentially serious one. The idea that Nature is opposed to grief is Senecan (see *Consolatio ad Marciam*, vii, 3; *Epistulae Morales*, ii).

36 There are signs that for the Middle Ages this might have a more sinister sense than it would for us. The unsuccessful lover who wanders in the wood is often depicted as not merely sad but also mad. This is the case with Lancelot, Tristram, Ywain and Amades. Similarly, the speaker in a Middle English lyric swears that if his lady does not satisfy his desires he will 'wyht in wode be fleme', where something more damaging than a country ramble is clearly meant ('Lenten ys come wiþ loue to toune', line 36, in Carleton Brown, ed., *English Lyrics of the Thirteenth Century* [Oxford, 1932]).

37 C. S. Lewis, *The Allegory of Love* (Oxford, 1948), p. 164.

2 New themes in the love vision

1 The *Parlement* has been treated at length by several scholars comparatively recently, and it will be obvious that the present discussion owes much to their work, while, I hope, it still offers its own approach. The most important books and papers on the subject are: J. A. W. Bennett, *The Parlement of Foules: An Interpretation* (Oxford, 1957); D. S. Brewer, ed., *The Parlement of Foulys* (London, 1960); D. Everett, 'Chaucer's Love Visions with particular reference to the *Parlement of Foules*', in *Essays on Middle English Literature*, ch. 4; Clemen, 'The Parliament of Fowls', *Chaucer's Early Poetry*, ch. 3. Here, as elsewhere in this book, I must ask for the acceptance of a general acknowledgement of my very great debt to earlier critics, in order not to burden the reader with too many notes containing detailed references to agreements and disagreements with other writers.

2 Chaucer would certainly have regarded this as one of the most important sources of poetic material, since – English poetry apart, in which love lyric and romantic love story were already flourishing – his fashionable French and Italian models made so much use of it. As we have seen, however, moral-philosophical and purely religious poetry were also demanded of a poet who aimed at a sophisticated audience in the fourteenth century.

3 See Bennett, *Parlement*, pp. 45 ff.; Brewer, ed., 26 ff.

4 Cicero writes of the fate of the souls of those 'qui se corporis voluptatibus dediderunt' (*Somnium*, II, xvii) and uses the term 'libido' for the passion which rules them. As Bennett points out (*Parlement*, pp. 41–2), in Classical Latin 'libido' meant 'sensual passion'. It later, however, came to mean 'sodomy', i.e., the perversion which is castigated in the *de Planctu Naturae*. Chaucer's use of 'likerous' suggests that he may have preferred the more general sense and had in mind the medieval vice of *luxuria*, which, although it might include sodomy, is generally contrasted with the productive and virtuous love of marriage.

5 On this phrase see complete edition, I, pp. 160–2.

6 See H. Rackham, ed., *de Natura Deorum* (Cambridge, Mass., 1951; Loeb ed.), II, xxiv: 'Suscepit autem vita hominum consuetudoque communis ut beneficiis excellentis viros in caelum fama ac voluntate tollerent.' ('Human experience, moreover, and general custom have made it a practice to confer the deification of renown and gratitude upon distinguished benefactors.') Cf. *Tusculan Disputations*, I, xii. On this view of the gods in the Classical and medieval period see J. Seznec, *La Survivance des Dieux Antiques* (London, 1940).

7 For Plato's account of the creation see A. E. Taylor, *A Commentary on Plato's Timaeus* (Oxford, 1928). Macrobius's use of the *Timaeus* and its neo-Platonic commentators is discussed, with full bibliographical

references, by W. H. Stahl in the introduction to his translation of the *Somnium Scipionis* (*Macrobius: Commentary on the Dream of Scipio*, Records of Civilization, Sources and Studies, XLVIII [New York, 1952]). See also the footnotes to this translation. A. O. Lovejoy, *The Great Chain of Being* (Harvard, 1936), chs. 2 and 3, discusses many of the ideas involved, in relation to both Greek and medieval philosophy.

8 See pp. 160 ff.

9 See complete edition, I, pp. 175 ff.

10 Chaucer could have taken this term from either the *de Planctu* (cols. 453, 476, 479) or the *Roman* (16782, 19507) or both. He uses it in a more restricted sense of Nature's power to make and adorn (*'forme and peynten'*) earthly creatures in the *Physician's Tale* (*CT* VI, 21). Here he is careful to state that God is the ultimate source of all forms ('formere principal', line 19). When Chaucer addresses the Blessed Virgin Mary as 'vicaire and maistresse / Of al this world' (*ABC*, 140–1), he is presumably thinking of her in relation to grace, and so to reformation, not formation.

11 I. P. Sheldon-Williams and Ludwig Bieler, eds., *Iohannis Scotii Eriugenae Periphyseon* (*De Divisione Naturae, Liber Primus*) *Scriptores Latini Hiberniae*, VII (Dublin, 1968). All quotations are from the text and translation of this edition.

12 See pp. 160 ff.

13 *Man of Law's Tale* (*CT* II, 1131); *Clerk's Tale* (*CT* IV, 1129, 1132, 1136); *Franklin's Tale* (*CT* V, 760). In all these, married love and its results are in question.

14 *De Planctu Naturae*, in Thomas Wright, ed., *The Anglo-Latin Satirical Poets*, II (London, 1872), p. 451. This echoes the 'rerum concordia discors' of Horace, *Epistles* xii, 19 (of the Empedoclian doctrine of nature as a perpetual conflict of love and strife).

15 *Somnium*, I, vi.

16 *Ibid.*, I, vi.

17 *Ibid.*, I, vi.

18 (*Parlement*, 381). As Bennett points out, the normal meaning of 'even' in the phrase 'even number' in the fourteenth century would be 'exact' (p. 133). The only support for the sense 'not odd' comes from *Piers Plowman*, B, XX, 268: 'Heuene hath euene noumbre, and helle is with-out noumbre.' It is true that, according to Revelation, the number of the blessed is even, in the modern sense – *viz.* 144,000; but, in the context, Langland means that a definite, exact number is given for heaven, while hell, on the authority of Job 10:22, has 'nullus ordo' (cf. *Parson's Tale*, *CT* X, 218, where this is associated with number). This enables Langland to make a jibe against the Friars: they have no fixed number of members, in keeping with their ability to support them, and in this respect they resemble Hell, not Heaven. See R. W. Frank Jr, *Piers Plowman and the Scheme of Salvation* (New Haven and London, 1957), pp. 112 ff.

19 The whole of chapter vi in Book I of the *Somnium* is relevant. This passage contains the idea expressed by Chaucer's phrase 'of accord', although he was probably also thinking of the wording of Alanus: 'quatuor elementorum concors discordia' (*de Planctu*, in Wright, ed., *Anglo-Latin Poets*, II, p. 451). Boethius's 'noumbres proporcionables' (in Chaucer's translation of *de Consolatione Philosophiae*, III, m. ix, 18–19) are also three and four: the four elements and 'the mene soule of treble kynde'.

20 According to all Classical and medieval musical theory, musical harmony depended on numerical relationships which reproduced those of the music of the spheres. See E. Wellesz, *A History of Byzantine Music and Hymnography* (Oxford, 1962, 2nd ed.), ch. 2.

21 See *de Planctu*, in Wright, ed., *Anglo-Latin Poets*, II, pp. 475 ff. It is significant that in the *Parlement* Chaucer combines in one figure Venus with the flaming torch (the Venus of sexual passion from the *Roman de la Rose*) and the 'blysful lady swete', Cytherea, corresponding to the Venus to whom he elsewhere (notably in the *Troilus*, III, 1 ff.) appeals as a cosmic force.

22 *De Planctu* in Wright, ed., *Anglo-Latin Poets*, II, 445 ff.

23 See *Roman de la Rose*, especially 18947 ff. Nature, however, first appears at 15891 ff. Jean de Meun's treatment of the material is extremely diffuse.

24 *Ibid.*, 19021 ff.

25 For their stories see Robinson, notes. Hercules' love was a criminal one insofar as it was adulterous; and his death was the result of Deianira's jealous action. Chaucer nowhere shows any tendency to regard adulterous love as justifiable. In his one comparatively sympathetic treatment of love outside marriage, the *Troilus*, the lovers are, respectively, widowed and unmarried.

26 The vestal virgin breaks a deliberate vow to serve the gods in a certain way. Diana's nymphs pass from her service to that of Venus as part of a natural process in which virginity is converted to fruition. For Chaucer, Diana was a goddess of fruitfulness as well as Venus (see p. 147).

27 It is true that the phrase 'serve Venus ne Cupide' can be taken as a mere formula, meaning no more than 'love' (see Brewer, ed., *Parlement*, note to 652); but its position is emphatic, and in a poem which, as I believe, turns on the relations of Venus and Nature, it is appropriate that Nature's favourite bird should refer to her relationship to the other goddess.

28 Chaucer has combined the single gate and single inscription of the *Inferno*, III, 1–3 (whose cadence his own inscription echoes), with the two gates from which issued the true and false dreams of the *Aeneid*, VI, 893 ff. These have no inscriptions, but do have the contrary import of the gate of the *Parlement*.

29 Two recent full-length studies of the poem are J. A. W. Bennett, *Chaucer's Book of Fame: An Exposition of 'The House of Fame'* (Oxford,

1968), and B. G. Koonce, *Chaucer and the Tradition of Fame: Symbolism in the House of Fame* (Princeton, 1966). To the first of these books I must acknowledge a general debt, although, once again I have not noted every agreement or disagreement in the course of this chapter. I do not think that I owe much to the second, which takes a totally different viewpoint.

30 It is, however, nearer to the style of Ovid than of Virgil. The emphasis falls on the unhappy figure of Dido and her long complaint. For a detailed analysis of Chaucer's rehandling of the *Aeneid*, IV, see Bennett, 'Venus and Virgil', *Chaucer's Book of Fame*, ch. 1.

31 *Ibid.*, ch. 1, and see further pp. 72–4.

32 Even the grotesque and comic rumours are, like the eagle, 'wynged wondres' (*House of Fame*, 2118).

33 As, for example, Muscatine seems to do when he criticizes the 'grotesque stylistic disharmony with its narrative context' of parts of the *House of Fame* (*French Tradition*, p. 109).

34 The *descriptio* of Fame is analysed at length by Bennett, *Chaucer's Book of Fame*, pp. 128 ff. On the linking of Fame with poetry, see pp. 136 ff. Koonce's statement (*Chaucer and the Tradition of Fame*, p. 5) that 'in its simplest reduction, the theme of the *House of Fame* is the vanity of worldly fame' seems to oversimplify this passage.

35 Chaucer's attitude to Homer in the *House of Fame* (1475 ff.) is a little doubtful; although he attributes criticism of him to envy, he is obviously well aware of the tradition that, as the translator of the *Destruction of Troy* puts it, placed all 'poyetis of prise' among those who 'dampnet his dedys and for dull holdyn' (47 ff.). His opinion of Homer seems to have changed for the better by the time he wrote the *Troilus*, since he mentions him with respect at the end.

36 Skeat–Sisam, ed., *Havelok*. There is no positive evidence to show whether or not Chaucer knew this romance.

36ᵃ This refers to the complete edition.

37 Smithers, ed., *Kyng Alisaunder*, EETS, O.S., 227 (1952 for 1947) and O.S., 237 (1957 for 1953). On the lyrical 'headpieces' of this poem, see O.S., 237, pp. 35 ff. Such passages, at least as far as content is concerned, are to be found in Old French and medieval Latin narrative poems.

38 Bliss, ed., *Sir Orfeo*. I quote from the Auchinleck text, which may have been known to Chaucer. See Laura H. Loomis, 'The Tale of Sir Thopas', in *Sources and Analogues*, pp. 486 ff. and the references there given.

39 The nearest to Chaucer's own day is Guido delle Colonne, who made a Latin prose redaction of the much more important work in French of Benoît de Sainte-Maure, the *Roman de Troie*. Chaucer evidently considers the use of the two great languages of the Classical past important in the selection of the basic upholders of fame. 'Englyssh Gaufride' is unlikely to break this series. He is, almost certainly, Geoffrey of Monmouth, who, of course, wrote in Latin.

40 This structure is not dictated by the French love vision. The opening on sleep and dreams can be found there – that of the *House of Fame* is, in fact, closely imitated from a poem of Froissart (for details see Robinson, notes). The device of a tale told at length is not developed by French writers, although they do make use of *exempla*. Since the core of the love vision in French is the didactic speeches, which give instruction concerning Love at length, the descriptions and settings are necessarily subordinate, and there is nothing to compare with Chaucer's thematic use of these parts of his work. It might even be possible to see an element of literary satire in Chaucer's insistence on the elusive love-tidings which are never actually spoken. Such reticence is, at any rate, markedly unlike the normal practice of the French poets.

41 The tablet of brass seems to have an inscription on it consisting of, at least, the opening lines of the *Aeneid* (the 'Thus writen' of line 142 is, clearly, followed by a quotation). What happens next is not so clear, but line 149, 'And tho began the story anoon', could indicate a different method of representation, and the repeated use of 'saw' (lines 151, 162, 174, 193, etc.) suggests pictures. 'Graven' (e.g. line 193) is ambiguous and could mean either 'drawn' (sculpted or incised) or 'inscribed', but at line 211 the unambiguous 'peynted' is used. I think that the tablet of brass is either to be taken as providing the title lines for the series of paintings that accompanies it, or, in the manner of a dream, as dissolving and giving way to the more vivid method of painting. For a discussion of the passage and its various possibilities see Bennett, *Chaucer's Book of Fame*, pp. 13–14.

42 I do not, therefore, think that the iconography, typical and untypical (in the case of the comb), of Chaucer's treatment has much significance for the rest of the work. He seems to me merely to take over a set piece found in convenient form in the *Teseida* and to treat it cursorily. More emphasis is placed on the function of Venus in the poem in Bennett, 'Venus and Virgil', *Chaucer's Book of Fame*, ch. 1.

43 For Chaucer's use of the machinery of the gods in the *Troilus*, see complete edition, I, pp. 165 ff., and in the *Knight's Tale*, see Chapter 4.

44 The implication and Chaucerian associations of the desert are discussed at length by Bennett, *Chaucer's Book of Fame*, pp. 47 ff.

45 See complete edition, I, pp. 169 ff.

46 The same idea is implied in lines 1209–13. 'Craft', 'skill in art', counterfeits or copies nature; 'smale harpers', on the contrary, can only imitate other artists 'as an ape'. According to a common conceit, any artist, however great, is of course 'the ape of Nature' – *simia naturae*.

47 Virgil, *Aeneid*, IV, 188–90, is the basis of the description of the flying rumours ('nocte volat caeli medio, terraeque per umbram / stridens'. *Aeneid*, IV, 184–5) in the third book of the *House of Fame*.

48 Cf., e.g., *Havelok*, lines 886–94, 909 ff.

49 The only deficiency seems to be that there is no description of the

goddess to whom the House of Rumour belongs. One would expect a set piece parallel to the *descriptio* of Fame. This would, of course, present difficulties, since much of the material belonging to *Fama* = Rumour has been used in the description of *Fama* = Renown, and what is left has been used for the flying rumours. The 'lytel laste bok', too, has run into considerable length already, and there would seem little space for another full-scale *descriptio*. If, however, this was the conclusion Chaucer had in mind, it would account for his failure to finish, in that it was a difficult and exacting task, worth the putting off. It is hard to see why even as confirmed a non-finisher as Chaucer should have postponed the writing of a few concluding lines of the sort proposed by Caxton.

3 *Troilus and Criseyde*

1 The relative dates of the two poems are, of course, uncertain. A date for the *Parlement* of 1393, which is definitely later than the *Troilus*, has recently been suggested by North, 'Kalenderes Enlumyned', pp. 270 ff. This depends on the interpretation of the description of Venus's temple and its attendant figures in astronomical terms. The argument, however, seems of dubious validity in view of the fact that most of these details are taken over from the *Teseida* or the *Roman de la Rose*. As far as our understanding of Chaucer's thought is concerned, the question of which poem came first is not really crucial. The *Parlement* undoubtedly gives in summary form ideas that are more fully developed in the *Troilus*, whether Chaucer proceeded from a brief statement to a fuller one or *vice versa*.

2 See K. Young, *The Origin and Development of the Story of Troilus and Criseyde*, Chaucer Society, 2nd series, 40 (1908); C. S. Lewis, 'What Chaucer Really did to *Il Filostrato*', *Essays and Studies*, XVII (1932), pp. 56 ff.; Sanford B. Meech, *Design in Chaucer's Troilus* (Syracuse, 1959). Ida L. Gordon's study *The Double Sorrow of Troilus* (Oxford, 1970) came to hand too late for reference here; I am glad to find much agreement between us, though I think our main theses differ a little.

3 *The Filostrato of Giovanni Boccaccio* text and trans. by N. E. Griffin and A. B. Myrick (Philadelphia and London, 1929), pp. 114 ff. All quotations are from this edition.

4 *Ibid.*, iii, st. 28 ff.

5 *Ibid.*, pp. 126–7.

6 At II, 606, she considers the possibility 'of peril, why she ought afered be'. In lines 708–14 she seriously contemplates the fear of standing 'in worse plit' if she were to earn the hatred instead of the

favour of such a powerful man as Troilus. At III, 76, it is, thus, his 'lordshipe' that she comes to beg for. Even in the consummation scene, Pandarus harps on the same string: 'Nece, se how this *lord* kan knele!' (III, 962).

7 Cf. III, 1210–11. Her reproaches to Pandarus next morning are hardly serious. She answers his enquiry as to how she is, with a colloquialism typical of their friendly exchanges: 'Nevere the bet for yow, / Fox that ye ben!' (III, 1564–5).

8 V, 956 ff.

9 Pandarus the ready-tongued is finally completely silenced: 'Astoned', 'as stille as ston; a word ne kowde he seye' (V, 1728–9). His attempts to convert Troilus to his own way of thinking are unsuccessful (IV, 393 ff., and V, 330 ff.).

10 IV, 547 ff.; V, 43 ff.

11 The phrase 'make in som comedye' suggests that the term does not refer to a literary kind, but to the nature of the subject.

12 *CT* VII, 1973–81, 1991–6, 2761–6. For parallels and possible sources, see Robinson, notes.

13 For a somewhat different idea of the meaning of tragedy for Chaucer see D. W. Robertson Jr, 'Chaucerian Tragedy', *ELH* XIX (1952), pp. 1–37. This article also emphasizes the link between tragedy and Fortune.

14 See Howard R. Patch, *The Goddess Fortuna in Medieval Literature* (Cambridge, Mass. 1927; reprinted London, 1967: my references are to the reprint), pp. 10–14 give a brief account of Classical ideas.

15 See pp. 160 ff.

16 The concepts of Fortune and Nature, and even of Love, are very nearly related when they are used with reference to the results brought about by God's creative providence in the world. Thus Boethius, writing of Love, speaks (in Chaucer's version) of the 'atempraunce' which 'norysscheth and bryngeth forth alle thinges that brethith lif in this world; and thilke same atempraunce, ravysschynge, hideth and bynymeth and drencheth undir the laste deth, alle thinges iborn' (IV, m. 6, 34 ff.). This 'atempraunce' is the same as that by which Nature, in the *Parlement*, controls the elements. See Patch, *The Goddess Fortune*, pp. 75 ff., on Nature and Fortune, and 90 ff., on Fortune and Love.

17 *de Consolatione*, II, pr. viii, 11 ff.

18 In the *Divina Commedia*, the tour of heaven is ordered as a progression through the spheres, starting from that of the moon. In both the *Troilus* and the *Parlement*, Chaucer makes use of the clearer view afforded to the soul which mounts above the sphere of change. In the *House of Fame*, the Eagle's flight does not take him so far – Fame operates in the delusive sphere of Nature. For living men such flights are, of course, made 'wyth fetheres of Philosophye' (*House of Fame*, 974), that is, Reason is not subject to Fortune and change (cf. *de Consolatione*, IV, m. i).

19 *CT* I, 3072; cf. *de Consolatione*, II, m. viii 21 ff.

20 See complete edition, I, pp. 148 ff.

21 *de Consolatione*, IV, pr. vi and m. vi, *Inferno*, VII, 67 ff.; Chaucer, *Fortune*, 57–72.

22 For the implications of this passage in Chaucer's hands, see also complete edition, I, pp. 175–7.

23 E.g., at I, 968; and cf. I, 986; II, 316 ff. Criseyde echoes this praise at II, 703 ff. (and it is notable that Antigone's song develops the same theme, i.e., of a lover who is 'welle of worthynesse' at II, 841). Cf. III, 474 ff.; III, 1550 ff.

24 As described, e.g., in the very popular *Legenda Aurea*.

25 This dream, like that of Troilus concerning the boar at V, 1232 ff., could be intended as a true prophetic dream, in which future events are shown under allegorical disguise (one of Macrobius's categories); or we could take it as showing psychological insight on Chaucer's part – the dreaming mind, in both cases, admits as a *fait accompli* what the waking mind is not yet prepared to admit. The case for 'realism' in the depiction of dreams in Chaucer and other medieval authors has recently been discussed by Constance B. Hieatt, *The Realism of Dream Visions* (The Hague and Paris, 1967).

26 North, 'Kalenderes Enlumyned' pp. 142–3.

27 See Curry, *Chaucer and the Medieval Sciences*, ch. 10. 'Destiny in Troilus and Criseyde', North ('Kalenderes Enlumyned'), points out that Skeat's notes are usually a more reliable source than Curry's book for the analysis and interpretation of astronomical references.

28 For a contrary view see D. W. Robertson Jr, *A Preface to Chaucer* (Princeton and London, 1963) pp. 251 ff.

29 See pp. 130–3.

30 A. C. Cawley, ed., *Everyman* (Manchester, 1961).

31 *Piers Plowman*, B, XI, 60 ff.

32 E.g., I, 582; II, 323 ff.; II, 1355–8; IV, 344 ff.; IV, 427–31; IV, 872 ff.

33 Book II, 78 ff. and 1093 ff.

34 All mentioned in Book II; and cf. III, 614: 'He song; she pleyde; he tolde tale of Wade'.

35 IV, 680 ff. Throughout 'tho wordes and tho wommanyshe thynges . . . Hire advertence is alwey elleswhere' (694–8).

36 For this characteristic of the *fabliau* see Muscatine, *French Tradition*, p. 60.

4 The *Knight's Tale*

1 For the existence of an earlier, pre-*Canterbury Tales* version of the *Knight's Tale*, see Robinson, p. 669 (general note to the *Knight's Tale*).

2 *Ibid.*, p. 669, col. 2, for references to the main discussions of Boccaccio's sources.

3 For Chaucer's use of the *Teseida*, see *Sources and Analogues*, ch. 2, and R. A. Pratt, 'Chaucer's use of the *Teseida*', *PMLA* LXII (1947), pp. 598 ff.

4 Critics have varied in the degree of differentiation which they detect between them. For the moderate view that they are 'significantly differentiated' but not 'individualized', see R. Frost, 'An Interpretation of Chaucer's *Knight's Tale*', *RES* XXV (1949), pp. 290 ff., where references to other opinions are also given.

4ᵃ This refers to the complete edition.

5 See pp. 147 ff.

6 Cf. the dual aspect of Venus in the *Parlement* and also pp. 144 ff.

7 This aspect of Virgil's epic is made the basis of an illustration of the fall of Troy as related by Aeneas, which is found as early as 1502 in the form of a woodcut, in the Grüninger Virgil, Strassburg. This is more magnificently reproduced in Limoges enamel dated 1525–30 (see Plate II). The various gods Aeneas mentions in Book II are all depicted as playing their parts in the action. Venus is shown immediately behind Aeneas, advising him – she seems, indeed, almost to grow out of his more dominating figure. Jupiter is shown through the purely Christian iconography of the hand of God coming through a cloud and scattering lightning: he is thus, for this artist, as so often for Chaucer, placed, as Providence, on a different footing to the other gods.

8 Curry, *Medieval Sciences*, pp. 119 ff.

9 *Ibid.*, pp. 119 and 120.

10 *Thebaid*, I, 124.

11 Quoted and translated in Saxl, Panofsky and Klibansky, *Saturn and Melancholy*, p. 261. See Ficino, *Opera Omnia* (Basle, 1576), p. 534.

12 The importance of the theme of order in the *Knight's Tale* has often been pointed out. For a recent study see Paul G. Ruggiers, *The Art of the Canterbury Tales* (Madison, Milwaukee and London, 1967), pp. 151 ff., where references are given to earlier discussions.

13 In England this is clearly reflected in *Piers Plowman*. See P. M. Kean, 'Love, Law and *Lewté* in *Piers Plowman*', *RES* N.S. XV (1964), pp. 241 ff.

14 For Langland's use of the term 'conqueror' in relation to the ideas of kingship and justice, see P. M. Kean, 'Justice, Kingship and the Good

Life in the Second Part of *Piers Plowman*', in S. S. Hussey, ed., *Piers Plowman: Critical Approaches* (London, 1969), pp. 106 ff.

15 Robertson, *Preface*, pp. 264 ff.

16 This corresponds to the first three lines of st. lxxxv, Book II, of the *Teseida*, but the Italian is less specific:

> Mentre li Greco i lor givan cercando,
> e rivistando il campo sanguinoso,
> e' corpi sottosopra rivoltando . . .

17 See complete edition, I, pp. 165 ff.

18 See, however, Robinson, note to line 1167, where it is pointed out that Gower uses 'positive law' to refer to ecclesiastical restrictions on marriage (*Mirour de l'Omme*, 18469 ff.). If this is the sense here, 'in ech degree' may refer to degrees of kinship. This would, however, only mean that Arcite places the chief disrupting effect of love within the institution of marriage, which normally stands for the maximum unity and order (see further pp. 167–71).

19 In III, pr. ii. For a full comparison of the two passages see Bennett, *The Knight's Tale*, 117–18.

20 Book I, m.v. Details in Bennett, *The Knight's Tale*, notes to lines 445 ff.

21 *Teseida*, IV, especially st. xxviii.

22 See Bennett, *The Knight's Tale*, note to 503–20 and Robinson, note to 1372, for details and references.

23 A detailed discussion of melancholy as an illness is given in Saxl, Panofsky and Klibansky, *Saturn and Melancholy*, especially in the first two chapters.

24 Cf. *de Consolatione*, IV, pr. vi and m. vi. Chaucer uses the same material in *Troilus*, V, 1541 ff.

25 Providence and prescience are discussed and distinguished by Boethius in *de Consolatione*, V, pr. iv. Providence belongs to a chain of causality (cf. IV, pr. vi); prescience does not (V, pr. iv, beginning). Neither, as Boethius argues at length, are incompatible with free will.

26 Boccaccio could, no doubt, have seen the remains of an actual Roman building. He could also have used the description given by Vitruvius, *de Architectura*, V, iii, 3 (a work well known in the Middle Ages as well as in the Renaissance), or that of Isidore of Seville, *Etymologiæ*, XVIII, xlii–li (cf. the description of the Circus, XVIII, xxviii–xxxi).

27 See Paul Frankl, *The Gothic: Literary Sources and Interpretations through Eight Centuries* (Princeton, 1960); and George Henderson, *Gothic* (London 1967), pp. 19 ff. On Chaucer's buildings in the *House of Fame* (his most elaborate contributions to the fashion) see Bennett, *Chaucer's Book of Fame*, pp. 113 ff.

28 E.g., Westminster Abbey, rebuilt under Henry III; Westminster Palace, with many elaborate and magnificent murals (see Henderson, *Gothic*, p. 38). Royal patronage of the arts continued under Richard II on a scale sufficient to justify a modern art historian's comparing him

to the Duc de Berri (Henderson, p. 35). A brief account of notable buildings in Chaucer's London is given by D. W. Robertson, *Chaucer's London* (New York, 1968); unfortunately, many dates and factual details are inaccurate.

29 Architects are often shown in visual representations with geometrical instruments. See Henderson, plates 2 and 3. Vitruvius also stresses the importance of geometry, for example in Book I, i, of the *de Architectura*.

30 *Cligès*, ed. A. Micha (Paris, 1957), 5317–18.

31 See Henderson's discussion in 'The Gothic Artist', *Gothic*, ch. 1. Vitruvius also stresses the versatility needed by the architect (*de Architectura*, I, i.).

32 *Cligès*, 5316 ff.

33 Quoted in Henderson, *Gothic*, p. 22.

34 *Hexameron*, I, ii, 27, and I, ii, 25. The idea of the artificer-creator is, of course, Platonic. Cf. Cornford, *Plato's Cosmology* (London, 1937), p. 26. It would be possible to equate Theseus's circular theatre, more precisely, with the zodiac and the temples with the positions of the planets in a real configuration (see North, 'Kalenderes Enlumyned', pp. 150 ff.). If Chaucer had intended this, however, one would expect Saturn to have been included, since his relation to Venus is so important in the action – to say nothing of Jupiter. The *Knight's Tale*, it seems to me, owes its peculiar character and structure to a treatment of the gods which blends the idea of planetary power and pagan deity, and not to the kind of purely astronomical allegorizing which Chaucer used in the *Complaint of Mars*.

35 Good examples are reproduced in Saxl, Panofsky and Klibansky, *Saturn and Melancholy*, plates 31–4, 36–42. See also plates 77, 78, 100, 116 in M. Hussey, *Chaucer's World: a Pictorial Companion* (Cambridge, 1967). Chaucer also uses literary sources for his descriptions of the gods and probably draws indirectly on Petrarch's *Africa*, via the *Libellus de deorum imaginibus*, ascribed to Albericus. See W. H. Ernest, 'Descriptions of Pagan Divinities from Petrarch to Chaucer', *Speculum*, XXXII (1957), pp. 511 ff. See also J. M. Steadman, 'Venus' Citole in Chaucer's *Knight's Tale* and Berchorius', *Speculum*, XXXIV (1959), pp. 620 ff.; B. Nye Quinn, 'Venus, Chaucer and Peter Bersuire', *Speculum*, XXXVIII, pp. 479 ff.

36 Chaucer is probably drawing on Statius, *Thebaid*, VII, 40 ff., where the carter is, more heroically, a charioteer. If the change is deliberate, it must be intended to support the more realistic treatment of epic-heroic material which we so often find in the *Knight's Tale*. It is possible, however, that Chaucer actually has a chariot in mind, since medieval illustrators often rendered the Classical chariot as a kind of farm cart.

37 This detail is in the *Teseida*.

38 For example, in the careful attention paid to the hours (those appropriate to the various planets) at which the votaries offer their prayers.

39 Hanging, breaking on the wheel and punishment in the stocks are common features of the Children of Saturn illustrations.

40 Probably because labourers of all sorts are subject to Saturn. Otherwise a revolt would seem more appropriate to Mars.

41 The Saturnian man is repeatedly characterized as treacherous. See Saxl, Panofsky and Klibansky *Saturn and Melancholy*, especially pp. 127 ff.

42 Diseases, especially epidemic ones, were thought to be due to stellar forces. Hence, of course, the term 'influenza'. Arcite provides an instance of disease induced by Saturn.

43 Cf. especially *de Consolatione*, IV, vii: 'Omnem', inquit, 'bonam prorsus esse fortunam'. See also Chaucer's own *Fortune*.

44 See Saxl, Panofsky and Klibansky, *Saturn and Melancholy*, pp. 151 ff. The essential goodness of the planets was also part of Stoic doctrine. Cf. Cicero, *de Natura Deorum*, II, xx.

45 For the identification of Saturn with the Sun, see Saxl, Panofsky and Klibansky, *Saturn and Melancholy*, p. 155, n. 96.

46 See pp. 43 ff. and 162 ff.

47 See Saxl, Panofsky and Klibansky, *Saturn and Melancholy*, p. 157, n. 102.

48 Saxl, Panofsky and Klibansky, *Saturn and Melancholy*, p. 169.

49 Thomas Wright, ed., *de Natura Rerum* (London, 1863; Rolls Series), p. 41.

50 On this etymology see Saxl, Panofsky and Klibansky, *Saturn and Melancholy*, p. 177.

51 The Saturn page in the early prints shows the merging of ideas (see Plate III). Saturn is an old man, muffled up in flowing garments: he carries the symbolical scythe, but the genealogy itself implies an euhemeristic interpretation. For an account of Boccaccio's methods in the *de Genealogia*, see C. G. Osgood, *Boccaccio on Poetry* (Princeton, 1930; reprinted New York, 1956), pp. xvi ff.

52 Curry, *Medieval Sciences*, pp. 130 ff.

53 See, e.g., A. T. P. Byles, ed., *The Book of Fayttes of Armes and Chiualrye*, EETS, 189 (1937), p. 9, on the caution with which war should be regarded by the king. In *Sir Gawain and the Green Knight*, King Arthur is criticized by his court for unnecessarily exposing Gawain to danger (674 ff.).

54 Curry, *Medieval Sciences*, pp. 139 ff.

55 See *OED* 'Transmutation', 2.

56 The idea that man is a stranger in the world and life a journey is also a Stoic one. Seneca uses it, for example, in the *Consolatio ad Marciam*.

57 This long lapse of time is Chaucer's addition.

58 Full citation of the passages from Boethius which are used by Chaucer will be found in Bennett, *Knight's Tale*, pp. 146–7.

59 See pp. 43 ff.

60 This is the 'entrechaungeable mutacioun' (Chaucer's translation) of the elements in the *de Consolatione*, IV, pr. vi.

61 *Wanderer*, lines 64–5. Both this poem and the *Seafarer* show an interest in ideas concerning the organization of the physical world. Both (*Wanderer*, 62–3; *Seafarer*, 80 ff.) subscribe to the common view that it and all its inhabitants were undergoing gradual diminution – in contrast to the theory derived from Aristotle's system of compensatory changes (see pp. 164–6).

62 The argument for the existence of God from the perception of order and causality in the universe is derived in part from Plato, especially in the *Timaeus*, in part from Aristotle. Cicero was probably the most important link in its transmission to the later Middle Ages. He used the argument to refute the Epicurean thesis of a random universe in which the concept of Providence was impossible. See *de Natura deorum*, II, xxx.

63 See pp. 41 ff.

64 *F.Q.*, VII, especially 17 ff. The argument is even more fully deployed in Book V, ii, 39 ff.

65 I owe this reference and the one to Aristotle, which follows, to Miss E. G. W. Mackenzie.

66 The *consolatio* has recently been explored in relation to the *Pearl* by I. Bishop, *The Pearl in its Setting* (Oxford, 1968); on the use of 'consolatory topics' in the *Knight's Tale*, see pp. 21 ff. J. E. Cross 'On the Genre of the Wanderer', *Neophilologus*, XLV (1961), p. 69, notes that the fall of cities is a consolatory topic, and we must allow for a certain overlap between *solacia* and the philosophical argument on mutability.

67 At the end of the *Wife of Bath's Tale*, Chaucer ironically repeats the phrase 'parfit joye' of the Wife's conception of an ideal marriage.

68 It was generally agreed that virginity was the highest way of life for the individual, since this was the life lived by Christ on earth. Nevertheless, it is important to remember that the three possible ways of life – virginity, marriage and widowhood – were all valued, and chastity played a part in each (see the *Parson's Tale*, *CT* X, 940 ff.).

69 *CT* X, 882, and see Plate V.

70 St Ambrose, xi, 50, *de Paradiso*, in J. J. Savage, trans. *St. Ambrose: Hexameron, Paradise, and Cain and Abel* (New York, 1961), pp. 328–9.

71 St Augustine, *The Good of Marriage*, C. T. Wilcox, trans., *St. Augustine: Treatises on Marriage and other Subjects* (New York, 1955), p. 9.

5 The *Canterbury Tales*: the problem of narrative structure

1 A full discussion of the frame device will be found in *Sources and Analogues*, I, pp. 1 ff.

2 Dante, Boccaccio and Petrarch all wrote of poetry in a general way (but did not concern themselves with questions of structure) in works which Chaucer may have known. Apart from these, there were only the more technical treatises on rhetoric, to one of which, that of

Geoffrey of Vinsauf, he refers and which he must therefore have read. These, of course, were mainly concerned with details of style, in the use of figures of speech, and only cursorily with larger questions of organization. The most detailed modern work on medieval aesthetics is that of E. de Bruyne, *Études d'esthétique médiévale*, 3 vols. (Bruges, 1946). See also Dorothy Everett, 'Some Reflections on Chaucer's "Art Poetical" ', in *Essays on Middle English Literature*, pp. 149 ff., and the references there given. Chaucerian narrative structure has recently been discussed by R. M. Jordan, *Chaucer and the Shape of Creation* (Cambridge, Mass., 1967). See also R. O. Payne, *The Key of Remembrance* (New Haven and London, 1963).

3 The short narrative presents few problems, as it necessarily implies a closer structure. For the relation of narrative form to length and the suggestion that medieval romances are best classified by taking length and scope into account, see D. Mehl, *The Middle English Romances of the Thirteenth and Fourteenth Centuries* (London, 1968).

4 See complete edition, I, pp. 28–9.

5 *OED* 'Tenor', sb.[1], I. 1.

6 For Humanist poets like Boccaccio or his countryman Salutati, the poetry itself, with which Classical authors clothed their versions of the stories, was valuable. It seems likely that Chaucer shared their viewpoint. On the division between the Humanists and the Moralists, who were only interested in what could be made of the content of Classical poetry, see R. H. Green, 'Classical Fable and English Poetry in the Fourteenth Century', in D. Bethurum, ed., *Approaches to Medieval Literature* (New York and London, 1960), pp. 110 ff. The fourteenth century was often critical of the content of Classical narrative. Chaucer shows knowledge of the historical criticism applied to the versions of the story of the Trojan War which lead to the condemnation of Homer (see complete edition, I, pp. 28–9, 164 ff.). He was not alone in considering the relation of the various Dido stories to the facts, although he does not seem to have known – or perhaps did not care to use – the historical 'research' which proved her to have been a virtuous widow who resisted the charms of Aeneas, or even showed that she never met him, since she could be proved to have lived three hundred years earlier. Petrarch held the first, the Englishman John Ridevall the second of these views. See Beryl Smalley, *English Friars and Antiquity in the Early Fourteenth Century* (Oxford, 1960), pp. 130–1 and 293.

7 As, e.g., in Salutati's *de Laboribus Herculis*. Boccaccio, too, in the *de Genealogia*, provides figurative interpretations of many of the stories; although this work is primarily an encyclopaedia of Classical mythology, it is an interpretative encyclopaedia.

8 See 'Classical Fable and English Poetry'. Many examples of the allegorization of Classical stories are given in Smalley, *English Friars and Antiquity*; see especially the chapter on Thomas Waleys's attitude to the classics, pp. 102 ff.

9 Cf.:   And shortly, outher he wolde lese his lif,
          Or wynnen Emelye unto his wyf.
          This is th' effect, and his entente pleyn. (*CT* I, 1485–7)

Here, 'effect' is used of the purpose which is to shape Palamoun's future course.

10 For example, Dorigen supports the contention that a woman had better die than be dishonoured by a long list of Classical heroines (*CT* V, 1399 ff.); and in the *Nun's Priest's Tale* appeals are made to Classical (and Biblical) examples as well as to the verses of 'Daun Burnel the Asse'.

11 *Heroides*, I, vii. Ovid makes Dido refer to the voices of the nymphs in the cave, but not to Venus and Juno, and only with scepticism to the divine order which summons Aeneas to leave her (lines 95–6, 139 ff.).

12 See pp. 123–4.

13 Although the term 'coniunx' is only used of Dido's first marriage, and she finally offers herself to Aeneas on any terms:

'si pudet uxoris, non nupta, sed hospita dicar;
dum tua sit, Dido quidlibet esse feret.' (167–8)

14 It certainly fails as an effective summary of the *Aeneid* and hardly achieves a successful abstraction of part of Virgil's material (as Ovid does). Chaucer has not really solved the problem of combining his two sources. The white swan passage, for example, from *Heroides*, I, vii, 1–3, is abruptly tacked on at the end, as if, glancing back, he found it too good to miss, but did not care to integrate it effectively into his version.

15 This topic is developed at length in the *Roman de la Rose*, 20817 ff. (cf. the discussion of art *versus* nature in lines 16005 ff.). Chaucer also uses it in the *Physician's Tale* in a way which shows that he understood its implications (see complete edition, II, pp. 179 ff.).

16 The possible stylistic influence of Chrétien, direct or indirect, is discussed by Muscatine, *French Tradition*, Ch. 2.

17 Except, perhaps, in the *Squire's Tale* (see pp. 183–4).

18 *Sources and Analogues*, XX, pp. 486 ff.; see also the discussion in complete edition, I, Chapter 1.

19 *Ibid.*, p. 490; full references in notes 1–3, pp. 490–1.

20 See H. L. Savage, *The Gawain Poet* (Chapel Hill, North Carolina, 1956), pp. 31 ff.; J. A. Burrow, *A Reading of Sir Gawain and the Green Knight* (London, 1965), pp. 71 ff.

21 *Sir Gawain and The Green Knight*, 1178–9, 1319, 1468–9, 1560–1.

22 See North, 'Kalenderes Enlumyned', p. 151.

23 E.g., *Sir Percevall*, 1057–60, 1121–5; *Ywain and Gawain*, 869–70; *Eger and Grime*, 721–2. Examples could be multiplied.

24 For the probable scope of the *Squire's Tale*, see *Sources and Analogues*, XIII, pp. 357 ff.

25 Cf. *OED* 'Process', sb. 4 and 5 ('a course or method of action'), both well attested for the fourteenth century.

26 See pp. 126 ff.

27 For Chaucer's knowledge and use of English lyric, see also pp. 206–7.

28 See Robinson, notes, for references. Dorothy Everett, 'Chaucer's Good Ear', in *Essays on Middle English Literature*, pp. 140–1, suggests that *Partonope* is likely to have been written in imitation of the *Knight's Tale*, as far as these lines are concerned.

29 Lines 3525 ff., and see R. M. Smith, 'Three notes on the *Knight's Tale*', *MLN*, LI (1936). Passages like these, which seem to preserve something of the actual movement of the alliterative line, are rare; but many romances use alliterative phrases in passages describing fighting, partly, no doubt because of such natural collocations as: 'helm', 'hauberk', 'hew'; 'shaft', 'shield'; 'spark', 'spring'; or, if the initial letter alone is accepted as sufficient (which it would not have been in O.E. verse), 'sword', 'spear', 'smite'. Some of these occur, for example, in *Guy of Warwick*, a romance which normally avoids alliteration: e.g., Auchinleck MS, 1442, 1485–6, 1506–67, 1961; and cf. Auchinleck MS, 1403–4, 1962.

30 This method goes back to OE battle poetry. Cf. *Battle of Maldon*, 108–10; *Judith*, 220 ff.; *Finn Fragment*, 28 ff. In ME it is found, e.g., in *Ipomedan*, 7811 ff., 7988 ff.; *Alliterative Morte Arthure*, 2807, 2910–11, 4113 ff., 3615 ff. (adapted to a sea battle); *Guy of Warwick*, Auchinleck MS, 1403–4, Caius MS, 2181 ff.

31 *Guy*, Auchinleck MS, 1393, 1979, 1983, 2967; Caius MS, 2187; *Havelok*, 2328–33.

32 A different interpretation of the function of the framing passages will be found in Jordan, *Chaucer and the Shape of Creation*, pp. 161 ff.

33 Chaucer may also be remembering Boccaccio's introductory *sonetto*, which gives the general argument for the whole poem. This passes straight from Arcita, as the subject of Books IX, X and XI, to Emilia, as that of the last book.

34 See pp. 137–8.

35 See pp. 124 ff.

36 For the characteristics of the 'Breton lay' see Bliss, ed., *Sir Orfeo*, pp. 36 ff.; Mehl, *Middle English Romances*, pp. 40 ff.

37 On this point see further pp. 215 ff.

38 See pp. 215 ff., 267 ff., 276 ff.

39 This is certainly the case with *Piers Plowman*, which becomes more intelligible as critics concentrate increasingly on the development of the poet's thought, rather than on the attempt to discover the kind of consecutive structure which would be normal for realistic narrative. In the same way, the *Roman de la Rose* may seem 'spoilt' by Jean de Meun unless the structural function of the so-called digressions is understood.

40 How far we can see, in the *Confessio Amantis*, consistent allegory, rather than a sequence of tales bound together by a framing device, is debatable. J. H. Fisher, *John Gower* (London, 1965), pp. 135 ff., has recently argued for an 'inner consistency in purpose and point of view' not only

in the *Confessio Amantis*, but in all three of Gower's major poems, which, he suggests, can be read as one continuous work.

41 R. A. Pratt and Karl Young, 'The Literary Framework of the Canterbury Tales', in *Sources and Analogues*, I, pp. 1–81.

42 The episode of the daughters of Minyas in Ovid's *Metamorphoses* (IV, 1–415) is an important prototype here. The stories are told for sheer entertainment; the frame provides the occasion, and brings the tellers together. See *Sources and Analogues*, pp. 9 ff.

43 This is, for example, the case with Boccaccio's *Ameto*, which Chaucer may have known, where all the stories are to be about the experiences in love of their tellers.

44 The most important are, of course, the *Decameron* of Boccaccio and the collection of *novelle* made by Sercambi. It is, however, impossible to prove that Chaucer knew either. See *Sources and Analogues*, pp. 13 ff.

45 So, for example, F. Tupper, 'Chaucer and the Seven Deadly Sins', *PMLA* XXIX (1914), pp. 93 ff., argued that the tales were intended to treat systematically the seven deadly sins. See Robinson, notes, p. 650, for further references. Two more recent critics have, in different ways, argued for a similarly consistent moral purpose in the plan of the *Canterbury Tales*. These are B. F. Huppé and Trevor Whittock, both of whose books are entitled *A Reading of the Canterbury Tales* (respectively, New York, 1964, and Cambridge, 1968).

6 The *Canterbury Tales*: Chaucerian comedy

1 There are, of course, other comic elements in these poems which have already been discussed. The figure of the Dreamer, too, might well be included among their comic ones.

2 See pp. 242 ff.

3 In the case of the Man of Law and of the Physician, for example, much of the criticism of their characters and activities is stock material. For details, see Robinson, notes.

4 Walter Raleigh, *Some Authors* (Oxford, 1923), p. 5, quoted in Lawlor, *Chaucer*, p. 105, in an illuminating chapter 'Tales and Tellers'.

5 There is a further stylistic nuance here in the use of alliteration in the last two lines. By this Chaucer reminds us of the tradition of alliterative writing and suggests some of its weighty seriousness as applied to social criticism.

6 Muscatine, *French Tradition*, pp. 59 ff.; although the selection of realistic and practical descriptive detail is also characteristic of much earlier romance writing.

7 See complete edition, II, Chapter 6.

8 See p. 283.

9 The Harley Lyrics are close to the mood and the actual wording of Nicholas's pleas; cf. G. L. Brook, ed., *The Harley Lyrics* (Manchester, 1948), pp. 44, 33.

3ef me shal wonte wille of on,
Þis wunne weole y wole forgon,

and:

Bote he me wolle to hire take,
For te buen hire owen make,
Longe to lyuen ichulle forsake,
Ant feye fallen adoun.

10 There is a suggestion here of the sophisticated form of the *aubade*, which Chaucer, of course, uses seriously in the *Troilus*. Here, however, the flatness and triteness of the formulae suggest a more popular version.

11 The Prologue to the tale describes the Summoner's anger with the friar, and this is allowed to enter into the tale itself. Thomas's revenge is the result of his pent up anger with the intolerable friar, who reacts with the same vice. It does not, however, follow that Chaucer intended to use this device systematically in the *Canterbury Tales*.

12 See Everett, 'Chaucer's Good Ear', in *Essays on Middle English Literature*, p. 145.

13 This is so convincingly carried out that a modern critic has, or so it seems to me, momentarily found himself inside the story. Cf. Ruggiers, *The Art of the Canterbury Tales*, p. 82, where he associates the Monk's sudden flush (an involuntary acknowledgement of the implications of his equivocal speech to the Merchant's wife) with modesty – which is to take it, literally, at its face-value.

14 A useful and moderate discussion of the problems involved in an attempt to assess the 'coherence' of the *Canterbury Tales* will be found in Lawlor, *Chaucer*, pp. 109 ff.

15 It is, of course, true that the personality of the Knight is of great importance in his tale not only as a reinforcement of the viewpoint of Theseus, but also as a living exemplification of some, at least, of the 'noble' aspects of the story. It may well be, too, that the peculiar limitations of the Prioress's religious sensibility are reflected by her choice of subject and handling of it in her tale – though I find this a more doubtful proposition.

16 The Summoner's vice of anger has already been mentioned. In the same way, the Merchant's preoccupation with his own misfortunes in marriage contributes to the near-obsessiveness of his tale. The Wife of Bath's interest in marriage, which extends to her tale, is also a personal one, and the Pardoner is implicated in his tale in a peculiarly complex way (see pp. 216 ff.).

17 See pp. 247–8.

18 *CT* VI, 960 ff., and *CT* II, 1170 ff. The latter is the epilogue to the *Man of Law's Tale*. Although its position in the series is very uncertain (see Robinson, notes, pp. 696–7), there seems no reason to doubt the authenticity of the exchange between the Parson and the Host. The second speech, telling the Parson not to preach here, is attributed in

most MSS to the Squire, to whom it seems inappropriate. The minority attributions of this speech to the Shipman or the Summoner seem likely to reflect Chaucer's second, and better, thoughts.

19 The heroine of *Le Bone Florence of Rome* is typical of this type of semi-hagiographical figure. Not only does she beat out the teeth of a would-be ravisher with a stone, found conveniently by her bed, but she brings upon a seaman, who makes an attempt on her virtue, first a storm at sea and secondly a hideous disease.

20 See p. 241.

21 See complete edition, II, pp. 173–5.

22 Perhaps most fully and recently by Whittock, *A Reading of the Canterbury Tales*, pp. 77 ff.

23 For the various sources on which Chaucer might have drawn, see *Sources and Analogues*, pp. 207 ff.

24 Not given as a source in *Sources and Analogues* (see pp. 333 ff.).

25 For a discussion which throws much light on figures of this kind, see Tuve, *Allegorical Imagery*, pp. 173 ff.

26 Although verbal reminiscences of the *Roman* are few. See *Sources and Analogues*, pp. 409–11, where the passages closest to the *Pardoner's Prologue* are reprinted.

27 *Piers Plowman*, B, II, 52 ff.

28 Although to be successful such figures need to be presented as fully and strikingly concrete. Rosemond Tuve points out that an essential part of allegory of this kind, is 'the spate of colloquial specificity, by means of which the abstraction shines through as a living form' (*Allegorical Imagery*, p. 175).

29 The question of Chaucer's authorship of the fragmentary English translation is still unsettled (for references see Robinson, notes, pp. 872–3). Fragment C has always been considered least likely to have been written by him, since (like B) it contains non-Chaucerian dialect forms. Its rhythms, too, although they have some affinity to the *House of Fame*, seem, for the most part, un-Chaucerian.

30 For a recent discussion of these movements, with full references to earlier studies, see Gordon Leff, *Heresy in the Later Middle Ages*, 2 vols. (Manchester, 1967).

31 For Langland, see R. W. Frank Jr, *Piers Plowman and the Scheme of Salvation* (Newhaven, 1957), pp. 45 ff. It has been suggested, notably by Morton W. Bloomfield, *Piers Plowman as a Fourteenth Century Apocalypse* (New Brunswick, N.J., 1961), that Langland was influenced by Joachimite ideas – a thesis which I do not find fully convincing. It seems clear, at any rate, that such an influence was not felt by Chaucer.

32 *Roman de la Rose*, Chaucerian version, C, 7127 ff.

33 Jean de Meun devotes lines 4221–6900 to Reason's attempt to convert L'Amant.

34 Luxuria (often identified with Venus) as a naked woman swimming in the sea goes back to the *Mythologies* of Fulgentius. She is transmitted through the *Ovide Moralisé* (C. de Boer, ed. [Amsterdam, 1938], V,

p. 402). Cf. Seznec, *La Survivance des Dieux Antiques*, plate 31. Robert Holcot reproduces the idea in one of his 'pictures'; see Smalley, *English Friars and Antiquity*, p. 175.

35 This latter passage is usually accepted as genuine, since the MS authority is good, but as cancelled, because of its overlap with the passage quoted above. See Robinson, p. 755, for details and references.

36 The venom and directness with which he goes straight to the Pardoner's most obvious weak point in lines 952–5 are in keeping with his later admission that his prevailing sin, like that of the Summoner, is *ira*: 'For I am perilous with knyf in honde' (VII, 1919). Chaucer has not drawn a simple figure of a genial host in Harry Bailey.

37 Curry, *Medieval Sciences*, pp. 54 ff.

38 This is clearly seen in the confessions of the sins in *Piers Plowman*; the device of the confession, indeed, presupposes a kind of consciousness in the vices of their converse. In the same way, the motif of the abandonment of the soul by its vices, often used in the morality plays, depends on acknowledgement of the fact that they stand opposed to their corresponding virtues.

39 See pp. 267 ff., 276 ff.

40 *The Book of Courtesy*, st. 49 (quoted in Spurgeon, *Chaucer Criticism and Allusion*, p. 67).

7 The *Canterbury Tales*: major themes

1 T. W. Craik, *The Comic Tales of Chaucer* (London, 1964), p. xiv.

1[a] See complete edition, II, pp. 165–85.

2 *Piers Plowman*, B, XIII, 272 ff.

3 See pp. 51 ff.

4 I would therefore modify a little the view of Barbara Bartholomew, *Fortuna and Natura: A Reading of Three Chaucer Narratives* (The Hague, 1966). She sees Fortune and Nature as fundamentally and permanently opposed.

5 For a recent study of the medieval genre of the saint's life, see Rosemary Woolf, 'Saints' Lives', in E. G. Stanley, ed., *Continuations and Beginnings: Studies in Old English Literature* (London, 1966), pp. 37 ff. The date of the *Man of Law's Tale* is uncertain, and I do not necessarily suggest that it was written later than the *Knight's Tale*. The astronomical evidence for date is examined by North in 'Kalenderes Enlumyned', pp. 426 ff; he would place it late, in 1394, although he regards the evidence as doubtful.

6 See Mehl, *The Middle English Romances*, pp. 120 ff.

7 The horoscope is fully discussed by North, 'Kalenderes Enlumyned', p. 426.

8 See p. 239.

9 *Troilus*, III, 1819. There is poignancy in Chaucer's persistent use of words meaning rest and stability in reference to a love which is necessarily as transient as the natural world of which it forms a part. There may also be a more particular philosophical implication in his use of such formulae (see complete edition, II, pp. 174–5).

10 Cf. *Truth*, 8–10, and see pp. 10–12.

11 This is, of course, the substance of Boethius's complaint against Fortune (see pp. 131–3).

12 Chaucer uses this topic, in relation to the inevitable reversal brought about by death in the *Knight's Tale*, in Theseus's speech on the First Mover: 'He moot be deed, the kyng as shal a page' (*CT* I, 3030). The crowned king is often depicted attached to Fortune's wheel in MS illustrations.

13 The figure of Griselda brings together the Stoic virtue of patience in adversity and the Christian virtue of patience which is a branch of fortitude, that is, of persistence, in a general way, in the Christian life. (Much relevant material is collected by Tuve, *Allegorical Imagery*; see Virtues and Vices, Patience, and Fortitude in her Index.) In *Piers Plowman*, the allegorical figure Patience has reference to the living of the Christian life in general. For something nearer the Stoic view, in which Patience is opposed to the assaults of particular vices, see, e.g., the illustration to a ninth-century *Psychomachia* from Leyden University Library reproduced as plate V of A. Katzenellenbogen, *Allegories of the Virtues and Vices in Medieval Art* (London, 1939); this dominating, militant (and male) figure is shown standing, self-sufficient and unharmed by the slings and arrows of the small and ineffectual looking Vices.

14 The topic of the three states of human life, and the perfection appropriate to each, is handled at length in *Piers Plowman* B, XVI, 60 ff. All discussions are based on I Cor. 7.

15 See his note to this line. Salter, *Chaucer: The Knight's Tale and the Clerk's Tale*, pp. 48–9, notes several Biblical echoes in the *Clerk's Tale*, but does not comment on this one.

16 E.g., in Rolle's *Meditations on the Passion*, I, 54–5 (H. E. Allen, ed., *English Writings of Richard Rolle* [Oxford, 1931], p. 21).

17 Isaiah 53:7: 'He shall be led as a sheep to the slaughter and shall be dumb as a lamb before his shearer, and he shall not open his mouth.'

18 The fourth book of Thomas à Kempis's *Imitation of Christ* has much, especially concerning the soul's need for endurance and patience *vis-à-vis* its divine lover, which is of interest in relation to the *Clerk's Tale*, as have many other works on mystical love. The differences, however, between such works and Chaucer's poem are as striking as the similarities.

19 R. M. Wilson, ed., *Sawles Warde* (Leeds, 1938), p. 2. The English writer follows, with some modifications, Hugh of St Victor, *de Anima*, xiii (reprinted in *Sawles Warde*, p. 3).

20 See Henderson, *Gothic*: the discussion on 'Gothic for Art's Sake' (ch. 3) is illuminating. For a contrary view of the significance of secular decoration in the religious art of this period see Robertson, *Preface*, passim.

21 This was not the only possible view. St Augustine considered that free will consisted in the ability to do either evil or good, and he appears to have been followed by Langland (*Piers Plowman* C, XVII, 193–4). See the discussion by A. V. C. Schmidt, 'Langland and Scholastic Philosophy', *Medium Aevum*, XXXVIII (1969), pp. 134 ff.

22 Brook, ed., *Harley Lyrics*, p. 44.

23 'Mysgovernaunce', *CT* VIII, 2012. Of Lucifer, the Monk says:

> For though Fortune may noon angel dere,
> From heigh degree yet fell he for his synne.
>
> (2001–2)

24 As, for example, Robertson (*Preface*, pp. 251–2) seems to do. J. D. North ('Kalenderes Enlumyned', pp. 418 ff.) finds an underlying astronomical allegory in the poem. But this, too, seems unconvincing.

25 The emphasis at the beginning is on the political (and, of course, missionary) aspects of the marriage (see especially 232 ff.); and Constance's son Maurice does, in fact, become a good and Christian emperor (1121 ff.). On the whole, however, the political implications of the marriage are subordinate to the Christian ones in this tale.

26 This is especially obvious at the beginning, when failure to marry is cited as a fault in Walter as a prince. He finally marries in answer to the pleas of his people (92 ff.) and carefully chooses a wife capable of furthering the 'commune profit' (431).

27 See G. L. Kittredge, 'Chaucer's Discussion of Marriage', *MPh* IX (1911–12), pp. 435 ff. This was the pioneer study, to which many have since been added. Some of the most important contributions are conveniently listed by R. Schoeck and J. Taylor, *Chaucer Criticism*, I (Notre Dame, Ind., 1960), p. 158, n. 1; Kittredge's article is also reprinted in this book.

28 See pp. 168–71.

29 It is, of course, the case that much of L'Ami's advice is cynical, and even this is double-edged: L'Amant can take it one way, we can take it another.

30 With the proviso, of course, that the *Knight's Tale* does make considerable play with the 'service' of love – an irrational proceeding (according to Theseus) and a contributory factor to the discords which are finally resolved by the marriage.

31 Used, e.g., in the *Knight's Tale*, 1164, where Chaucer is quoting Boethius: 'Quis legem det amantibus?' (*de Consolatione* III, m. xii, 47). See also *Troilus*, IV, 618, and the Chaucerian *Roman*, 3432 ff. Closest to the *Franklin's Tale* is L'Ami's dictum 'Car il couvient amour mourir / Quant amant veulent seignourir', which Chaucer doubtless had in mind.

32 *Roman*, 4221 ff. On the place of *amicitia* in love and marriage, see Gervase Mathew, 'Ideals of Friendship', in J. Lawlor, ed., *Patterns of Love and Courtesy: Essays in Memory of C. S. Lewis* (London, 1966), pp. 45 ff.

33 J. J. Parry, ed., *The Art of Courtly Love by Andreas Capellanus* (New York, 1941), p. 102. The women speakers in the dialogues generally show a common sense which points up the unscrupulous logic of the men who try to seduce them. 'Courtly' in Parry's title renders *honeste*.

34 *Ibid.*, p. 103.

35 A phrase which may carry sophisticated connotations: the implication here is of a law compatible with marriage and the 'law of Kind', instead of the reverse. Andreas Capellanus makes frequent reference to the laws or rules of love, e.g., I, dialogue v, where they are listed (*ibid.*, pp. 81–2), and Marie de Champagne's letter (*ibid.*, p. 107).

36 *Roman*, 14471 ff.

37 E.g., *Roman*, 12761 ff., 12857 ff.

38 Huppé, *A Reading of the Canterbury Tales*, p. 135.

39 At line 163 'Up stirte the Pardoner', but only to make a personal application of her words to himself. The Summoner (832 ff.) merely seizes on a chance to quarrel with the Friar. He is, evidently, satisfied with the 'disport' provided and resents interruptions.

40 *Roman*, 9091 ff.

41 See complete edition, I, pp. 168 ff., and II, pp. 175–8.

42 See complete edition, II, pp. 165 ff.

Short list of books on Chaucer published since 1972

Charles Muscatine, *Poetry and Crisis in the Age of Chaucer* (Notre Dame, Ind., 1972).

Ian Robinson, *Chaucer and the English Tradition* (Cambridge, 1972).

Sheila Delany, *Chaucer's House of Fame: The Poetics of Skeptical Fideism* (Chicago, 1972).

Jill Mann, *Chaucer and the Medieval Estates Satire: the Literature of the Social Classes and the General Prologue to the Canterbury Tales* (Cambridge, 1973).

George D. Economou, *The Goddess Natura in Medieval Literature* (Cambridge, Mass., 1973).

John Norton Smith, *Geoffrey Chaucer* (London, 1974).

J. A. W. Bennett, *Chaucer at Oxford and Cambridge* (Oxford, 1974).

Alice S. Miskimin, *The Renaissance Chaucer* (New Haven, Conn., 1975).

Henry Ansgar Kelly, *Love and Marriage in the Age of Chaucer* (Ithaca, N.Y., and London, 1975).

Alfred David, *The Strumpet Muse: Art and Morals in Chaucer's Poetry* (Bloomington and London, 1976).

Lorraine Y. Baird, *A Bibliography of Chaucer 1964–73* (Boston, Mass., 1977).

Derek Brewer, *Chaucer and His World* (London and New York, 1978).

David Aers, *Chaucer, Langland and the Creative Imagination* (London, 1980).

Index

313